LONDON 2001

TITLES OF RELATED INTEREST

The carrier wave
P. Hall & P. Preston

Cities and telecommunications
M. Moss

The city in cultural context
J. A. Agnew *et al.* (eds)

*Cost-benefit analysis in urban and
    regional planning*
J. A. Schofield

Development and the landowner
R. J. C. Munton & R. Goodchild

Environmental groups in politics
P. Lowe & J. Goyder

Environmental impact assessment
P. Wathern (ed.)

Housing and urban renewal
A. D. Thomas

Gentrification of the city
N. Smith & P. Williams (eds)

Greenprints for the countryside
A. & M. MacEwen

High tech America
A. Markusen *et al.*

Intelligent planning
R. Wyatt

Land use planning
D. L. Dent *et al.*

Landscape meanings and values
D. Lowenthal &
    E. C. Penning-Rowsell (eds)

London's Green Belt
R. J. C. Munton

*Migration and depopulation of the
    metropolis*
W. Frey

Planning the urban region
P. Self

Policies and plans for rural people
P. J. Cloke (ed.)

Property before people
A. Power

*Regional development and
    settlement policy*
R. Dewar *et al.*

Regional dynamics
G. Clark *et al.*

Regional economic development
B. Higgins & D. Savoie (eds)

Remaking planning
T. Brindley *et al.*

*Rural land-use planning in
    developed nations*
P. J. Cloke (ed.)

Silicon landscapes
P. Hall & A. Markusen (eds)

*Slums and slum clearance in
    Victorian London*
J. A. Yelling

*Technological change, industrial
    restructuring and regional
    development*
A. Amin & J. Goddard (eds)

Town and country planning in Britain
J. B. Cullingworth

Urban and regional planning
P. Hall

Urban problems in Western Europe
P. Cheshire & D. Hay

Western sunrise
P. Hall *et al.*

LONDON 2001

Peter Hall

London
UNWIN HYMAN
Boston   Sydney   Wellington

Published by the Academic Division of
Unwin Hyman Ltd
15/17 Broadwick Street, London W1V 3FP, UK

Unwin Hyman Inc.,
8 Winchester Place, Winchester, Mass. 01890, USA

Allen & Unwin (Australia) Ltd.
8 Napier Street, North Sydney, NSW 2060, Australia

Allen & Unwin (New Zealand) Ltd in association with the
Port Nicholson Press Ltd
Compusales Building, 75 Ghuznee Street, Wellington 1,
New Zealand

First published in 1989
Revised paperback edition 1989

British Library Cataloguing in Publication Data

Hall, Peter, *1932–*
    London 2001.
    1. England. south-east England. Regional
    planning.
    I. Title
    361.6'1'09422
    ISBN 0–04–445161–X
    ISBN 0–04–445556–9 pbk

Library of Congress Cataloging-in-Publication Data

Hall, Peter Geoffrey.
    London 2001 / Peter Hall.
        p.   cm.
    Includes index.
    ISBN 0–04–445161–X (alk. paper)
    ISBN 0–04–445556–9 pbk
    1. City planning—England—London.   I. Title.
    HT169.G72L64615   1989
    711'.4'09421–dc 19   88–23543
                                                            CIP

Typeset in 10/12 Palatino
Printed in Great Britain at the University Press, Cambridge

For
John Vaizey
Baron Vaizey of Greenwich
1929–1984

in memoriam

Preface

Twenty-five years ago, I published a book called *London 2000*. To my surprise and gratification, it received a great deal of notice. That, doubtless, was due less to its merits than to its timeliness. It appeared at a time when planning, above all the long-term strategic planning of activities and traffic, had just become a major issue, perhaps *the* major issue, of the day; the newspapers and television screens were full of it. In quick succession, after the book's publication in July 1963, there followed the Buchanan Report, *Traffic in Towns* (November 1963) and the first sketch of a strategic plan for South-East England, the *South–East Study* (March 1964). For any planner, Bliss was it in that dawn to be alive, But to be young was very heaven!

Not so a quarter-century later. For planning, above all strategic planning, is under a cloud. No one seems to have a good word for it. The Prince of Wales and the Prime Minister, who do not seem to agree on much else, concur that it is responsible for the awfulness of our cities, in particular London's. Everyone seems to agree that in those golden years of the 1960s, when planners ran wild, they wreaked havoc on the sensitive fabric of our cities and towns. The fact – that, often enough, the planners were not even present – is not allowed to mar the enjoyment of the witch-hunt.

In particular, long-term strategic planning is dismissed as some kind of irrelevant game; we no longer need it, we will no longer pay for it. The inconvenient fact – that other countries and other countries' cities, which seem to have done at least as well as ours over the long haul and maybe even better, have done so on the basis of planning – is conveniently ignored. Few look over the water at Paris, the most obvious comparison, which has continued over two decades to implement its audacious development plan – and has done so steadfastly, come left-wing government, come right-wing.

There is an historical comparison. In the 1950s, too, planning in Britain was under a cloud. Then, too, it was reduced to a negative, residual, role. Quite suddenly, at the start of the 1960s, there was one of those perceptual sea-changes that transform the whole political landscape: almost overnight, planning was seen as both desirable and necessary. And this affected people of every political persuasion; that most consummate of politicians, Harold Macmillan, sensed it early and sailed with the tide. Hence the notable fact that, during the years 1961–2, it was a Conservative government that initiated such classics as the Buchanan Report on *Traffic in towns* and the *South-East study*. Hence the huge swell of interest that, incidentally, caused *London 2000* to be commissioned.

History is not always cyclical. But a quarter-century later, as I started work on this book, my hunch was that there would be another turn of the wheel. If I am wrong, this new book may prove an historic curiosity. If I am right, it may make another modest contribution to the debate. As I finish it a year after I started, bombarded by newspaper articles and television specials about the crisis of planning in the South East, I think that my hunch was right.

It is a new book. It shares with *London 2000* only a similar title and a similar structure. There are a few sentences culled from the old book, in Chapters 1 and 9, mainly in the form of quotations. There are also passages culled from presentations I have made on the question during 1987–88; extremely assiduous readers may recall them in fugitive publications.

The first objective is to look back at that youthful work, full of naive hope and burning evangelism, and ask: What, if anything, was achieved? How much of the vision of the early 1960s did we get, how much hope was betrayed, and why? The second aim is to take stock of where we are now, to map out the problem landscape, and to suggest some solutions as a contribution to a new debate. Essentially, then, *London 2001* shares with *London 2000* something else: its purpose.

In an old-fashioned way, which many critics will doubtless find fuddy-duddy, I try to insist that, like its predecessor, this book is apolitical. Though the idea of planning itself has latterly become the subject of fierce political controversy, it is perhaps worth remembering that the founding father of the new conservatism, von Hayek, thought that the word and the concept were worthy of a better fate.

Three days before the manuscript went to press, the London Planning Advisory Committee published its consultation draft, *Strategic Planning Advice for London: Policies for the 1990s* (London Planning Advisory Committee 1988). It is a hopeful sign that such a body has produced a comprehensive and balanced review. It is less hopeful that the media gave it so little attention. This book should have given it much more, but in the circumstances that was impossible. Some key points have however been noted.

Preface

London 2000 was dedicated to John Vaizey, who inspired it and persuaded me to write it. He spent his too-brief life as fierce crusader for independence of thought, for ideas that flew in the face of the conventional wisdom, for a continuous attack on what he liked to call the forces of cant and humbug. It is all too appropriate that this successor should be dedicated to his memory.

PETER HALL
Berkeley, California, and London
May–June 1988

Acknowledgements

Sheila Dance of the University of Reading Department of Geography drew all the maps for this book, producing work of superb quality against impossible deadlines, as so often before.

Figs 3, 4, 8, 10, 13 and 14 draw on material from research by SERPLAN. It is a pleasure to acknowledge SERPLAN's continuing contribution to our understanding of regional change.

My thanks to the following suppliers of illustrations: Hunting Aerofilms (Plates 4a, 8 and 11); British Road Federation (Plate 7); Olympia and York Canary Wharf Limited (Plates 1(a) and 1(b)); David Crewe Associates (Plates 10(a) and 10(b)); Eurotunnel (Plates 12(a) and 12(b)); JAS Photographi 2 (Plate 9); and London Regeneration Consortium PLC (Plate 4(b)). The remaining plates are my own work.

Contents

List of Tables

List of Figures

List of Plates

Introduction

The first problem with London is to define it. London has never taken kindly to attempts at delimitation, whether by people who wanted to govern it, or by those who just wanted to fix it statistically; every time this was done, London promptly outgrew its administration or its figures.

Thus began *London 2000*, in 1963; thus, 25 years later, begins *London 2001*. If anything, the problem is more intractable now than then. The 1981 Census gives figures for a unit that in 1988 no longer exists: the 620-square-mile *Greater London Council*, now the area of the City of London and the 32 London boroughs. It corresponds very roughly to the continuously built-up area of London, which however snakes out beyond it in certain directions, especially along the busier commuter lines. It is thus roughly co-terminous with the London of 1938, and it is bounded by the Metropolitan Green Belt, an idea first fixed by legislation in that very year in a vain attempt to halt the spread of the metropolis into the fields of surrounding England, and properly realized only after the Second World War.

Greater London includes at least three smaller units, commonly used in comparative statistics, which fit inside each other like Russian dolls. The smallest of all is the 677-acre ancient *City of London*, which – as *London 2000* predicted – survived both the administrative holocaust of 1965, which brought the GLC into being, and that of 1986, which eliminated it. Around it is an area ten times as large, the 10-square-mile *central area* embracing the City, the West End, and such specialized areas as the 'Museum Quarter' of Kensington. It is a convenient shorthand for the area that contains the biggest concentration of employment in Britain, and one of the three or four largest in the world.

Finally there is *inner London*: the area of mainly older and denser housing, corresponding very roughly to the built-up area of London in 1914. Confusingly, there are two different definitions of it. One is the area that still – as this book is finished, but not for long – is administered for educational purposes by the Inner London Education Authority: it corresponds to the old *London County Council*, which administered London from 1888 until the GLC supplanted it.

1

The other, widely used for statistical purposes, chops off an ILEA borough in south-east London – Greenwich – but for good measure adds two others: Haringey in the north and Newham in the east. Because this is the definition commonly used in the statistics, I shall use it here.

That much is relatively simple. The real problem, as *London 2000* pointed out, was that even by 1963 Greater London was no longer great enough: as early as the 1950s, it was declining in population, while a wide ring around – up to 45 or 50 miles from the centre – was the fastest growing part of Britain, growing by nearly 1 million people, 29 per cent, in only ten years. Statisticians and planners were just then learning to call this the Outer Metropolitan Area. It went on growing, but at diminishing speed: nearly 19 per cent in the 1960s, 8 per cent in the 1970s, between 2 and 3 per cent in the 1980s.

It was not that population growth had ceased, though: the growth was just rolling farther out. In the 1950s, as already noted, the belt of maximum growth was between 15 and 30 miles from the centre. In the 1960s it was already 35–70 miles distant, and had begun to break up into conglomerations corresponding to major urban groups: Reading–Basingstoke, Southampton–Portsmouth, Milton Keynes. In the 1970s it was even farther distant, and even more broken. By the early 1980s it had lapped outside the South-East region as defined for statistical purposes, into the neighbouring South-West, East Midlands, and East Anglia regions (Figs 6(a)–(d) below).

Small wonder then that during the early 1980s the official statisticians stopped using the concept of the London Metropolitan Area, and hence the Outer Metropolitan Area outside Greater London; instead they referred to the entire South East, and to ROSE (the Rest of the South East), again outside Greater London. 'Roseland', as some commentators call it, is still one of the fastest-growing areas of Britain. But its growth too is slowing, a product of that same outward roll: its percentage increment was over 18 per cent in the 1960s, 6 per cent in the 1970s, but less than 6 per cent in the 1980s. What we need now is a concept no one has officially recognized, though it was first described in a 1983 report by the Regional Studies Association: a Greater South East, incorporating the entire official South East and the fringe of fast-growing counties, 10 or 20 miles wide, around it. In 1986 this area had an estimated population of 19.8 million, just under 40 per cent of the total for England and Wales (Table 1 and Fig. 1).

The real growth in this extended South East has recently occurred right at its edge, much of it outside the official South-East region, in what Table 1 terms the 'South-East Fringe'. In terms of counties, the

Table 1 Definitions of London and the South East

	Population				
	1961 Census	1971 Census	1981 Census	1981 Estimate	1986 Estimate
'Greater South East'	18 217 529	19 484 079	19 615 233	19 859 800	20 266 300
South East	15 993 116	16 930 630	16 795 756	17 010 400	17 264 600
Greater London	7 992 443	7 452 346	6 713 165	6 805 700	6 775 200
Inner London	3 492 879	3 031 935	2 497 978	2 550 200	2 511 700
Outer London	4 499 564	4 420 411	4 215 187	4 255 500	4 263 500
Outer Metropolitan Area	4 390 087	5 206 831	5 461 918	5 513 600	5 581 000
Outer South East	3 610 586	4 271 453	4 620 673	4 691 100	4 908 600
ROSE	8 000 673	9 478 284	10 085 591	10 204 700	10 489 600
South East Fringe	2 224 413	2 553 449	2 819 477	2 849 400	3 001 700
ROGSE	10 225 086	12 031 733	12 902 068	13 054 100	13 491 300

Source: Office of Population Censuses and Surveys (1984, 1987).

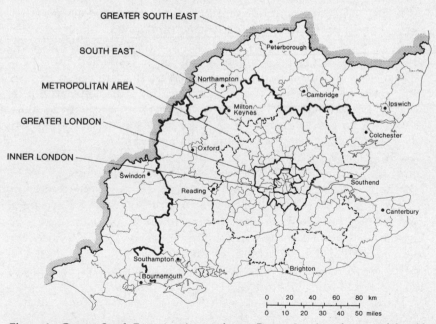

Figure 1 Greater South East: constituent rings Greater London, the area of the old Greater London Council, is part of a much larger London Metropolitan Area. But growth has now rippled right outside even this latter area – even, in fact, beyond the official South-East region, making it necessary to talk of a Greater South East.

3

'Golden Belt' of the 1980s runs from Dorset on the south coast, via Wiltshire, Oxfordshire, Buckinghamshire, Northamptonshire, and Cambridgeshire to Suffolk on the east coast, at distances of 60 to 110 miles from central London. And the official statisticians in the Office of Population Statistics and Surveys expect this pattern to continue down to the end of the century: the 'Fringe' will have far higher growth rates than areas closer to London (Fig. 11(a) below). Within this belt, growth is highly concentrated in a few key city regions: Bournemouth–Poole, Swindon, Milton Keynes–Northampton, Peterborough–Huntingdon, and Ipswich.

So the wider London, big enough and confusing enough in 1963, is now bigger and more confusing by an order of magnitude. According to this widest definition, it now extends from Poole Harbour to the Suffolk coast, from the middle of Northamptonshire down to Sussex. The fastest-growing parts of that region, in the 1980s, were the borders of the South East and the neighbouring South West, East Midlands, and East Anglia regions. Within that fringe, certain urban areas were showing extraordinary dynamism. The question must be: what, if anything, has this vast region in common, apart from having London at its rather eccentrically positioned centre?

Clearly, it is not continuous bricks and mortar. Perhaps that might have been true if we had seen unplanned, unconstrained urban growth over these past forty years; but ever since the historic 1947 Planning Act, urban England has been contained. The best estimates we have, set out and compared by the late Robin Best in 1981, relate to the period 1961–70; at that time, the 'official' South East had between 13 and 19 per cent of its total area urbanized (Best 1981, 65). The figures for the South West and East Anglia were much lower, though there has been some urban growth since then. So the view from the aeroplane is no optical illusion: most of the extended South East is green, the towns relatively few and far between.

Perhaps, then, what the region has in common is a set of functional relationships, above all with London itself. Geographers have long liked to plot commuter flows, or trips to shop for what they call 'comparison' goods, or the catchment areas of local newspapers or radio stations, as indicators of the sphere of influence that a city or town exerts over its surrounding countryside. The latest and most sophisticated exercises of this kind have come from John Goddard's Centre for Urban and Regional Development Studies (CURDS) at the University of Newcastle-upon–Tyne (Champion *et al.* 1987). This CURDS regionalization of Britain has a particular value in analysing the parts of the country that are most heavily and complicatedly urbanized, because it is hierarchical: it shows not merely the immediate spheres around the smaller places, but also their relationship with larger higher-level catchments.

In it, London's immediate metropolitan region – with 7.8 million people in 1981, little bigger than the area of the Greater London Council – is surrounded by no less than 30 other Local Labour Market Areas (LLMAs), forming a contiguous group and occupying much of the South-East region, which are classed as 'subdominant' to the capital (Table 2 and Fig. 2). Together they form the London Metropolitan Area, with well over 12 million people at the Census of 1981. Additionally, two other places in the South East-Brighton and Portsmouth – qualify under the CURDS system as independent, freestanding metropolitan regions. Over and beyond these, the outer parts of the South East contain no less than 25 other LLMAs based on cities and towns, of which three – Luton, Oxford, and Southampton – have the title of Southern Freestanding City, indicating that they have considerable importance in their own right. And, beyond the regional limits but within our Greater South East, Bournemouth, Swindon, Northampton, and Ipswich all attract this appellation. Within the South East, only one Local Labour Market Area – Didcot in Oxfordshire – is classed as 'Rural'. Within the East Anglian fringe, there are rather more: here the major growth centres are separated by quite wide areas, where the central places – Huntingdon, Newmarket, Woodbridge – still do not qualify as fully urban on the CURDS criteria. But these areas are few and far between.

To summarize, the functional London region, joined together by complex ties of commuting and other kinds of dependence, is a vast area of over 12 million people, stretching from Basingstoke to Chelmsford, from Bishop's Stortford to Horsham. Contiguous to it, but not so strongly linked, is a whole series of other areas stretching

Table 2 Local labour market areas (LLMAs) in the South East

	No. of LLMAs	Population 1981 ('000)	Example
London	1	7 836.9	London
London subdominant cities	7	1 740.2	Southend
London subdominant towns	23	2 794.9	Maidenhead
London Metropolitan Region	*31*	*12 372.0*	
Freestanding metro areas	2	727.7	Brighton, Portsmouth

Source: Champion *et al.* (1987)

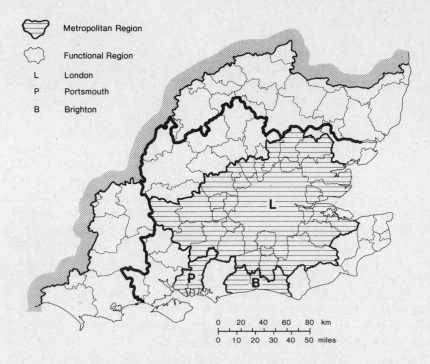

Metropolitan Region

Functional Region

L   London

P   Portsmouth

B   Brighton

```
0    20   40   60   80  km
|--+--|--+--|--+--|--+--|--+--|
0   10   20   30   40   50 miles
```

Figure 2   Greater South East: metropolitan regions and functional regions   As defined by the CURDS group at the University of Newcastle-upon-Tyne, London's metropolitan region stretches far beyond Greater London itself, even beyond the officially defined Metropolitan Area (Fig. 1). It is surrounded by a host of smaller functional regions based on the region's major towns. Portsmouth and Brighton constitute separate metropolitan areas in the CURDS scheme.

out to the South-East boundary and beyond. And these definitions are based on the functional relationships as long ago as 1971. We know from more recent analysis by the London and South East Regional Planning Conference (SERPLAN), that between 1971 and 1981 London's own commuter sphere extended relatively little (Figs 3(a)–(c)). Perhaps, since then, it has shown a quantum outward leap: in 1987 and 1988 the press was full of reports of huge increases in long-distance commuting from places like Diss in Norfolk, 80 miles from London, and Grantham in Lincolnshire, 105 miles distant. All this may be just another example of media (and estate agency) hype; maybe not.

What we do know is that by 1981, virtually the whole of the South East outside London consisted of a complex set of commuting relationships into, and between, the major centres – CURDS' London

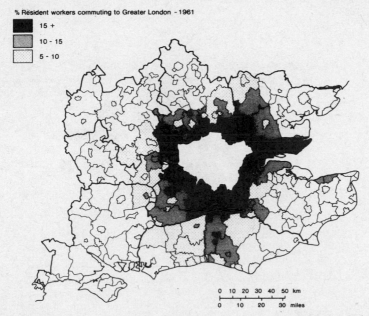

% Resident workers commuting to Greater London - 1961

- ■ 15 +
- ▨ 10 - 15
- □ 5 - 10

0 10 20 30 40 50 km
0 10 20 30 miles

Figure 3(a) The London commuter area, 1961 The commuter field of 1961 formed a fairly tight ring between 15 and 25 miles from central London, but stretched down the Brighton and Southend lines to the coast. Figs 3(a)–(c) are based on research by SERPLAN.

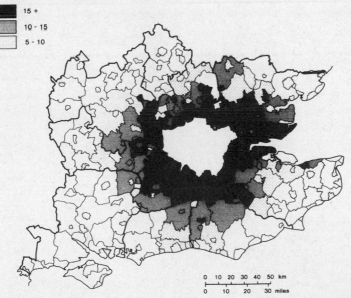

% Resident workers commuting to Greater London - 1971

- ■ 15 +
- ▨ 10 - 15
- □ 5 - 10

0 10 20 30 40 50 km
0 10 20 30 miles

Figure 3(b) The London commuter area, 1971 The commuter field extended steadily during the 1960s into the 30–40-mile belt, and in some sectors even beyond that.

7

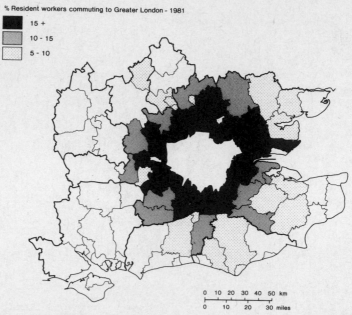

% Resident workers commuting to Greater London - 1981

- 15 +
- 10 - 15
- 5 - 10

0 10 20 30 40 50 km
0 10 20 30 miles

Figure 3(c)   The London commuter area, 1981   During the 1970s the commuter field extended far less dramatically – and even contracted in some places, indicating a development of local labour markets around the major towns of the home counties.

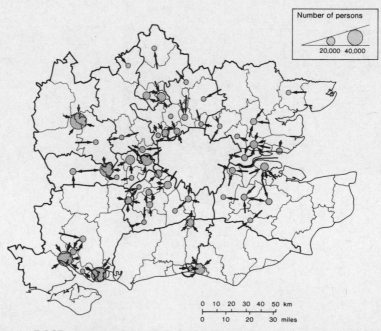

Number of persons

20,000 40,000

0 10 20 30 40 50 km
0 10 20 30 miles

Figure 4   ROSE commuter fields   By 1981, with the decentralization of employment, many of the major centres in the rest of the South East were extending their local spheres of influence over belts 10–15 miles around, which in places - especially west of London - overlapped. This map is based on research by SERPLAN.

Subdominant Cities and Towns – in such a way that one place linked itself to the next, and it in turn to the next, almost in the form of a chain (Fig. 4). This is the contemporary reality of life in the South East; and, as mobility increases, it is becoming more interdependent, and thus more complex, every day.

1

London's Problems

The central burden of this book, as of its predecessor, is this: in theory, and in popular myth, since the great Town and Country Planning Act of 1947, this vast area has been planned. The critical decisions – as to the what, where, and how much of the different activities and land uses – have been taken out of the hands of the market and given into the care of a group of professionals called planners. Like disinterested philosopher–kings, they have taken their decisions on what is best for the region, and its people, as a whole. Eschewing narrow sectional interests, they have taken into account only such considerations as efficiency, convenience, aesthetics, the conservation of the countryside and the architectural heritage, and equity as between one citizen and another.

Of course, everyone knows that it has not been like that at all. If it had, we might have or might not have liked the results, but they would have been very different from what we have. In 1963 it was already clear that planning, in this abstract sense, was not operating as its founding fathers had intended: its pure waters had been massively muddied by sectional interests, by politics, by the continuing operation of the market and the search for profit. In 1988 it is clearer than ever. The result is that what we see now, as then, is a muddle. In some respects planning has made a huge mark; in others, it hardly seems to have touched the way London and its region look or work. One might say – some have been tempted to say – that either it should have been made to work better, or the attempt to plan should have been abandoned. *London 2000* was in essence a passionate plea to make it work better. It ended with a vision – born out of youthful idealism and not a little naîvety – of the London of 2000 that might be. These were its last words:

> This London is the result of a set of positive planning actions by the community, which it need not have taken. It need not have built these New Towns; these motorways; these new shopping and office sub-centres. Indeed, it would have been easier to turn the blind eye; to prepare wholly specious and impracticable alternatives on paper, and to fail to make plans where plans would be effective. In that case we should have a different London 2000. It also would be recognizable; but chiefly through the ugliness and frustrations which have been maintained, and intensified, from the London we know now. We could have a formless, inadequately planned sprawl of offices out from central London, as suburbs sprawled between the wars; traffic gradually congealing to a stop in the centre and along the main arteries; ugly, dispiriting suburbs springing like fungi from every old town within sixty miles of St Paul's. These things are not possibilities; if my argument is correct, they are also certainties, unless the community acts soon, to recognize the practicable limits of planning, and within these limits to devise a new concept of planning, more total and effective than that which it produced in those intense wartime and early postwar years.
> Which?

Fine rhetoric, perhaps; but to little effect. Everyone knows which alternative we mostly got. As the Chinese would say, it was about 20 per cent good and 80 per cent bad. We got three New Towns (and at least three Expanded Towns – Swindon, Andover, and Basingstoke – which were New Towns in all but name). We got most of the motorways outside the capital (save, oddly, the New Kent Motorway on which the fictional citizens travelled; but, in 1988, that is due to start any moment now), yet hardly any in London itself. We got some new shopping centres, with more promised. But we also got plenty of traffic congealing to a stop, offices spreading in every direction, ugly suburbs springing like fungi, and the other horrors. So the first

11

task, this time around, must be not to look into the glorious future, but to conduct a *post mortem* on the less-than-glorious recent past; not Which?, but Why?

Hypertrophy in the Middle: London Bridge

That was the heading in *London 2000*; it still is, though both the location and the cause have changed. People are still struggling through the tube stations – but the place to see it at its worst is perhaps no longer Oxford Circus, centre of one of the big office building boom areas of the 1960s, but London Bridge. Here, the British Rail tracks from South-East London and beyond still converge to a bottleneck on their onward route to Charing Cross. Here, thousands fight their way on to the Northern Line, dubbed the 'Misery Line' because of its breakdowns and cancellations, to make their onward journey into the City.

All around, not only in the City itself but now also on this south bank of the Thames, is evidence of London's newest office boom: the one that has accompanied the Big Bang, the deregulation of the financial services sector, in October 1986. The new offices of the 1980s are quite unlike the classic high-rise model of the 1960s and 1970s, which – after a building cycle of only 25 to 30 years, shortest in London's history – they are now beginning to replace: unlike the slim Natwest Tower, London's highest; unlike Richard Rogers's glistening high-tech Lloyd's building, which users are condemning for its inadequacies barely a year after it was finished. The new buildings are fairly low by their predecessors' standards, only eight or ten stories; but no amount of post–modern architectural cladding can disguise the fact that they are extremely broad and squat. One of the most knowledgeable office architects around, Frank Duffy, describes them as looking like pre-Sullivan Chicago (Marmot & Worthington 1987). They are designed around massive trading floors, with light admitted through atria from above; they are designed, above all, for the huge quantities of wiring packed between the floors.

And here is the source of a major new controversy, just coming on the boil in 1988: as much as the towers they replace, though in a totally different way, these structures will totally alter the traditional townscape of the City of London. They are totally incompatible with human-scale urban design and traditional architectural forms, the cause to which Prince Charles and fellow-conservationists have publicly committed themselves. The first major battle in this war was just about to be fought, in mid-1988, over the redevelopment of the Paternoster area immediately north of St Paul's Cathedral – itself one of the least-loved major rebuildings of the 1960s. It will not be the last.

Yet they house fewer workers than the structures they replace. In 1963, one of the major issues of the day – indeed, of the entire decade – was the apparently uncontrollable growth of office jobs in central London, a product mainly of a loophole in the Third Schedule to the 1947 Act, brilliantly exploited by the first postwar generation of property millionaires like Joe Levy and Harry Hyams. In the mid-1960s Harold Wilson's Labour government made desperate attempts to grapple with it: George Brown's ban on office building, in November 1964, was followed by a comprehensive attempt the next year to license new office building through the issuance (or denial) of Office Development Permits. It proved a fiasco: the City complained that invisible earnings were threatened, and shortages forced up rents and brought a bonanza to the developers.

Since then, a strange set of paradoxes has transpired. Office space in central London has grown – from 98.6 million square feet in 1974 to 114.7 million in 1981 and to 117.9 million in 1983 – but office employment has barely grown at all, while total employment has fallen: from an estimated 1.4 million in 1961, to 1.1 million in 1971, to only 947 000 in 1981. Numbers commuting to central London, 1.238 million back in 1962, actually diminished to 1.075 million in 1975 and to 998 000 in 1983, since when they have risen again to 1.103 million in 1986. Total passenger miles on the London Underground system have risen much faster than that: by nearly 70 per cent in only five years, from 2.3 billion in 1982 to 3.9 billion in 1986–7; and the system is now so overloaded, with journeys 50 per cent and more up on the peak years of the 1930s, that the management are contemplating higher fares just in order to limit the demand.

The explanation of these paradoxes is simple. Office workers in central London need more and more space, partly because of generally rising standards, partly because of the need to house new technology. That last factor has become especially significant in recent years, because of the rapid advances in information technology within the financial services sector, which have demanded a new kind of wired office. At the same time, central London rents have risen dizzily, and with them the differential *vis-à-vis* anywhere else in Britain; in 1987, good central London floor space was renting at up to £60 per square foot, four to five times its equivalent in outer London or in a major South-East centre like Reading. Small wonder, then, that in the interim – enormously facilitated by the Location of Offices Bureau, set up by the then government in

13

1963 to promote outward movement from London, and summarily abolished two decades later – thousands of routine office jobs, and some headquarters, left central London for good.

But patently, the effect on central London's streets, and in its tube stations, has been negligible. The main reason is tourism. Now one of the country's major industries, it attracts 20 million overseas visitors a year. Close on half these – 8.9 million in 1986 – head for London, spending a record £3.55 billion. Government has encouraged them by massive promotion and by subsidizing a crash hotel building programme in the mid-1970s. London Transport likes them because they travel between the peak hours, spreading the load; to encourage them, and to promote off–peak travel generally, it has vigorously promoted cheap off-peak travel cards, which offer unlimited travel at zero marginal cost. The travel cards have succeeded beyond management's wildest dreams, and the result is almost a management nightmare – particularly when it is combined with a genuine fear for safety on the system, highlighted in the tragic fire at King's Cross in November 1987 when 32 people lost their lives. Meanwhile, the streets are clogged by tour buses, which crawl past the standard list of sites, or clog all available kerbside space.

The issues, then, are not very different from those 25 years earlier. Since the Big Bang of 1986 was followed by the Big Crash of 1987, there is of course no guarantee that the recent upturn in office jobs, particularly in the City, will continue. But suppose it does: may it not mean a big increase in demand for new commuter links, and if so, what will be their cost? Are there ways of diverting the demand to other parts of London? Given the nature of the financial services sector, not much of it could be diverted very far – which means to the City's fringes, as on the South Bank at Hay's Wharf, the Fleet Street area, the Barbican, Spitalfields, and – the most spectacular, most controversial development of the late 1980s – Canary Wharf in the middle of London's Docklands.

Docklands and Deptford: Revival and Recrimination

There can be no doubt about the most dramatic planning show in town during the 1980s: it is the transformation of the 8 ½ square miles of former Port of London Authority dockland, down stream from Tower Bridge, by the London Docklands Development Corporation (LDDC). So spectacular indeed is it, that the ride on the Docklands Light Railway, from Tower Gateway next to the Tower of London, via Limehouse and the Isle of Dogs Enterprise Zone to

Island Gardens at the southern tip of the Isle of Dogs opposite Greenwich, became an obligatory tourist itinerary almost from the day of opening. With the completion of the gigantic Canary Wharf development in the mid-1990s, Docklands in effect will join the twin cores of the City of London and the City of Westminster, to become London's third City.

The critics are all agreed on that. They are in vehement disagreement on almost everything else. One group, which happens to be pro-business and in general a supporter of the Thatcher government, concludes that this is an outstanding example of economic transformation and wealth creation: a totally derelict area, almost apparently without prospects, has been transformed within a mere seven years into a new town intown, with new jobs, new homes, a sparklingly new urban landscape on the water. The other group, which just happens to be pro-Labour, argues that this is the quintessence of the unacceptable face of capitalism: rampant financial speculation, creation of a Yuppie paradise, total disregard of the needs of the existing population for new jobs and low-cost housing.

There might just be a third group, though it certainly does not much get heard: it might say that what has happened was for the most part inevitable, was not all that bad, but could have been better. True, the dockers' jobs were gone, and to dream them back into existence is a pipedream; true, government policies have virtually ended low-cost council housing programmes anyway, here and everywhere else; true, the LDDC has provided plenty of land for low-cost starter housing for sale, in a virtual new town at Beckton at the far east end of the project, which all too few visitors ever see because they never get that far. But true too, much of the housing is cramped and mean, and may not even sell if the market weakens; too much of it wastes the splendid opportunities the riverfront offers; when the huge Canary Wharf office development – 45 000 workers, as big as the centre of a major English town – is finished, the Docklands Light Railway (DLR) will be near its capacity limits; true, there ought to be more shops and pubs and entertainment. Some of these represent opportunities lost until the next rebuild, whenever that may be; some people think it may be sooner than anticipated. Others merely await arrival of the right entrepreneurial spirits. In 1988, judgement on Docklands really needs to be suspended.

The point about Docklands is that, like it or not, it is so dazzling that it casts the rest of inner London's 124 square miles into a kind of deep shade. And admittedly, that is where many of those square miles naturally belong. The astonishing fact about Victorian London, in 1988, is just how much of it seems to have been visited

15

by a holocaust – not by the German bombs of 45 years ago, though almost unbelievably some of those scars are still visible, but by a more recent disaster: the great deindustrialization of the 1970s and early 1980s, which took away 255 000 manufacturing jobs, 45 per cent of the 1971 total, and another 132 000 jobs in trade and transportation industries in inner London between 1971 and 1981 alone (Hall 1987). The effect is ironically most marked in just those areas that bore the brunt of the Blitz: the manufacturing and port boroughs of east and south-east London, in the great horseshoe of what not long ago (Hall 1962) was called the Victorian manufacturing belt. Here, huge swathes of land lie derelict and still, the gaunt shells of past factories and warehouses standing as isolated ruins amidst the weeds and the rubble. Some of them – the great goods yard north of King's Cross station, the triangle of land between the railway tracks south of Deptford – are almost like mini-Docklands in themselves.

Eventually, these all seem destined to generate equal controversy. For in and around every one of them is a local community, battered and resentful at its fate, committed to defending traditional jobs and traditional ways of life, bitterly hostile to what it sees as grasping commercial developers. One such epic battle so far (Docklands) was effectively won by the development forces; another (for the Coin Street area next to the National Theatre on the South Bank) was – rather surprisingly, and only after an epic battle – won by the community. At Spitalfields Market north east of the City, the next such site, the developers seem to have secured victory again; at the King's Cross goods yard, a far bigger prize, the protagonists are girding their loins.

Around these sites, the astonishing fact is how little seems to have changed in a quarter century. The rows of yellow stock-brick housing, made by baking the excrement of Victorian Londoners and their horses, survive; so therefore does the curious informal domestic coziness of this traditional London landscape, which the Danish observer Steen Eiler Rasmussen so acutely noticed in the 1930s (Rasmussen 1937). In between them, the brave new 1950s world of the towers of the old LCC Architects' Department, those self-conscious homages to the memory of Le Corbusier, have somehow been absorbed; so have the efforts of their borough imitators, often less inspired and now equally problematic.

We too easily ignore, perhaps, that this is the landscape imagined by Patrick Abercrombie, London's most distinguished planner, when he co-authored the definitive County of London Plan in 1943 (Forshaw & Abercrombie 1943). Frederic Osborn, that sedulous campaigner for London's New Towns, condemned him for it at the time, and never ceased his battle against the high-rise reconstruction of London; but his was a lone voice in the wilderness. We know better now, with the benefit of hindsight. The fact was that we knew then, if anyone had cared to read. Osborn spelt out, month after month, that high density and high rise was a solution that nobody wanted, built at too high a cost. *London 2000* quoted him at length on that, and suggested that London might be rebuilt at densities allowing everyone a house and garden. But that would have meant massive overspill of the London poor to New Towns, and so ran right up against the political prejudices of both the urban left and the rural right; it was simply not on, and both Osborn and *London 2000* were crying for the moon. Thus, indeed, are the ordinary people betrayed by those they trust to run their lives.

It is, of course, water under the bridge now; at least, until the next rebuild, which – for some of these blocks – could be closer than we think. So it is not too soon to pose the question, How can we do it better? At what density, and in what way, should we redevelop inner London? What is the right use for the remaining tower blocks? Suitably rehabilitated, many might make superior housing for the dinkies (double income, no kids) who, so the pop sociologists tell us, are an increasing part of London's population. To get it right, we need not merely crude demographics, but also – even harder – forecasts of future life-styles.

Stuck in the Gluepot: The Problem of Mobility

One thing has not changed at all in a quarter-century: the average Londoner is still hopelessly stuck in a traffic jam. If anything, it has got worse. In December 1987, three vehicles collided near Blackfriars Underpass – itself a major traffic improvement of the early 1960s – on the Thames Embankment. Traffic immediately came to a virtual standstill, and the paralysis spread. As the rush hour approached, there was a burst water main in Hampstead and a gas leak in nearby Finchley Road. Together they caused the traffic progressively to lock in increasing circles. By about 7 in the evening, an estimated 50 000 cars were stuck in a motionless jam that stretched from Hendon in the north to New Malden in the south.

This, mercifully, was rather special. But the facts speak for themselves: total car-miles in inner London up 16 per cent between 1972 and 1986, in Greater London as a whole up 25 per cent; peak traffic up 22 per cent from 1975 to 1985; and, despite increasingly sophisticated computer traffic controls, peak period speeds down to just over 12 miles per hour, 11 per cent slower than in 1968 (Movement for London 1987). One newspaper, recently seeking to reconstruct Phineas Fogg's epic 80-day journey around the world by sea and land, ruefully commented that his first stage – from home to the station – would be no faster now than in 1873.

That the traffic was moving at all was a tribute mainly to the skill of the software writers. It certainly was not due either to increased roadspace, or to effective regulation of what limited roadspace there was. Since the Greater London Council made its historic decision in April 1973 to axe the 800-mile, £2000 million motorway programme for the capital, very little roadbuilding had been done, mainly in the form of radial motorways extended to distances between 6 and 12 miles from the centre. Instead, the funds were diverted to construction of the world's longest bypass: the 117-mile M25 orbital motorway around London, opened by Mrs Thatcher in October 1986 after ten years of construction, only a small part of which penetrated Greater London itself. The end of 1987 saw one major opening, of a 6-mile extension of the North Circular Road in east London: a major programme is promised in that sector between now and the mid-1990s, together with the comprehensive upgrading of the North Circular along virtually its whole length from Chiswick to Woodford. But that will do nothing at all to resolve the intractable problems of the gluepot ring in the rest of inner London, above all inner south London.

So London makes do with what it has got. It does not make much of it. Because human resources are pathetically inadequate – 800 traffic police, plus 1800 overextended and inadequately managed wardens – the existing parking and waiting regulations are widely disregarded. The main roads, long ago dubbed 'clearways' and supposed to be entirely free of standing vehicles at peak hours, are almost universally clogged with thousands of parked vehicles, which no one makes much effort to remove. Though 2.5 million parking tickets are issued every year, they seem to make little difference. Wheel-clamping – introduced as an experiment in parts of central and inner London, and now extended – has proved a fairly effective deterrent, but of course does not remove the obstructive vehicle. By late 1987 the Commissioner of Police for the Metropolis, Peter Imbert, was again canvassing the idea of a supplementary licence to enter central London – an idea, ironically, which was invented by staff of the Greater London Council in the early 1970s, rejected there as politically too dangerous, and then borrowed most effectively (and with acknowledgement) by Singapore, which made it world-famous.

Meanwhile, critical land use decisions were everywhere being taken with apparently complete disregard for the traffic consequences. In the Greater London Development Plan of 1970, the second comprehensive attempt ever made in London's history to plan the capital comprehensively (the first was Abercrombie's), seven sites, spaced roughly at equal intervals around the ring 4 to 6 miles from the centre, were dubbed 'major strategic shopping centres'. Chosen for their access to public transport and for their potential access to the future high-quality road system, they were to be built up into the equivalent of the major shopping centres of provincial British cities, thus taking the pressure off the overloaded West End.

The outcome, as so often in London, has been ironic. Only one, Brent Cross, planned from the start as a new American-style mall, had adequate access to a good-quality highway. (Just before Christmas 1988, with the opening of the North Circular extension in east London, a second, Ilford, achieved this also.) The others continued to extend willy-nilly. At Ealing, where a major new precinct was completed in the early 1980s, car-based shoppers leave the gridlocked North Circular Road – still untouched by improvements, at this point, in the past half-century – and thread their way through a succession of formerly quiet suburban streets until they reach a dead end, from which a right-angle bend leads into a multi-storey car park. No more eloquent comment could be found on the complete breakdown of planning in London, the failure to follow through from strategic concept to local execution, than this pathetic example.

Just down the road, speculative office blocks of the 1960s and 1970s line the Uxbridge Road, replacing the grand Victorian villas that once graced the Queen of the Suburbs. They look rather as they have been dropped here by parachute; no planning principle seems to have intervened. The car parks around them are jammed, and parking spills out on to the neighbouring residential streets, to the woe and fury of the residents. Studies show that whether rail transport is accessible or not - here it is, but only at some distance – the bulk of the workers in these suburban offices come by car; the fact is that their location makes journeys by public transport very indirect, slow, and inconvenient. So the workers here simply pour out onto the already congested roads of west London, desperately rat-running through quiet suburban back streets, in a vain search to cut their lengthening commuter trips.

Traffic and transport, then, produce another host of questions. Does London after all need new roads? Where and how they should be built? How should they be financed? How do we improve regulation on the existing network? What kinds of traffic restraint policies could prove acceptable and effective? Is it possible to plan major concentrations of offices and shops so that they are accessible to good public transport from all directions, thus making it a real alternative to the car? These were questions addressed in *London 2000*. The answers provided then did not prove acceptable; but the problem has not gone away, and it is more than time for another look.

The Land of Bypass Variegated

Beyond an invisible but significant boundary, on average about six miles from the centre, Victorian London gives way to neo-Georgian London: not the inner-London gracious landscape of squares built under the first four Georges, but the outer-London landscape of arterial roads and mock Tudor semi-detached that spread and sprawled under the fifth. Ever since writers like George Orwell vilified it in prose and Osbert Lancaster so brilliantly parodied it in his cartoons, it has been the accepted fashion to find it either irredeemably vile or patronizingly funny. Only lately is a new generation of writers coming to accept that it may have its merits. It provided good, cheap, basic housing with gardens for people who could never earlier have aspired to anything like it. It has proved adaptable to change, absorbing numerous remodellings and improvements. Its landscape has softened since the trees have matured. Now that successive generations have got used to the fact of commuting first 30, then 50, now 100 miles, the 8- or 10-mile trip on the tube to town seems of no consequence at all. Interwar suburbia, now the motorways have bypassed the bypasses, has even absorbed mass motorization – for which, contrary to what many think, it was never designed.

There are some snags about it, minor for the most part. The houses are not as big as they might have been, and – especially down market – the rooms are pokey. (But many compare well with what the same spec-builders are offering today, 40 or 50 miles farther out: an apt comment on human progress.) The road layouts are sometimes inconvenient and often unimaginative, since – again, especially at the lower end of the market spectrum – the aim was to build fast and build cheap. The shopping parades around the tube stations do not adapt well to hordes of traffic; the retailers are increasingly responding to that by developing superstores on redundant industrial and warehouse sites, but there are sometimes problems of access there too. Yet the irony is that these parts of London, vilified since they were built, have worn about the best.

But here, too, there are some questions. The suburbs will not last for ever. In the late 1980s, they are between 50 and 70 years old. Not all were well built; not all have been well maintained. The cost of maintaining them will surely rise, and their owners may not all be able to meet it. Some may well degenerate into the new slums, and the question of clearance and rebuilding will then loom large. The shopping parades, which will prove increasingly unattractive to car-based shoppers, will demand reconstruction; indeed, some, such as Harrow, are already undergoing it. Some of these questions may wait awhile; others will not.

Green Belt and Outer Ring: Plans and Half-Plans

About 15 miles on average from the centre, suburbia abruptly ends; all of a sudden, the lines of semi-detached houses give way to green fields. The speculative builders of the 1930s were stopped in their tracks, first by the Second World War, then by the imposition of the postwar planning system. The great Town and Country Planning Act of 1947, passed by Attlee's reforming Labour government, effectively nationalized the right to develop land, and transferred this power to the local planning authorities. Thus, for the first time, they were able simply to say no to development, without fear of ruinous compensation claims; and say no they did. Following the lead in Abercrombie's great regional plan of 1944, and encouraged by government in a celebrated circular – Number 42 of 1955 – they created a massive Green Belt, 5–10 miles wide, around the metropolis. Beyond Edgware, you may still see traces of the Northern Line extension, started before the war but abandoned after it, when it became clear that the passengers would never be there; the vast Aldenham Garage, standing anomalously in the middle of the Green Belt, was intended as the car sheds.

Developers have constantly tried to nibble at the Green Belt; for forty years, with few exceptions, they have been relentlessly fought back. It is true that the M25 and its vast interchanges have eaten up a goodly part of it; but Abercrombie himself had proposed a recreational parkway here. It is true also that very little of the Green Belt is actually available for the recreation of the Londoner, and that bits of it are not very prepossessing. The point, as one minister said long ago, is that it may not all be very beautiful and it may not all be very green, but without it the town would never end; the very essence of the Green Belt is that it is a stopper (q. Hall *et al*. 1973, II, 58).

21

Beyond it, the fields roll on: here, in what Abercrombie called the Outer Country Ring and the statisticians used to call the Outer Metropolitan Area, the idea is what both Abercrombie and his predecessor Raymond Unwin called Towns against a Background of Open Country. Here are the eight original New Towns for London: a main element in Abercrombie's 1944 regional plan, begun between 1946 and 1950 under the New Towns Act of 1946, and faithfully planned to follow the precepts of Ebenezer Howard's *Garden Cities of To-morrow*, perhaps the most influential book in the modern history of town planning (Howard 1898). They have long ceased to be new; most were effectively completed in the mid-1960s, and two whole generations have been born and grown up in them. They have been the subject of minor criticisms over the years: social facilities were scarce at the beginning, and new residents were said to suffer 'New Town Blues' (though ironically, that journalistic conclusion was based on a study that was not of a New Town at all, but of a peripheral housing estate); the architecture was said to be bland, and the planning insufficiently urban.

But most of the hard words are forgotten, and no one now seems to have anything but good words for the New Towns. They have achieved what they were meant to achieve: they are self-contained towns for living and working; they have achieved a rough social balance; they have provided good homes with plenty of green space; their town centres are lively and bustling; they have more than repaid the public investment in them. Similar in character – in fact, indistinguishable to the eye – are two major town expansions built under different parliamentary powers, those of the 1952 Town Development Act (Basingstoke and Andover south-west of London), plus a host of much smaller expansions of country towns, most of them in the rural heart of East Anglia.

Much farther out – 50 and more miles from London – are the three New Towns, more properly New Cities, of the 1960s: Milton Keynes, Northampton, and Peterborough. These have a different character: they are much bigger; two of them are built around existing old towns; these same two are even outside the boundaries of the South-East region: and none is yet complete. Similar in size and position is Swindon, which happens to have been built under the 1952 Act but is in effect the fourth New City of the South-East fringe.

Important and visible as the New Towns and New Cities are, perhaps the most significant fact about them is that, in terms of hard numbers, they are a relatively unimportant part of the great ring of growth around London. In total, between their designations and the end of 1986, they have housed a net additional population of 606 000

(Table 3). Swindon might add about 40 000 to that figure, Andover 20 000, Basingstoke 50 000: say 700 000. That compares with a total population increase in ROSE, between 1951 and 1986, of no less than 3 725 000. The New Towns and Cities have housed less than one-fifth of the additional people.

The other four-fifths, together with a goodly part of the new jobs that have accompanied the population growth, have gone into suburban growth around the existing towns and even villages. For the most part, the planning system has worked to concentrate as many as possible into suburban fringe developments around the major towns of the Outer Metropolitan Area: places like Reading, Aylesbury, Luton, Chelmsford, Southend, Rochester–Chatham–Gillingham, Maidstone, Horsham, Guildford, and Aldershot–Farnborough–Fleet. Nearly all these places lie in a ring 30–40 miles from London, thus about 10 miles farther out than the eight Mark I new towns. They were already substantial market and industrial towns before the Second World War; several of them were county towns. They have expanded dramatically since 1945, some of them nearly doubling their population when contiguous suburbs are taken

Table 3 New Towns in the Greater South East

Name	Date of designation	Date of completion	Population Original	Population End-1986
Basildon	1949	1986	25 000	103 000
Bracknell	1949	1982	5 100	50 800
Crawley	1947	1962	9 100	72 900
Harlow	1947	1980	4 500	78 000
Hatfield	1948	1966	8 500	25 200
Hemel Hempstead	1947	1962	21 000	77 100
Stevenage	1946	1980	6 700	75 700
Welwyn Garden City	1948	1966	18 500	40 500
Total Mark I			98 400	523 200
(Net growth)				(+424 800)
Milton Keynes	1967	1992	40 000	133 000
Northampton	1968	1985	133 000	170 000
Peterborough	1967	1988	81 000	132 500
Total Mark II			254 000	435 500
(Net growth)				(+181 500)
Total New Towns			352 400	958 700
(Net growth)				(+606 300)

Source: Potter (1987)

---

into account. But, unlike the new and expanded towns, there has been far too little accompanying public investment in the necessary roads and other infrastructure.

The results are all too plain to see. Reading, 40 miles west of London, is a particularly melancholy example. Until 1939 it was a typical Wessex county town – it actually appears in Hardy's *Jude the Obscure* – serving its local rural population, and dependent on its three basic industries of Beer, Bulbs, and Biscuits. Then, because it lay in the very centre of what came to be known as the M4 Corridor, it attracted high-tech industry relocating from London and new spin-off firms; later, the pool of skilled labour and technical services, together with nearness to Heathrow airport, brought major American multinationals like Digital (Hall *et al.* 1987). Excellent train services to London – including British Rail's first InterCity 125 service, inaugurated in 1976 – helped attract service industries relocating their routine activities from London, making it eventually the fourth office centre in South-East England after the City, the West End and Croydon. In 1970 the official *Strategy for the South-East* designated it as the centre of one of five major growth areas intended to house the lion's share of the region's population growth down to the year 2000. That brought bitter local resistance across the whole area, but particularly from the rural areas outside Reading. There was an interim compromise: the first major share of growth, homes for about 20 000 people, would go into Lower Earley, a new suburb south east of the town, itself forming an extension of a huge suburban outgrowth of the 1960s and 1970s.

The result, in the late 1980s, is a mess. For twenty years the town centre has looked like a building site, which it is. It still does. Everywhere new office blocks are separated by vast open lots used as temporary car parks, waiting their turn to become more office blocks. There is a half-finished inner distributor road, full of spaghetti junctions, which plunges its traffic into an immovable mass of cars trying to get out of the town. The necessary radial links, long planned and promised, still do not exist. With luck, they may arrive in the early 1990s.

Commuters to Lower Earley grind their way home along the old road to Aldershot, an upgraded country lane. Since there is no direct access to the suburb, they must make a vast dog-leg around Whiteknights Park, a huge country park now swallowed up by the town, which is the home of the university. Many try to take short-cuts through the campus. Extricating themselves from a half-mile jam outside the university entrance, from which campus traffic pours, they go through two more dog-legs onto more country lanes.

Within the suburb, the planned roads were all cut in half as an economy measure. Dense traffic flows pass along narrow 7-metre roads between high brick walls, immediately behind which are the bedrooms of the new brick boxes. Small wonder that they are festooned with estate agents' 'For Sale' signs; presumably, their residents have already had enough. There are no pubs, no restaurants, no meeting places; no shops, apart from one superstore, which is perversely reached from a blind T-junction, stuck at the top of a hill. The whole thing looks as if it had been planned by accident, or as if someone had got the plans mixed up.

That, notice, is the result of planning – or of what passes for statutory town planning after more than thirty years of practice. It is only the most spectacular example of what is going on all over the South East, in every town up to 100 and more miles from Charing Cross. Not all are this bad. Nor even, to be quite fair, is Lower Earley as bad as much of what was done in the 1950s and early 1960s, pilloried in *London 2000*: the houses are grouped around cul-de-sac courts from which through traffic is excluded; there is an attempt to provide a segregated system of safe routes for pedestrians and cyclists, especially important in a community that contains so many mothers and children; and so on.

But there are too many mistakes that ought not to have happened. And the basic reason is significant: it is a combination of lack of money, which always means a botched job, and a desperate anxiety to squeeze the last house onto the available land. The private developers of course wanted that, because they had paid dearly for the land; the planners were willing to let them have it, because every brick box shoehorned in here was one less angry protest somewhere out there in the well-heeled villages.

Just how shrill and well orchestrated those protests could be emerges from the saga of Heseltown. With Lower Earley well into construction, the problem was to find a location for the next tranche of new housing for Berkshire. The Central Berkshire Plan was revised; the minister at the time, Michael Heseltine, in 1981 amended it to include 8000 more houses. The favoured site was north of Wokingham and Bracknell. The residents fought the proposal, and the local district council simply refused to incorporate it into its own plans.

Meanwhile the next round of the battle is just beginning. In 1988 Nicholas Ridley, Heseltine's successor as Secretary of State for the Environment, modified the new Berkshire Structure Plan by adding provision for 7000 new homes, raising the total from 36 500 to 43 500. Four thousand of these would go on to the bitterly fought ground north of Bracknell, where Ridley added another 2500 to the already-contentious 1500 in the plan. This provoked a storm of protest from the locals, who demonstrated by blocking a local road, and from their MPs; by May 1988 it had become national headline news.

Meanwhile, a few miles to the south west in Hampshire, Consortium Developments – a group representing nine of the country's biggest builders, some of whom built Lower Earley – have proposed a new town, or new community, for 12 000 people on a 710-acre site ten miles south of Reading at a place called Foxley Wood. It went to public inquiry in June 1988 just as this book was being completed. Only five miles to the south another group proposes another community at Hook, a place rejected as a site for a New Town for London overspill after another battle as long ago as 1961. To the north, yet another development group proposes a major satellite just south of Reading itself; and another has unveiled a scheme next door to it, which would provide a kind of foil to Lower Earley on the town's south-west flank. Each of these will be bitterly fought, as will similar proposals across the face of the South East. But some at least are almost certain to succeed. Perhaps some of them will manage to avoid Lower Earley's mistakes. Whether this game of roulette by public inquiry is the best way of securing orderly, high-quality, urban development is of course another matter altogether. It is one of the main questions this book must address.

The Central Problem

So that rhetorical question, posed at the end of *London 2000*, has to receive a melancholy answer: *yes*, we did have a formless, inadequately planned sprawl of offices out from central London; *yes*, we did have traffic congealing to a stop in the centre and along the main arteries; *yes*, we did get ugly, dispiriting, demoralizing suburbs springing like fungi from every old town within sixty miles of St Paul's. True, there were some credit items on the balance sheet too: three more New Towns, and some town expansions, of high quality; the radial motorways at last linked by the M25 orbital, as Abercrombie had planned as long ago as 1944; a score of country parks; quite a lot of sympathetic new development; a much more sympathetic attitude to urban conservation. But they were not enough. We could have done much better; we still could.

The question is, How? What mechanisms would be needed? In particular, what combination of public and private money, through what kind of administrative organization? That, again, was a subject that deserved, and got, extended attention in the original *London 2000*. Like so much else there, there was little result. But again, the problem has failed to go away; and the results of the failure to act are all too plain to see.

The extraordinary fact, then, is that so much of it went on happening as it had happened before: badly. And among a complex skein of reasons, there was one in particular, the one with which the opening chapter of *London 2000* concluded, and with which this successor must also conclude. The question was, and is, *Shall London Grow?* All along, ever since people became concerned about the planning of London in the 1930s, there has been a powerful body of opinion that has basically wanted London to stop growing. That was a central tenet of the Barlow Report of 1940, which set the framework for much of the subsequent postwar planning of the London region; it was a central assumption of the Abercrombie 1944 plan, which saw the construction of the new and expanded towns as a strictly limited once-for-all decentralization measure, after which London and its region would relapse into some sort of steady state; it has underlain much of the policy thinking in the counties around London ever since that time.

But, of course, it has not happened. London itself has not grown, because the Green Belt would not let it; but instead, its growth has leapfrogged the Green Belt, moving out in ever-widening circles, 30, then 50, now 100 or more miles from the capital. And the fact that growth in the South East appears to be slowing down is a pure optical illusion: the zone of growth is now lapping out beyond the boundaries of the region, into the South West and the East Midlands and East Anglia; hence the need for an extended definition of the region.

Yet it has been resisted every inch of the way. The inhabitants of the shires, particularly the rural inhabitants, want only to pull up the drawbridge: NIMBY, Not In My Back Yard. They fought the New Towns; they have fought every suburban expansion large and small. Their attitude is comprehensible and logical enough: most were not born there, but came there to enjoy a rural way of life; they do not want it disturbed. But, extended across the region, it has dire consequences for all those others who seek a place to live. It means that they are fobbed off with homes that are smaller, meaner, and dearer, in suburbs that are environmentally poorer, than need have been the case. During 1987, report after report from the building societies spoke of the vast and growing divergence in housing prices between the South and the North of England; one estimated that the average price in London was rising £53 a day. Eventually, of course, this must have serious consequences not merely for the people who bear the brunt, but also for their actual or potential employers, who are faced with the need to pay an escalating southern premium in order to attract staff at all.

Some have argued – eloquently, during the 1970s – that the answer was to divert the population flow back into London. While we were covering the Home Counties with bricks and mortar, this argument ran, there was increasing urban wasteland in the heart of London. Redevelop this, and much of the apparent problem will go away. Arguments like these led to the major shift in government policy in the Callaghan Labour government of the late 1970s, represented in the White Paper of 1977 and the Inner Urban Areas Act of 1978, which effectively switched money from the New Towns programme to inner-city revitalization in such areas as London Docklands. The evidence is now coming in: it is that such schemes are at last helping to stem the outflow of people from London, but that there is no way that they can serve as a long-term substitute for new building in ROSE. Indeed, with the completion of Docklands in the early 1990s, much of this once-for-all opportunity will be gone, and the outward drift will continue as strongly as ever.

Others might argue – indeed, ministers are rumoured to argue – that this is just a matter of old-fashioned market economics: let the price rise, and sooner or later firms will relocate to the North, thus re-equilibriating the British space economy. But this ignores that the price system is not fixed in a free market: ever since we passed that fateful 1947 Act, for good or ill, land and house prices are the direct result of the planning system. And the evidence, to be later presented, is fairly overwhelming that its effect has been to drive prices up artificially: otherwise, why should prices be so much higher in the South East than in the North West, though the latter has far less available building land?

Attitudes to growth, then, remain the central problem. Despite the new political climate of the 1980s, with the emphasis on wealth creation and economic freedom, in the sphere of planning, ministers have never dared take the dash for growth that they have so long promised. They have made forays into enemy territory, in the form of speculative White and Green Papers; but, come time for the frontal attack, they have failed to blow the bugle. That of course only demonstrates the size and strength of the army that faces them. Unless this issue can be resolved, we shall continue to muddle through with the curious half-planning that we have used since the 1940s; and the results will continue to be as melancholy. So it must be the first question now to address.

2
London's Growth

To understand better London's present problems, above all to understand the problem of its growth, some history is needed. To do it justice would need another book. So this must be selective.

London: The Unique City

That was the title that Steen Eiler Rasmussen gave in 1937 to his study of London's growth and character, still the most perceptive and most sympathetic study of the subject ever written (Rasmussen 1937). Rasmussen's point was that London had grown in a way completely unlike the other great cities of Europe. Because of England's early political stability, from medieval times onward it did not have to be constricted by a city wall. The ancient City of London, the famous Square Mile, sprawled out beyond the Roman gates of Aldgate, Bishopsgate, Moorgate, Aldersgate, and Ludgate. What Rasmussen could not know, what no one knew until archaeologists unearthed the fact in 1987, was that the first Saxon London was outside the Roman walls too, along the Roman road that is now the Strand. Then the Saxon kings established their royal palace on an island in the marshes, at what became Westminster. From that time on, London grew as a two-centred city:

29

the commercial city in the east, and the political city to the west, joined from earliest times by the Saxon city that became a kind of suburb to both.

Still, for centuries London did not need to exploit its freedom much. It remained a remarkably small place by our standards. It had an estimated 35 000 people in 1377, perhaps 200 000 in 1600. Then, with its growth as a world trade centre, began its really meteoric rise. It doubled its population in the 17th century, to 550 000 in 1700, doubled it again during the 18th century, to 1 million at the first Census in 1801, and doubled it again in the first half of the 19th century, to close on 2 million; it had 4.5 million by 1881, 6.5 million by 1911.

But, down to about 1861 – the point can be fairly precisely dated – it did not expand much physically. Indeed, during the first half of the 19th century, people packed themselves in more and more closely; densities actually increased. The reason was transport, or rather the lack of it. The rich had hackney carriages, the middle class had horse buses or stage coaches, but most of the population had to walk to their work and to everything else: Dickens, in *Sketches by Boz*, gives a graphic picture of the great morning flows of pedestrians converging on the City. Since most jobs then were in and around the City, and since there is a limit to human endurance, this meant that most of mid-19th century London's 2 million people were crowded within three miles, or one hour's walk, of the centre. That limit comfortably circumscribed the great upper-class squares of Mayfair and Marylebone and Belgravia, the solid middle-class areas of Bloomsbury and Barnsbury and Bayswater, the artisan quarters of Pimlico and Lambeth, the teeming rookeries of St Giles and Shoreditch and Wapping.

But then, rapidly, London's growth underwent a major change. Some of the railway companies introduced season tickets. Others were forced to introduce workmen's fares, as a condition of extending their lines through areas of demolished working-class housing. The world's first underground railway, a shallow steam–hauled subway, opened in 1863; 21 years later it had been extended to form a continuous circle linking the more affluent inner suburbs with the City. From 1855, the London General Omnibus Company developed a network of horse bus routes; from the 1870s, horse trams supplemented them in the inner suburbs.

London was now free to spread; and spread it did, in long tentacles up to 8 or 10 miles along the railway lines and a few main radial highways, more evenly where the horse buses and trams trundled. The villa builders created scores of new suburbs within a few years: Highbury and Hornsey, Bedford Park and Brondesbury Park, Streatham and Sydenham, and many many more. Most were for the solid Victorian middle class. But in North-East London, where the Great Eastern Railway was compelled to offer cheap workmen's trains into Liverpool Street, there developed huge working-class suburbs: Tottenham and Edmonton and Enfield, Walthamstow and Leyton. Thus, while continental cities grew through high-density apartments, London could grow via single-family homes for rich and poor alike.

At this time, however, it remained an ideal: many poor families were still trapped in central slums, still lived in a single room. Technical limitations continued to put limits on London's growth. Horse trams and buses moved at only 6 or 7 miles per hour, little more than a brisk walking pace. Steam trains accelerated slowly, so stations were widely spaced. Feeder-buses were often few, so suburbs developed within a few hundred yards of the stations. The big change came after 1890, with electric traction. At the same time, new tunnelling techniques allowed the construction of deep-level tube railways through the London clay. Three of the tubes were built by an American buccaneer capitalist, Charles Tyson Yerkes, who clearly intended them as a vehicle for massive land speculation; but he died before they opened. Rather more slowly than in Germany or America, after 1900 the tram lines were electrified too. The London County Council, under socialist management, developed a dense network in South London and in North-East London, with cheap workmen's fares, creating new working-class suburbs; here the trams were patently the 'gondolas of the people', in Richard Hoggart's graphic phrase. In west London a commercial company, the London United Tramways, developed feeder-services radiating from the tube stations; it was duly taken over by the tube company. The London General Omnibus Company motorized itself, and was in turn taken over by the tubes. All this happened in a very short time, between 1890 and 1910.

The Creation of Modern London, 1919-39

Now all was in place for the creation of modern London. It was essentially the creation of two men, Albert Stanley (Lord Ashfield) and his lieutenant Frank Pick. As chairman and commercial manager of the London Underground group – and, after its creation in 1933, London Transport – they inherited Yerkes's empire, and realized the plan that he had doubtless intended. Between the two world wars

they extended their tubes out into open country, planned bus routes
to fan out from the new stations, and waited for the builders. They
did not have to wait long. South of the river the Southern Railway,
under the equally dynamic leadership of Herbert Walker, electrified
itself and did the same thing (Hall 1988).

The circumstances, it must be said, were uniquely favourable.
World-wide depression had cut the costs of building materials,
and of building labour, to an historic all-time low. Agricultural
depression, too, made farmers anxious to sell their land: the best
crop, as one observer put it at the time, was a crop of bungalows.
Furthermore, interest rates were at a minimum, making mortgage
payments readily bearable, even for families with modest incomes.
A flourishing building society movement provided the funds. The
growth of white-collar employment in London, a product of the
increasing bureaucratization of industry and the growth of government, provided a huge market with stable incomes, even in the
depths of the Depression. And of course, planning controls were at a
minimum. Though Parliament passed Town Planning Acts – in 1909,
1924, and 1932 – they basically empowered local councils to make
town planning schemes for new suburban areas, which if anything
facilitated the task of the building industry. Because the problem of
compensation still proved insuperable, these authorities could do
nothing to stop the onward march of the speculative builders.

By the late 1930s, the results were worrying many in what might be
called the thinking classes. Some, like the geographer Dudley Stamp,
showed that bricks and mortar were eating up much of our top-
quality agricultural land, especially in the fertile market gardening
plain west of London. Many more, like Patrick Abercrombie and his
fellow-founders of the Council for the Preservation (later Protection)
of Rural England, deplored the loss of traditional countryside.
Frederic Osborn and his fellow–campaigners for Garden Cities,
who followed the precepts set out by Ebenezer Howard in his
classic *Garden Cities of to-morrow*, argued that the people would be
more happily housed in places like the pioneer Garden Cities of
Letchworth, 35 miles north of London, or Welwyn, 20 miles away.
Others contrasted the growth of London with the depressed poverty
of areas like North-East England and South Wales, where up to 40
or 50 per cent of the work-force remained idle; why should not the
new industries, then burgeoning along the North Circular Road and
the Great West Road, be somehow persuaded to locate in Jarrow or
Merthyr Tydfil instead? Many others, as already noticed in Chapter 1,
simply deplored the taste of the builders and their lower-middle-class
clients: they did not like the look of it.

Barlow, Abercrombie and After, 1940-59

The coalition – which united left and right of the political spectrum, Garden City enthusiasts as well as the rural squirearchy – proved irresistible. Early in 1937, as one of his first acts on becoming prime minister, Neville Chamberlain – who had taken a passionate interest in planning questions ever since he was mayor of Birmingham – appointed a Royal Commission on the Geographical Distribution of the Industrial Population, under the chairmanship of Sir Anderson Montague Barlow. It reported in January 1940, not a propitious time. But it proved to be the most important single influence in the creation of the modern British planning system. On London, it concluded:

> It is not possible from the evidence submitted to us to avoid the conclusion that the disadvantages in many, if not most of the great industrial concentrations, alike on the strategical, the social, and the economic side, do constitute serious handicaps and even in some respects dangers to the nation's life and development, and we are of opinion that definite action should be taken by Government towards remedying them.... The continued drift of the population to London and the Home Counties constitutes a social, economic and strategical problem which demands immediate attention (Royal Commission 1940, paras. 413, 428)

It must be said – *London 2000* said it – that this conclusion was based on flimsy and contradictory evidence. Many of the disadvantages of the 'great industrial concentrations', such as poor housing and low levels of public health, did not even then apply to London. Others, like overcrowding, traffic congestion, high land values, and long journeys to work, undoubtedly did; so, presumably, did the strategical disadvantages, which the Commissioners – sitting at the time of the Munich crisis of 1938 - heard in camera, and which may have proved decisive. In any event, it was a conclusion fortified by the prejudices of many who gave evidence; and in turn it fortified the prejudices of its readers. The fact is, as *London 2000* argued, that many of these ills might have been put right by better planning *within* the London region, rather than by trying to divert its growth altogether; but this seems not to have been considered.

Finally, though, Barlow went much wider, and vaguer. The Commission accepted implicitly the London County Council's testimony that Greater London 'is already larger than is desirable on proper planning principles or in the interests of the population of the county of London' (1940, para. 171), a view based on the fundamentalist dogma that the right-sized London was that within the old LCC boundaries. But underlying this was a principle that seemed to have affected much of their thinking: a concept of *national balance*:

> The concentration in one area of such a large proportion of the national population as is contained in Greater London, and the attraction to the Metropolis of the best industrial, financial, commercial, and general ability constitute a serious drain on the rest of the country. (Royal Commission 1940, para. 171)

At a time when the North/South divide is again the topic of the hour, this argument deserves taking more seriously than I took it in *London 2000*. Other countries, like West Germany and the United States, have strong independent regional cities: we do not, with the partial exception of those quasi-capitals, Cardiff and Edinburgh. The fact is that the way to help build them is through a genuine decentralization of economic and political power to the regions. This has been endlessly debated, in particular during the great devolution debate of the 1970s; the debate came to an effective end when the people of Scotland did not support even the weak form of devolution that was proposed. We shall doubtless return to a national debate on the issue; meanwhile we must do the best we can, by building up one or more northern centres – above all through better transport and communications – to provide real competition to London for high–level service functions. The Town and Country Planning Association proposed just such a strategy in November 1987: Greater Manchester, they suggested, should be developed as a major northern counter-magnet, exploiting its commercial pre-eminence and its air traffic linkages, through improved high–speed rail services and advanced telecommunications (TCPA 1987).

Barlow, half a century ago, did not propose anything like that. The interesting reason was that the Commissioners were obsessed by manufacturing industry, and that this obsession passed over into postwar planning policy. The report noticed that London and the home counties had attracted a disproportionate share – 42 per cent – of new jobs between 1923 and 1937. It attributed this to the pull of the home and export markets which were so strongly concentrated there, and thought that in the absence of action the trend would simply continue. It failed to appreciate, perhaps because the then data were deficient, that many of the extra jobs were not in manufacturing but in services, particularly in offices. So, instead of proposals to reorganize national commercial and political life, the report suggested regulation of new factory jobs. A majority of Commissioners wanted this for the South East; a radical minority – including the influential Abercrombie – for the entire country. The minority won: the Distribution of Industry Act of 1945 established national control over factory industry, new and extended, through a system of Industrial Development Certificates from the then Board of Trade.

More or less enthusiastically, dependening on the winds of political change, the Board and its successors administered the controls until they were swept away by the Thatcher government in the early 1980s. Detailed study has now made clear that the controls were not nearly as effective as was hoped. For good economic and strategic reasons, many growing firms – above all in the high-tech electronics field – were given certificates to relocate out of London not to the Development Areas, but into the western crescent of Hampshire, Berkshire, and Buckinghamshire, there creating the nucleus of what came to be known as the M4 Corridor. Offices and office work were totally outside national regulation until an Act of 1965, and – as already seen in Chapter 1 – that proved ineffectual. So the great bulk of employment growth escaped the controls altogether.

The Barlow Commission did not merely propose controls on employment. It also called for effective physical limits on London's growth, through a more efficient town and country planning system, to be realized via an attack on the problem of compensation and betterment. After the Second World War, the Attlee government grasped the nettle. As already seen in Chapter 1, the 1947 Town and Country Planning Act effectively nationalized development rights and then re–vested them in the new county planning authorities, which were thus effectively empowered to stop development altogether. These authorities used the new powers enthusiastically to implement the main lines of Abercrombie's Greater London Plan of 1944, which had called for the establishment of a Green Belt to halt London's further growth and – a result of redevelopment of blitzed and blighted areas – the planned decentralization ('overspill') of 1 033 000 people and their jobs away from the capital to new and expanded towns beyond it. With very minor exceptions, London's growth was halted; slowly, and in the first years painfully, first the New Towns and then the Expanded Towns came into being, the former under the powers of the New Towns Act of 1946, the latter under the Town Development Act of 1952. Almost unbelievably, the dreams of the utopians seemed to have come to pass.

That, perhaps, was because the utopians had finally found such an effective spokesman. Abercrombie was 65 years old – academic retirement age – when he was called upon to undertake the great labour of his life. He triumphantly rose to the occasion. The point about his plan is its extraordinary cartoon-like simplicity, which conceals great subtlety. London, that most chaotic, that least organized, of all the world's great cities, was at last to have an order imposed upon it. But it was to be an organic order: it would arise almost naturally, out of the old London, because it was an order that was lurking just underneath the chaotic surface. London, Abercrombie argued, was – just like the cliché – a collection of villages. They could no longer be easily recognized; but by building a hierarchy of new arterial and sub-arterial highways, you would not only relieve traffic congestion and make the streets safer, you would also define the edges of London's local communities. And the really major ringways would additionally define critical breaks in London's physical and functional structure: the edge of the central area, the edge of the densely built-up inner Victorian London, the edge of suburbia against open countryside.

Further, this organic structure was to be continued far out, across the rest of the region. But now it was to be turned inside out, rather like one of those black–white optical tricks: instead of urban communities separated by highways in park strips, now there would be self-contained exurban communities – the new and expanded towns – against a continuous background of open space (Fig. 5). It recalled, once again, the easy organic character of the country town nestling in the womb of its surrounding countryside. No one, whether red radical or true blue conservative, could be against it. It rallied people of good will, of every shade of persuasion.

The Search for a New Strategy: 1960–79

It was, of course, too good to be true. Two things went wrong, almost from the beginning. First, as noted, there was no way of stopping further job growth in London and the surrounding area. This attracted in-migrants, something Barlow and Abercrombie had thought must not and assumed would not happen. Second, completely unexpected by the demographers and therefore by the planners, from 1955 to 1964 the birth rate rose. By the mid-1960s the national population was increasing by (as the phrase then had it) 'a Bristol a year', that is about 700 000 annually.

Almost half of this net gain – 1.1 out of 2.4 million between 1951 and 1961 – was in the South East. During that decade, it formed a

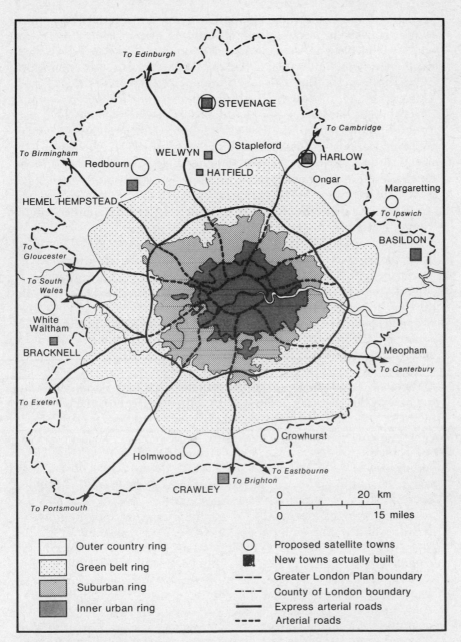

Figure 5   The Abercrombie Plan 1944   Abercrombie's Greater London Plan provided for a Green Belt to contain London's further sprawl, and for an overspill of more than a million people to New and Expanded Towns. A series of radical and circumferential highways would define London's neighbourhoods and, outside London itself, link the entire complex together.

37

solid ring of growth around London, roughly 15 – 35 miles from the centre, and spilling down the Brighton line to the south coast (Fig. 6(a)). By the 1960s the growth had slackened to about 36 per cent of the England and Wales total; it had moved farther out, to form a wide but discontinuous ring some 25-70 miles from the centre (Fig. 6(b)). This slackening of growth was in large measure due to accelerating population decline in London, which lost some 165 000 people in the 1950s but 0.5 million in the 1960s. The Outer Metropolitan Area was the main beneficiary, gaining 1 million in the 1950s, 800 000 in the next decade. As already seen in Chapter 1, the New and Expanded Towns took only a small part of the growth. Much more went into suburban accretions to the existing towns of the Outer Metropolitan Area, which took the form of speculative housing, much of it innocent of much plan or design.

Clearly, something had to be done. From 1960 onwards there was a complete review of government policy, resulting in a cascade of official reports. The first, the *South East Study*, caused a popular sensation in 1964 with its forecast that between 1961 and 1981 the South East (including East Anglia) would gain 3.5 million extra people. To help house them, the *Study* proposed new cities at Bletchley, at Newbury, and between Southampton and Portsmouth, and what it called big new expansions at Ashford, Ipswich, Stansted, Northampton, and Swindon.

These proposals met very different fates. Bletchley became Milton Keynes, Newbury was dropped (and the centre effectively transferred to Swindon), while it was determined that South Hampshire would grow without much encouragement; the Ashford, Ipswich, and Stansted proposals all disappeared, but Northampton and Peterborough joined Milton Keynes as Mark II New Towns, designated in 1967-8. Meanwhile, in 1967 the South East Economic Planning Council – a new advisory body – suggested joining London to the major growth centres by discontinuous corridors of growth; in the resulting furore, the government set up yet another study in co-operation with the local planning authorities. In 1970 it produced a *Strategic Plan for the South East*, the definitive successor to the 1944 Abercrombie Plan and the most important regional planning document for the region to appear since then.

The *Strategic Plan* reiterated the message of the 1964 *Study*: come what may, the region must continue to plan for growth. Between 1966 and 2001 it forecast an increase in population from 17.0 to 21.6 million. Since Greater London would continue to suffer marginal losses before stabilizing in the 1990s, all must be housed in the Outer Metropolitan Area, a gain of 3.1 million, and in the Outer South East,

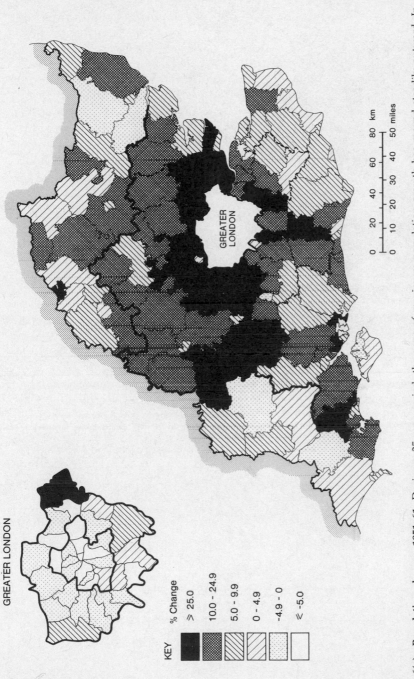

GREATER LONDON

KEY

% Change

▨ ≥ 25.0

▨ 10.0 – 24.9

▨ 5.0 – 9.9

▨ 0 – 4.9

▨ -4.9 – 0

☐ < -5.0

0   20   40   60   80 km
0 10 20 30 40 50 miles

Fig 6(a) Population change, 1951–61. During a 35-year period, the zone of maximum population growth has moved steadily outward. In the 1950s it formed a tight ring immediately around London, including the eight original New Towns, but extending further westwards into the central Berkshire growth zone.

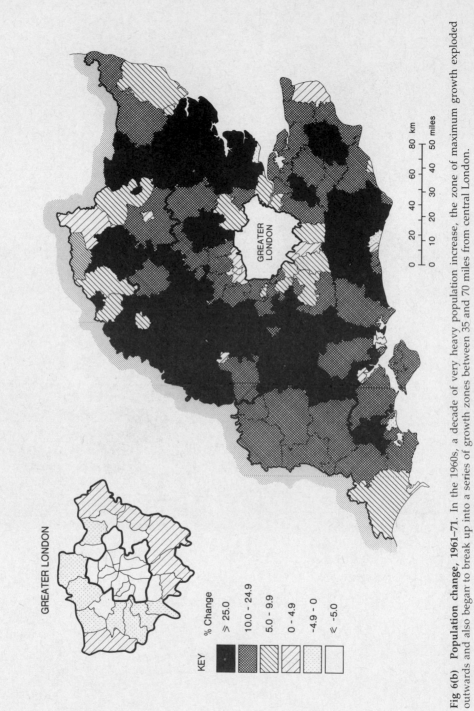

GREATER LONDON

KEY

% Change

≥ 25.0

10.0 – 24.9

5.0 – 9.9

0 – 4.9

–4.9 – 0

≤ –5.0

80 km

50 miles

0   20   40   60   80
0 10   20   30   40

GREATER
LONDON

Fig 6(b) Population change, 1961–71. In the 1960s, a decade of very heavy population increase, the zone of maximum growth exploded outwards and also began to break up into a series of growth zones between 35 and 70 miles from central London.

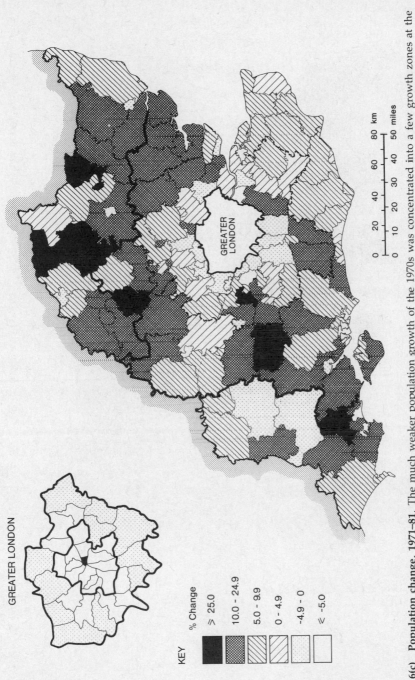

GREATER LONDON

KEY

% Change

⬛ ≥ 25.0

▨ 10.0 – 24.9

▧ 5.0 – 9.9

▤ 0 – 4.9

⬜ -4.9 – 0

⬜ ≤ -5.0

GREATER LONDON

0   20   40   60   80 km

0   10   20   30   40   50 miles

Fig 6(c) Population change, 1971–81. The much weaker population growth of the 1970s was concentrated into a few growth zones at the edge of the South-East region and beyond, including south Hampshire, Milton Keynes, and Peterborough–Huntingdon.

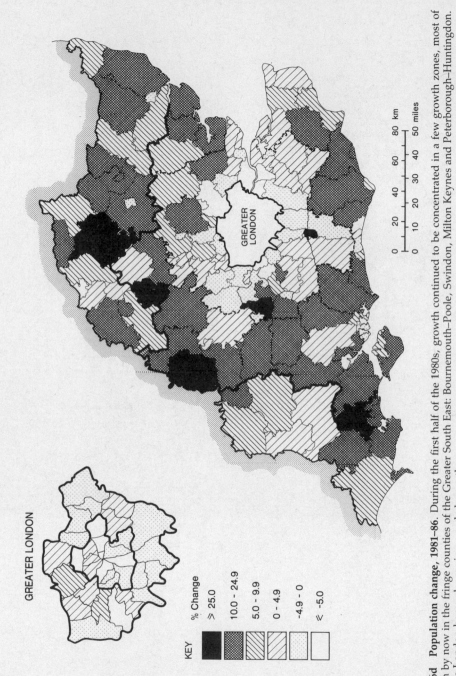

GREATER LONDON

KEY

% Change

■	≥ 25.0
▨	10.0 – 24.9
▨	5.0 – 9.9
▨	0 – 4.9
▨	–4.9 – 0
□	≤ –5.0

GREATER LONDON

0	10	20	30	40	50 miles
0	20	40	60	80 km	

Fig 6d **Population change, 1981–86.** During the first half of the 1980s, growth continued to be concentrated in a few growth zones, most of them by now in the fringe counties of the Greater South East: Bournemouth–Poole, Swindon, Milton Keynes and Peterborough–Huntingdon. Some London boroughs again recorded growth.

Table 4 The South East strategic plan proposals, 1970

(a) Population, actual and planned

	Population ('000)				
	1966	1981	1991	2001	1966–2001
South East	17 000	18 700	20 100	21 600	+4600
Greater London	7 800	7 300	7 000	7 000	− 800
Outer Metropolitan Area	5 100	6 400	7 400	8 200	+3100
Outer South East	4 000	4 900	5 700	6 400	+2400
ROSE	9 100	11 100	13 100	14 600	+5500

(b) The major growth areas

	Distance from London (miles)	Population ('000)		Population growth ('000), 1966–2001
		1966	2001	
Reading–Wokingham–Aldershot–Basingstoke	30–50	500	1 200	+ 700
South Hampshire	70–90	800	1 400	+ 600
Milton Keynes–Northampton	60–80	300	800	+ 500
South Essex	30–40	600	1 000	+ 400
Crawley–Burgess Hill	30–40	200	500	+ 300
Total, 5 areas		2 400	4 900	+2500
Total, South East		17 000	21 600	+4600

Source: South East Joint Plan Team (1970).

a gain of 2.4 million (Table 4(a)). It argued that the best way to do this would be to develop large planned urban regions, which – by proving attractive to decentralizing factories and offices, and by offering a wide range of jobs, social opportunities, and entertainment – would function as effective counter-magnets to London. There would be five of these major growth centres, at distances of between 40 and 80 miles: one to the south-west, one due west, one to the north-west, one to the east, and one to the south, with eventual populations of between 0.5 million and 1.5 million – equivalent to major British provincial agglomerations like South Yorkshire or Tyne and Wear. They would in fact take an actual majority of the entire projected regional growth, 2.5 out of 4.6 million (Table 4(b) and Fig. 7). Thus, the character of the South East would profoundly change: from being a unicentric region based on London, with a whole ring of relatively

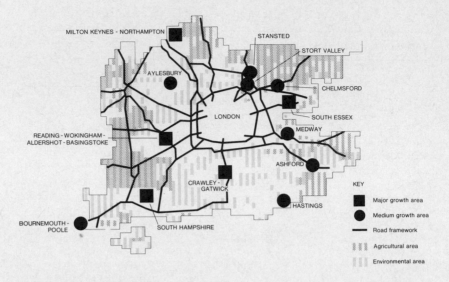

Fig 7   The Strategic Plan for the South East, 1970   This, the logical successor to the 1944 Abercrombie Plan, recognized the outward movement of people, and sought to channel it into five major growth areas and seven smaller ones. Though it engendered major controversy and no longer provides official guidelines for the region, it has exerted a strong influence over county planning policies.

small satellites, it would become a polycentric city region rather like the Netherlands' Randstad Holland.

It was a revolutionary notion, but in some ways it was a logical reinterpretation of the principles that had guided Abercrombie's plan, or the thinking of Ebenezer Howard before him. Just as Abercrombie had reinterpreted Howard, proposing New Towns double the size of Howard's Garden Cities, so now the Strategic Plan team reinterpreted Abercrombie, arguing that social and economic change demanded much bigger units still. But there was this basic continuity: essentially, the major growth centres are what Howard called for in the almost forgotten penultimate chapter of his book (Howard 1898, Ch. 13), polycentric Social Cities against a background of continuous open countryside, which could expand virtually without limit.

After a great deal of argument and some detailed modifications, one year later the government accepted the broad principles of the 1970 Plan. But that did not cause the controversy to go away. For one thing, demography played another of its tricks: the birth rate began to come down almost as fast as it had earlier gone up, and with it went the future projections. A major Review of the Strategic

Plan, in 1976, made by the same government-local authority team, concluded that between 1975 and 1991 the population increase for the entire region, earlier put at 2.8 million, would be only 174 000: an apt comment on the problems of planning in uncertainty. But for another thing, London earlier expected to suffer marginal population losses, was in fact haemorrhaging: the *Review* predicted that its 1991 population, earlier set at 7.0 million, could be as low as 5.7 million. Therefore, paradoxically, the two changes cancelled each other out: the projected increase in ROSE over this 16-year period would be reduced only from 3.4 million to some 2.0 million. So the five major growth zones would still be needed, though not on the earlier scale. And the government's response of 1978 accepted this broad approach – though by then, as noted in Chapter 1, both government and the local authorities were happy to go slow on the growth areas in order to pump resources back into the regeneration of inner London.

The discovery of the inner-city problem, through the medium of the three major consultants' reports – on Liverpool, Birmingham, and Lambeth in 1977 – represented the major shift of government policy during the decade; indeed, during the entire postwar planning era (Department of the Environment 1977a, b). Strictly speaking, it was not a new discovery: observers like David Eversley and David Donnison had been writing about it for nearly a decade by then (Donnison & Eversley 1973). What was new was the official acknowledgement that this was a structural problem, marked by the accelerating deindustrialization of the great British cities, and by an apparently increasing concentration of major problems – economic, social, and physical – there. It found a powerful political constituency in support: left-wing councillors from east and south London boroughs were happy to make cause with right-wing politicians from the shire counties, since the new policies promised more resources for the former which might help relieve embarrassing pressures on the latter. So the resources were diverted; but the outward movement of people, and the steady erosion of urban jobs, continued.

The Advent of Minimalist Planning: 1979–

In 1979 came the arrival of a radical right-wing government, committed to minimalist planning. The new approach was clear enough in the first major governmental statement of August 1980: a mere three typewritten pages of A4 paper, replacing the main report and five supplementary study volumes of 1970. It stressed the priorities

45

of the new government: to promote economic recovery, to restrain
public expenditure, to stimulate the private sector, to sweep away
obstacles to commercial enterprise, to achieve more homeownership
and housing for sale. It repeated the 1970 policy: there was to be a
clear distinction between growth areas, where development was to
be concentrated, and areas of conservation, where restraint was to
be the rule. But underlying this was a profound change of policy: the
attempt to steer growth out of the prosperous South East and into the
North, maintained by successive governments since 1945 through
the Industrial Development Certificate, was to be abandoned.

Ironically, the urban riots of 1981 brought a new emphasis on
inner-city regeneration. The means were however different: Enterprise Zones, offering a holiday from local rates and a minimalist
planning regime, plus Urban Development Corporations – ironically,
modelled on the 1945 Attlee government's solution to building new
towns – to make the necessary public investments which would
bring private capital in behind. London Docklands represented the
most spectacular example of the new planning regime in action.

Undoubtedly, it represented an approach which the government
would dearly have liked to use elsewhere. The whole thrust of
government now was to set free the forces of commercial enterprise, including commercial development. Strategic planning, a
discredited notion of the 1960s, was out; the 1970 plan, or what
was left of it after savagery at the hands of the localities, was
forgotten. It was all easier than it might have been, since 1980–81
brought the most serious economic recession since the 1930s, which
not even the prosperous South East escaped; formerly fastidious
local planning authorities, which had been less than forthcoming
to proposals for new industry, wholesaling, and retailing, suddenly
proved much more flexible. The results are very plain on the face of
South-East England in the late 1980s: new factories and warehouses
and superstores at the urban peripheries, close to the interchanges
of the motorways and trunk roads.

And all the while, regardless of major shifts of planning policy
in Whitehall – now in favour of outward movement, now against it,
now in favour of planning, now not – the people went on moving
out. Whereas in the 1950s the belt of maximum growth had been
20–35 miles out from London and in the 1960s 35–45 miles out, in the
1970s it was up to 60–70 miles out and in the early 1980s even beyond
that, in the South-East fringe counties between 80 and 110 miles from
London (Figs. 6(c) and 6(d)). But, as the growth belt rolled outwards, it
increasingly concentrated in a few favoured city regions: some of
them, ironically, the designated growth areas of the ill-starred 1970

plan, like the Reading–Wokingham–Aldershot–Basingstoke quadrilateral or the Crawley–Gatwick area; some farther out, such as
Bournemouth–Poole, Swindon, Milton Keynes–Northampton, Peterborough–Huntingdon and Ipswich.

Yet, with the massive exception of the new and expanded towns
of the 1960s (e.g Swindon, Milton Keynes, Northampton, and Peterborough), what has not transpired, as seen in Chapter 1, has been
large-scale residential development. Clearly, in the early 1980s the
housebuilders, organized in a newly aggressive House Builders
Federation, were convinced that victory was theirs; assured by government statements about a massive simplification of the planning
system, they were preparing their plans for major developments.
In 1983 nine of the largest among them formed Consortium Developments, with the specific objective of developing new residential
communities in the South East. Their first foray, into the Essex
Green Belt at Tillingham Hall north of Tilbury, proved unfortunate:
after a 1986 inquiry, their appeal was rejected by the Secretary of
State. They are busy trying again, with proposals at Foxley Wood
south of Reading, at Stone Bassett east of Oxford, and – outside the
South East, but in that fast-growing South-East fringe – Wilburton
north of Cambridge. They will doubtless not be the last; and it is an
almost certain bet that some of them, better chosen than Tillingham
in relation to Green Belt and other objections, will succeed.

None of them, however, represents any kind of planning process;
with the exception of Wilburton, each has been predictably received
with howls of execration from the local planning authority. For its
part, the government, in a statement of 1983 presaging the abolition
of the Greater London Council and the five provincial English
metropolitan councils, roundly condemned strategic planning as
an outmoded concept of the 1960s. Later, in 1987, it announced
the abolition of County Structure Plans, effectively reducing County
Planning Departments – the mainstay of the 1947 planning system
– to a cipher.

The new-style vision of the English planning system, implied
by all this, runs something as follows. Truncated county planning
departments will co-operate, through the Standing Conference on
South-East Regional Planning (SERPLAN) and its equivalents in other
regions, to draw up regional advice to government. Another quango
– the London Planning Advisory Committee – will provide similar
guidance for Greater London, to be retailed both to the Secretary
of State and to the boroughs; its first draft report appeared in June
1988 (London Planning Advisory Commitee 1988). At intervals, the
government will respond through brief statements of regional policy.

These will provide guidance to the district authorities, which will do all the day-to-day planning. Developers will put their proposals to them, presumably with appropriate sweeteners in the form of Development Agreements (Section 52 Agreements, so-called after the relevant clause in the 1971 Town and Country Planning Act) to pay for much-needed infrastructure. If, nevertheless, the authority rejects the proposal, the developer will appeal and, after a public inquiry, may win. The best description is that it will be a system of planning by roulette. It may at last provide a mechanism by which developers can develop in the South East, and for this it should perhaps be praised. Whether it is the best means to achieve the end – good quality private development that will be liked by its customers – will presumably depend on one's visceral political views. Time will tell; but after eight years of promises and little realization, time is not on the side of the experiment.

The Current Impasse: 1988

The fact is that, after forty years of operating the present planning system in South-East England, we still seem as far away as ever from answering those fundamental questions, Shall London grow? and, How shall London grow? Abercrombie in 1944 provided one answer, on which for a time people of very different persuasions were able to agree; perhaps that reflected the unique circumstances of war's end, perhaps the fact that it appeared a once-for-all solution – after which, business would proceed as normal, that is, exceedingly slowly. The Strategic Plan Team of 1970 provided another solution, which proved exceedingly controversial and was never accepted at all by many people at the grass roots. So we are back with the old game of planning by roulette, which has been the dominant style over most years since the 1947 Act made development especially difficult but also especially profitable.

The question must be whose book it suits. Successful speculators in land, certainly; QCs and experts at public inquiries, too: but how many of those are there? And do we really plan for them? For the rest, it is unclear who benefits. Not the developers, certainly. Not the people who might buy their houses. Not even the beleaguered ruralites, because for them further turns of the wheel bring no certainty, no peace. The question must be whether a better ordered, a better articulated system would not be preferable for almost everyone. That is the vision that the remainder of this book will seek to spell out.

I shall spell it out, as best I may, in this logical order: first the employment base, because on this virtually everything else must depend; then people, their homes and the land they stand on; then the transport system that joins homes with jobs and with other opportunities – social, educational, cultural, recreational; then how to build the relevant parts of the new London super-region; then how to provide the system that regulates and governs it all; then how to pay for it; finally, the total picture into which it all fits.

3

Jobs 2001

Jobs are the key to most else in the planning of cities and regions, so
it is logical to start with them. And here comes the first truly big break
with *London 2000*. Twenty-five years ago, the problem seemed to be
how to control and guide the growth of jobs, which then seemed to
be submerging parts of the region – above all, its heart. As already
seen in Chapters 1 and 2, that is no longer true: London, and the
whole region around, have suffered a long loss of employment, to
which there seems as yet no end.

London 2000 was badly wrong here, though it was in good company. In 1963 there was no hint of what was to come: London's
economy seemed strong, because it was heavily weighted towards
the kinds of activities – both high-tech manufacturing and producer
services – that were growing nationally. Even by the early 1970s, no
one had grasped the change: at the inquiry into the Greater London
Development Plan the chief GLC planner, Bernard Collins, was still
talking about controls on floorspace at a time when there was less
and less demand for it. David Donnison and David Eversley were
the first to bring it to wide attention, at about that time (Donnison
& Eversley 1973).

The first step, then, is to lay bare the main lines of change; the
next, to try to interpret the reasons. Fortunately, the problem has
brought forth a mountain of research, from which this account will
freely borrow.

From Manufacturing to Services:
The Deindustrialization of London

The most important single feature of the British and the London economies during the last twenty years has been the shift out of manufacturing into services. In terms of employment, Britain is rapidly becoming a post-industrial economy, and in this respect London is merely an exaggerated example. In Britain as a whole, between 1963 and 1983 manufacturing fell from 34.8 to only 24.6 per cent of total employment, while services rose from 49.2 to 63.7 per cent; between 1973 and 1983 alone, manufacturing lost 2.2 million workers. Since the growth of service jobs added a little under 1.5 million new jobs, the result was a major loss of employment overall: more than 1.2 million jobs, 5 per cent of the 1973 total, were lost.

For the South East and for London, we have figures for the decade 1971–81, calculated by SERPLAN from the Annual Census of Employment (Table 5). They show that over that period the South-East region shed 104 000 jobs, a slightly lower rate of loss

Table 5 Employment changes, 1971–81

	1971	1981	1971–81 change	
			Nos.	%
Central London	1 104 699	946 755	−157 944	−14.3
Inner London	2 283 559	1 948 163	−335 396	−14.7
Outer London	1 653 693	1 562 402	− 91 291	− 5.5
Greater London	3 937 252	3 510 565	−426 687	−10.8
OMA	1 758 406	1 873 284	+114 878	+ 6.5
OSE	1 546 803	1 754 998	+208 195	+13.5
ROSE	3 305 209	3 628 282	+323 073	+ 9.8
5 growth areas	810 143	956 351	+146 208	+18.1
South Hampshire	316 251	343 857	+ 27 606	+ 8.7
Milton Keynes	30 028	56 359	+ 26 301	+87.6
Reading-Wokingham–Aldershot–Basingstoke	209 499	273 822	+ 64 323	+30.7
Crawley–Burgess Hill	85 833	105 455	+ 19 622	+22.9
South Essex	168 532	176 888	+ 8 356	+ 5.0
ROSE remainder	2 495 066	2 671 931	+176 865	+ 7.1
South East	7 242 461	7 138 274	−104 187	− 1.4
Great Britain	21 648 200	21 147 000	−501 200	− 2.3

Source: SERPLAN (1985a), based on Census of Employment 1971 and 1981.

than the country overall (1.4 against 2.3 per cent). But this conceals a loss of no less than 427 000 jobs in London itself, nearly 11 per cent of the 1971 total, and a gain of 323 000 jobs, just under 10 per cent, in the rest of the region. The gain in the Outer Metropolitan Area was some 6.5 per cent; that in the Outer South East, nearly double that. Throughout the different parts of the region, the story was the same: the job loss was a loss in manufacturing jobs. The only exception was London, where there was a marginal loss in service jobs also, and particularly inner London, where this loss was more than marginal. Outside London, in the Outer Metropolitan Area and the Outer South East, employment in services grew strongly, by about a quarter; and here also, as we progress out of London, the manufacturing loss diminishes, until in the Outer South East it is relatively slight (and, in the four growth areas of the so-called Western Crescent, negligible) (Table 6). Clearly, what was happening was a combination of two processes. The general secular decline of manufacturing and the rise of service employment was overlain by a relative decentralization of jobs from the region's core to its outer rings. We know that the latter has been important, because London's job decline has occurred despite its apparently favourable industrial structure: there is a differential 'London effect' at work (Buck *et al*. 1986, 66–7).

Table 6 Employment changes, sectors, 1971–81

	Manufacturing		Services		Total	
	'000	%	'000	%	'000	%
Inner London	− 186.7	−40.6	− 105.0	− 6.1	−318.3	−13.9
Outer London	− 192.0	−32.6	+ 98.7	+10.2	− 95.7	− 5.8
Greater London	− 378.8	−36.1	− 6.4	− 0.2	−414.0	−10.5
OMA	− 125.4	−18.4	+ 237.2	+25.0	+111.6	+ 6.3
OSE	− 15.3	− 3.5	+ 231.1	+23.9	+210.5	+13.6
ROSE	− 140.7	−12.5	+ 468.3	+24.5	+322.1	+ 9.7
Western Crescent *of which*:	− 11.1	− 3.0	+ 208.2	+32.1	+196.6	+17.6
4 growth areas	− 2.0	− 0.9	+ 133.6	+35.0	+134.0	+20.9
ROSE remainder	− 129.6	−17.2	+ 260.2	+20.5	+125.5	+ 5.7
South East	− 519.5	−23.9	+ 462.0	+10.0	− 91.9	− 1.3
Great Britain	−1963.2	−24.9	+1703.0	+14.5	501.2	+ 2.3

Source: SERPLAN (1985a), based on Census of Employment 1971 and 1981.

The position of inner London is particularly anomalous. It suffered massive manufacturing job losses, and – unusually, in terms of national trends – compounded these by losses in service jobs. This is quite contrary to the usual image of the dynamic information-processing financial and media centre of Britain. But it must be remembered that services include also a wide variety of jobs that handle goods other than information, and that these jobs – in docks, warehousing, and transport – suffered particularly badly from the closure of the London docklands and the associated activities. Table 7 presents detailed information on this point from a different source, the Census of Population. (Because of this, the detailed figures do not agree with Tables 5 and 6.) It demonstrates the huge losses in Greater London not only in manufacturing, but also in the goods-handling activities of trade and transportation. Altogether, goods-handling services lost nearly 110 000 jobs, and all goods-handling jobs (including also manufacturing and construction) lost 549 000, while information-handling services gained a mere 81 000 – only 15 per cent of the net loss on the other side of the equation. Table 8 supplements this by comparing the performance of inner London with that of the

Table 7 Employment changes, major sectors, 1971–81, by place of work

	Great Britain		South East		Greater London		ROSE	
	'000	%	'000	%	'000	%	'000	%
Primary	− 148.4	−14.5	− 19.2	− 4.5	+ 4.2	+41.8	− 23.3	−18.7
Manufacturing	−1958.4	−23.0	−590.1	−24.5	−418.6	−36.2	−171.7	−13.7
Constrn	− 63.3	− 3.9	− 20.3	− 3.7	− 24.6	− 9.9	+ 4.3	− 1.5
Services	+1337.4	+10.8	+300.5	+ 6.3	− 28.6	− 1.1	+329.4	+15.4
Trade	+ 199.2	+ 4.7	+ 25.7	+ 1.8	− 75.7	−10.3	+101.5	+14.8
Trptn	− 67.9	− 4.3	− 28.0	− 4.3	− 46.1	−10.9	+ 18.1	+ 8.0
FIRE	+ 537.1	+42.7	+212.4	+32.2	+ 80.3	+16.8	+132.1	+72.0
Pub Svs	+ 646.6	+14.1	+ 95.7	+ 5.6	+ 1.0	+ 0.1	+ 95.0	+10.7
Misc Sv	+ 22.5	+ 3.0	− 5.3	− 1.7	+ 11.9	+ 7.8	− 17.3	−11.2
'Goods'	+ 153.8	+ 2.4	− 7.6	− 0.3	−109.9	− 8.4	+102.3	+ 9.6
'Info'	+1183.7	+20.3	+308.1	+13.0	+ 81.3	+ 6.2	+227.1	+21.2
TOTAL	− 816.4	− 3.4	−339.7	− 4.5	−485.5	−11.9	+140.9	+ 8.7
'Goods'	−2016.3	−18.0	−637.1	−11.7	−549.0	−20.1	− 88.4	− 3.2
'Info'	+1183.7	+20.3	+308.1	+13.0	+ 81.3	+ 6.2	+227.1	+21.2
Ratios:								
Svs:Mfg		0.68		0.51		–		1.92
Info:Gds		0.59		0.48		0.15		2.57

Source: Hall (1987), based on Census of Population 1971 and 1981.

Table 8 Major British cities: changes in economic structure, 1971–81

	'Goods'	'Info'	Ratio
Inner London			
'000	−400.7	+56.5	0.14
%	− 27.2	+ 6.6	
Liverpool			
'000	− 79.3	+12.9	0.16
%	− 32.5	+16.3	
Birmingham			
'000	−122.3	+30.7	0.25
%	− 25.3	+26.1	
Glasgow			
'000	− 70.7	+20.0	0.28
%	− 22.2	+17.3	
Manchester			
'000	− 56.1	+17.0	0.30
%	− 23.3	+18.4	
Bristol			
'000	− 24.6	+18.4	0.75
%	− 15.4	+33.2	
Cardiff			
'000	− 15.0	+11.6	0.77
%	− 15.1	+26.4	
Edinburgh			
'000	− 12.9	+18.6	1.44
%	− 8.9	+22.2	

Source: Hall (1987), based on Census of Population 1971 and 1981.

major 'inner-city' economies of the rest of the country. It reveals the startling fact that inner London's performance was actually the worst of any – worse even than Liverpool's. Its relatively minor gains in informational service jobs made up only 14 per cent of the net loss in all goods-handling activities, as against 16 per cent in Liverpool, 25 per cent in Birmingham, 28 per cent in Glasgow, and 30 per cent in Manchester, the worst-hit provincial cities.

Nor are these losses a relatively new phenomenon of the 1970s. Table 9, based on analysis from the ESRC's inner-city studies, demonstrates that the loss of manufacturing jobs from London has been a long-continued process, beginning early in the 1960s and continuing almost without pause to the early 1980s. And it has been fairly consistent. The countervailing gains in service employment, in contrast, have been very irregular, occurring in two short bursts in the early 1970s and the early 1980s; otherwise, as already seen, service employment has actually contributed to the general contraction.

Table 9   Employment changes per annum in London, 1951–84

	All industries	Manufacturing	Production industries other than manufacturing	Services
1951–61	+17 700	+ 400	− 1 400	+18 700
1961–66	−14 300	−30 700	+ 4 700	−11 700
1966–71	−54 300	−38 400	−13 200	− 2 700
1971–74	−30 800	−49 200	− 6 200	+24 600
1974–78	−41 800	−33 100	− 5 100	− 3 600
1978–81	−34 800	−24 500	− 4 500	− 5 800
1981–84	−33 900	−32 300	− 7 900	+ 5 400

Source: Buck *et al*. (1986), based on various sources.

One particularly important element in the growth of service employment, stressed by many commentators, is the so-called producer services, including financial services, legal and accountancy services and the like. It is in this sector, so the myth runs, that the unique continuing strength of the London economy lies. Here, detailed analysis by the CURDS team at the University of Newcastle-upon-Tyne shows that, indeed, London has the strongest national concentration of producer service employment, as measured by the Location Quotient. But its employment gain in this sector during the 1970s was by far the lowest of any of the major kinds of urban centre distinguished by the CURDS team, and it was the only type of centre whose Location Quotient actually fell during the period. Significantly, some of the biggest gains were made by the centres in the region outside London: the London Subdominant Cities and Towns, forming part of the extended London metropolitan area described in Chapter 1 (Fig. 2), and the Southern Freestanding Cities, Rural Areas, and Service Towns (Table 10). These services, like so many other sectors of the economy, were showing a strong tendency to decentralize out of London into the surrounding towns of the Outer Metropolitan Area and the Outer South East.

To complicate the picture further, the job losses were heavily concentrated in certain parts of inner London. Manufacturing and goods-handling services suffered big declines in the old Victorian manufacturing and port belt, which stretches in a great horseshoe around the City to the east, from Islington through Hackney and Tower Hamlets to Southwark. After 1970, informational services, especially the more routine ones, left the City and West End. And at

Table 10 Types of urban area: producer service employment changes, 1971–81

	Location quotient 1981	Change in LQ 1971–81	Employment change (%) 1971–81
London	1.85	−0.19	14.73
London subdominant cities	1.21	0.04	59.42
Conurbation dominants	1.07	0.03	24.17
London subdominant towns	1.05	0.06	61.27
Provincial dominants	1.02	0.05	44.34
Southern freestanding cities	0.94	0.10	69.92
Southern rural areas	0.89	0.17	80.08
Southern service towns	0.84	0.02	59.74
Subregional dominants	0.84	0.16	62.26

Source: Gillespie & Green (1987).

this time, the decline of manufacturing also began to affect certain western outer boroughs, particularly Brent and Ealing, which were the homes of much of the interwar manufacturing development (Buck *et al*. 1986, 68, 71).

To summarize the statistical record, manufacturing jobs were on the decline, service jobs were on the rise. All kinds of activity were showing a strong tendency to decentralize out of London. These two trends combine in the statistics, demonstrating themselves in the differentially high rate of London manufacturing loss and the relatively weak performance of its service sectors compared with the rest of the region. The question is why this should be.

Towards Explanation: The Roots of London's Decline

We have the advantage of a very detailed analysis of the causes of this 'London effect', made as part of the ESRC's Inner Cities Programme (Buck *et al*. 1986). This considers four possible explanations of the poor performance of the London economy, and effectively rejects three of them:

(a) *Decentralization*: the thesis that London's economy is simply shifting outwards. No, say the ESRC researchers: London's losses were not balanced by Outer Metropolitan Area (OMA) gains, and firms' movements were not the main cause of the losses (Buck *et al*. 1986, p. 77).

(b) *Policy*: the thesis that planners put limits on London's industry and offices and gave incentives to firms to move out. No again: studies show that few moves to the Assisted Areas took place, and few firms responded to incentives (p. 79).

(c) *Comparative disadvantage*: the argument that London firms suffer higher costs, compounded by planning restrictions which have stopped them rebuilding to become more efficient. This seems true, but only in part: London costs are higher, but the differential has not widened; planning controls may have diverted dynamic firms out and caused others to close – the first mainly in outer west London, the second in the inner east – but this ceased to be true after 1978, when vacant premises became plentiful (pp. 81–5).

(d) *Restructuring*: the thesis that structural reorganization has encouraged a relocation of different parts of London firms: routine production to remote areas with plenty of labour and weak unions, R&D to environmentally good places in the OMA, headquarters to central London. This, the researchers think, was the most important cause; it accentuated after 1960, as firms were faced with a squeeze on profits and a need to become more efficient (pp. 86–7). All these operated with exceptional force from then until 1978; after that, the 'London effect' weakened, as constraints on growth in London became less evident with general recession. There is no room here, the ESRC researchers conclude, for optimism about the future: if growth resumes again nationally, London will again be squeezed (p. 88).

The London Paradox: Shrinking Jobs, Constant Unemployment

So far, so bad. The silver lining, the ESRC researchers find, is that the shrinkage of job opportunities in London has had virtually no perceptible effect on unemployment. London unemployment has risen, to be sure, but only in line with national trends; year after year, it has remained consistently about 1 per cent below national levels. The reason lies in the unique complexity of labour markets in the wider region, which we noted in Chapter 1. The region comprises 'a network of overlapping sub-market areas interacting strongly with each other', in which 'the long-term balance between supply and demand has produced more favourable aggregate outcomes than in most other parts of the country' (Buck *et al.* 1986, 90, 93). People

have moved out from London, shrinking the labour force by about
1 per cent a year; and 'Over the long term, this shrinkage in supply
has more or less balanced the faster rate of employment decline in
Greater London' (p. 97).

What seems to have happened was this. First, people moved out
and joined the tide of long-distance commuters back into London.
But before long, some of them – perhaps between 7 and 10 per
cent a year – got local jobs; after ten years a majority, perhaps
three-quarters, of the movers had found jobs closer to home. So,
in the longer term, the decentralization of people had a strongly
favourable effect in limiting the rise of unemployment in London
(Buck *et al*. 1986, 45, 97).

To this comforting conclusion there is, however, a massive and
unfortunate exception. This complex, overlapping character of the
labour market does not apply to everyone. At one extreme, top
professional people will move homes a long way out but are also
prepared to commute long distances (perhaps because they can
afford it). At the other extreme, unskilled workers are immobile,
partly because so many are in council estates which are concentrated in that Victorian industrial horseshoe east of the centre, and
also because many of them are black or brown. The kinds of jobs
they do are the ones that have disproportionately contracted, and
were traditionally concentrated in these same boroughs, close to
their homes. They always were in a weak labour market position,
but now it is relatively worse than ever. And this is especially
true for the younger first-time entrant totally lacking formal school
qualifications, still 40 per cent of the total, among whom West
Indian males are disproportionately represented, though they suffer
very high unemployment even when qualifications are controlled
for (Buck *et al*. 1986, 91, 98–104, 175–6). Thus, the researchers
conclude, there is

> an exceptionally high incidence of unemployment among the
> young, the less skilled, and the black population, and across
> much of Inner London. In general, high levels of mobility and
> 'efficient' labour market operations do not help these groups,
> because selection criteria work against them in competition for
> jobs with other Londoners and migrants from elsewhere. (Buck
> *et al*. 1986, 106)

This is not uniquely a London problem: it is a problem of every
great metropolis in the Western world. As long ago as 1968, the
American economist Charles Killingworth identified what he called

a 'twist' in labour demand, consisting of a long-term fall in demand for low-skill, unqualified, poorly educated labour and a long-term rise in the demand for high-skill, well educated labour, shifts that were occurring faster than the corresponding shifts in supply of labour (Killingworth 1968). John Kasarda and Jürgen Friedrichs (1986) confirm this in a comparison of the New York region with German cities, finding in both a 'mismatch' between labour demand and supply: urban economies are no longer supplying the entry-level jobs that could be performed by an unskilled, unqualified labour force.

That this must be true for London is suggested by a paradox (Fig. 8): the phenomenon of very large variations in local residential rates of unemployment between inner and outer London boroughs only a few miles apart, such as Hackney (24.5 per cent in September 1986) against Redbridge (8.7), or Lambeth (20.4) against Croydon (8.6) and Sutton (6.4) (SERPLAN 1987b). It is also suggested by the paradox of high rates of unemployment side by side with large numbers of vacancies for more skilled and even semi-skilled jobs, including jobs (as in public services) that combine low wages with unsocial hours. These are segmented labour markets; any reflation of the high-skill, high-wage economy will have little or no impact on the low-skill, low-wage one.

Future Prospects

There is not likely to be much change in this situation. To explain why would require a book in itself, and half of it would deal with theory. Not so long ago, geographers and urban economists discussed the location of economic activity by means of a checklist that had not altered much in decades. Now it has altered beyond recognition. In an economy dominated by producer services and high-tech manufacturing, many items have disappeared. What remains, what is enhanced, is the generation and exchange of information. And this comes in different ways, some traditional (the face-to-face exchange of the City or Fleet Street), some new (the electronic cottage). The key question is how far the new technology supplants the old processes. There are as many views on this as there are pundits: the best judgement is the old Scots one, Not Proven. Overall, traditional central areas of information exchange have not been rendered obsolescent by technology, but they have been weakened. It is *possible* to draw in information, to cogitate, to disseminate, anywhere in the world that has an adequate telephone system for

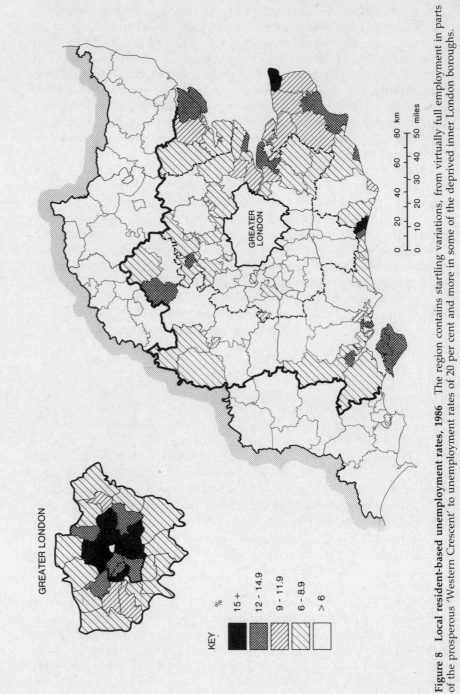

GREATER LONDON

KEY.

%

■ 15 +

▨ 12 - 14.9

▥ 9 - 11.9

▧ 6 - 8.9

□ > 6

GREATER LONDON

0   20   40   60   80 km
|——|——|——|——|——|——|——|——|——|
0   10   20   30   40   50 miles

Figure 8 Local resident-based unemployment rates, 1986 The region contains startling variations, from virtually full employment in parts of the prosperous 'Western Crescent' to unemployment rates of 20 per cent and more in some of the deprived inner London boroughs.

voice and data; whether it is *desirable* or *optimal* is another question altogether. The result is a set of tensions between old and new kinds of information exchange.

The resulting location of these jobs is governed by locational rules, subtler but no less binding than those of old. Some, the higher-level and better-paid ones, are tied together by traditional agglomeration economies: in an information society, the information you get in the corridor or the washroom or the cafeteria or the bar is still as useful as – often more useful than – the information that comes down the line and on the screen. The top HQ jobs are still in that old interactional world bounded by the regular cruising range of the London cabbie. The R&D jobs are in places where boffins and nerds feel secure and creative in each others' company. Other jobs are governed by cost constraints: they go to the point of minimum cost consistent with getting the job done properly. The clerical jobs are wherever large numbers of middle-class women, with the right skills and the right telephone voice, can be easily assembled from their outer suburban homes and can easily go out for lunchtime shopping on the local High Street. The blue-collar jobs, done not so long ago in Lambeth or Park Royal or in the centre of Reading, are anywhere and everywhere but there. Thus, while most of these jobs are information-based, many of them have no real need to be in central London, or even in Greater London; aided by advances in technology, especially the convergence of computing and telecommunications, they may be located anywhere in a wide metropolitan fringe.

At the same time, capital is concentrating: organizations are growing larger; and as they do so, they reorganize on functional grounds, putting the HQ in a traditional business centre, R&D in an environmentally attractive environment nearby, production and ancillary service functions almost anywhere that will satisfy tough cost constraints. Mapped on to South-East England, this gives a new economic landscape, partly similar to the old, partly different. Headquarters remain in the City or West End, perhaps decentralizing to the Isle of Dogs. Ancillary paper-processing functions, a big part of the old central pool of employment, go to Reading or Harlow. R&D is in a country house in the Thames Valley near Henley or Marlow; associated prototype manufacturing of high-tech goods is in a factory in nearby Bracknell; routine production moves perhaps to County Durham, perhaps to Scotland, perhaps to Malaysia or Brazil, dependent on available incentives. Around this core, there clusters a whole penumbra of service jobs, ranging from law and accountancy and gourmet meals to hamburgers and health services, and offering a variety of jobs from the professional to the casual.

Additionally, there are public service jobs catering partly for the daytime population, but very largely for a resident population that has been in long–term decline.

This schematic map implies that, within the South East, the available jobs will be overwhelmingly managerial/ professional, clerical, or scientific/technical; there is all too little need for blue-collar labour, except in the bottom-level service jobs. And the informational jobs, though partly still tied to traditional locations, are partly released from them by new technology. The future thus lies with the service industries, but their prospects in London itself are no better than those for manufacturing:

> Population and business decline in London serve to reduce the demand for many services; the costs and constraints of London cause many activities to move; new technology is likely to assist relocation and lead to *in situ* declines, particularly in office employment, though also in distribution; public expenditure constraints have halted the previous rise in public employment, and may also lead to declines. (Buck *et al*. 1986, 163).

And this spells further trouble for those at the bottom of the labour market: the jobs these groups traditionally held have disappeared, with the collapse of manufacturing and goods–handling services during the 1970s, and now with the squeeze on public sector spending in the 1980s (Buck *et al*. 1986, 172). 'In the near future, as in the past,' the ESRC researchers conclude, 'the major decreases in employment are likely to impinge most on male manual workers in London, and it is these which will have the greatest effect on unemployment at the local level' (p. 168).

All this suggests, first, that the best way of helping the unqualified unemployed may be to reflate the general economy. But there is a nasty snag here: since the depths of the recession in 1981 the world economy in general, and the British in particular, *has* been massively reflated, yet the results have been disturbing – indeed, without historic parallel. The effect on unemployment has been negligible; furthermore, the extra jobs that have been created have all been – as earlier indicated – in the service sector (Rajan 1987). True, as Rajan and others – Jonathan Gershuny in Britain, Stephen Cohen and John Zysman in the United States – argue, many of these service jobs may represent a restructuring of the manufacturing process, particularly the 'externalizing' of ancillary services (Gershuny & Miles 1983, Rajan 1987, Cohen & Zysman 1987). But this may not bring much comfort to the inner-city underclass, because, whatever the nature of the new jobs, they are not being created in the places where the old manufacturing jobs have been destroyed.

So, second and most importantly, such people will almost certainly do better in *expanding* local economies where new jobs are being created than in *contracting* local economies where they are being destroyed. Kasarda and Friedrichs conclude that, 'under conditions of sustained national economic growth, a locality with a moderate amount of unemployment has much better prospects of economically rebounding and further reducing its unemployment rate than a locality with substantially larger portions of its labour force unemployed' (1986, 245). And exactly the same conclusion is reached by the ESRC research in Britain: though the unskilled and unqualified do relatively as badly in the growth areas (mainly freestanding towns and rural areas in the southern half of the country) as in inner urban areas like London, they gain like everyone else: the 'standard male' in the growth areas was about 20 per cent less liable to unemployment than in Greater London, the 'standard female' about 35 per cent less so, and these relativities persisted through the different levels of qualification and skill. So the highly qualified person and the unqualified person alike will gain from living in Surrey Heath (unemployment 5.1 per cent in September 1986) rather than Hackney (24.5 per cent). The relativities apply, furthermore, to a *propensity* to unemployment that varies hugely, and cumulatively, from one group to another: the ESRC work suggests that an unqualified, unmarried, black worker, aged 16–19, in an unskilled manual occupation, living in council housing, would be *30 times* more likely to be unemployed than the 'standard male' (Buck & Gordon 1987, 99). So, the authors conclude,

> while much the same groups are liable to experience labour-market disadvantages in both growing and declining areas, they would tend to be much better off in the former, particularly in terms of exposure to unemployment. (Buck & Gordon 1987, 111)

Local job creation programmes for these groups, suggest Buck and Gordon, may be little use unless either the jobs are so unattractive that no one else wants them, or they are reserved for these people. The better strategy may be to try to protect the jobs they have as long as possible (Buck & Gordon 1987, 111–2). Otherwise, the best hope would lie in policies to encourage and assist them to move out to the growth areas. Not only would this directly help such groups; indirectly, and in the longer term, it would help the inner areas by reducing the concentration of disadvantaged people in them, thereby perhaps raising educational levels and making these areas more attractive to potential employers (Buck *et al*. 1986, 194).

That was a point made by quite a few people in the past, from Alfred Marshall and Ebenezer Howard onward, though admittedly in a very different economic context. The fact is that no programme, not even the New Towns programme of the 1950s and 1960s, has done very much to help the really disadvantaged to leave London; Ray Thomas's analysis conclusively showed that the main beneficiaries were skilled workers (Hall *et al*. 1973, II, 346–50). There have been too many political forces on the other side: an unholy alliance, in fact, of the Tory squirearchy and ex-urban middle class, who wanted to protect their countryside against invasion by the lower orders, and left-wing leaders in the London boroughs, frightened by the threat to their rating and voting base. They have proved decisive: as long ago as 1977, a survey for the Lambeth Inner Area study showed that a substantial minority would leave if they could, and the report advocated policies to help them (Department of the Environment 1977a, 41, 204). But it was much easier to do nothing. The London poor have remained segregated in their sink estates, because it was in no one's interest, save theirs, to help them move.

The Case for Action

There is of course a case for action. It is that the costs of inaction may be too horrible to contemplate. Begg, Moore, and Rhodes, in their analysis for the ESRC study, put it succinctly:

If, in the absence of policy action, the social problems associated with the concentrations of deprived groups grew cumulatively worse, and were passed on from one generation to the next, there might come a point when the social problems were so great that the costs of containing them grew disproportionately, compared with the costs of alleviating the same social problems of the individuals in a situation where the concentration had been dispersed. Possible consequences of prolonged deprivation might be severe alienation, crime and violence, extreme and widespread poverty, large-scale vandalism and physical dereliction, the eventual removal of the private sector from such areas, and a gradual deterioration

and breakdown of law and order and any sense of community.
(Begg *et al*. 1986, 12)

The authors suggest that there are ominous signs that we may be
drifting in this direction: the riots of 1981, the rise in violent crime
in inner-city areas, the fiscal stress of some urban local authorities,
the physical run-down of some inner-city localities. If anything,
events since they wrote have fortified their case.

What we would have to do is politically very difficult. To
paraphrase a celebrated statement, it may take a riot. It would be to
try to build a programme of dispersal of the unskilled and unqualified
into general programmes of dispersal. The first difficulty is that, with
the New Towns and Expanded Towns programmes nearly finished,
there is at present no mechanism by which this could be effected;
one would need to be recreated. In Chapter 4 I shall suggest one
such possibility. The second difficulty would be to sell it. I can
see one way, which is to provide sufficient incentive for someone
to do it. I will return to that point, also, in Chapter 4.

There are complementary programmes that could be easier,
though they too would be controversial. Their essence would be
to segment the urban underclass educationally, by trying to lift one
group rapidly out via the school system. The need to do so is evident
enough from the documented under-achievement of Afro-Caribbean
and some other groups in the London schools, so that experimental
treatment may be justified. Standardized test results from the Inner
London Education Authority show that in 1986 only 3.6 per cent
of Bangladeshi students and 4.6 per cent of Caribbean students
achieved 5 or more CSE1 or O-level A-C passes, against an overall
average of 9.8 per cent and a figure for Indian students of 20.7 per
cent; the same kinds of differential operated whatever the measure
(average performance scores: Bangladeshi 9.3, Caribbean 13.5, overall
15.2, Indian 22.0) (ILEA 1987, 6-7).

One way to overcome this would be through what the Americans
call 'magnet schools' in inner urban areas. These would be especially prestigious schools with high academic standards, but they
would be so located that they would attract low-income catchment
populations. The proposed city technology colleges could provide
one example. So, on the basis of some American evidence, could
schools managed by highly motivated minority group parents. True,
these courses of action carry high political risks. If successful, both
kinds of schools could cream off talent and motivation from the
remaining local authority schools. If unsuccessful, these schools
could perpetuate a ghetto culture, segregated from the mainstream

society and antagonistic towards it, especially if they fell into the hands of politically motivated governors. This remedy could just be worse than the disease.

There is another programme that should be tried: a more effective Youth Training Scheme, the present version of which – so reports clearly show – has been failing to deliver results for inner-city unemployed young people. The central problem is that the inner cities offer all too few good-quality work placements. So ethnic minorities – as usual, at the end of every queue – find themselves cut out and placed in college-based schemes, which notoriously offer few real technical qualifications and few prospects of real jobs afterward. As a result, they drop out of the schemes and become disillusioned. The government's response is to refuse them Supplementary Benefit unless they are registered with YTS. But, if the scheme is clearly failing to perform for them, the result – as in the inner-city school system – is likely to be nominal registration and effective truancy.

As of September 1988, the successor body to the Manpower Services Commission was said to be considering an alternative, more flexible, scheme that would allow trainees to drop in and out and to join shorter courses. The aim seems to be a system that could combine short college-based and work-based schemes. This may be difficult to reconcile with the government's intention to withdraw Supplementary Benefit from those who are not registered. In any case, the question is whether it will do anything to improve either the level of technical qualification or the future employability of those involved. That might – stress, *might* – be achieved by a longer, two-year course which combined a year of college, leading to credits towards a real technical qualification, with a year of work-related experience. And the latter might have to be outside the trainee's own inner-city locality – hence the need for an expensive lodging allowance.

All this would cost more money. And no one should assume that it will produce miraculous overnight results: mismatch is a real problem, and will not disappear in a day. But, again, we should consider the results of doing nothing.

Planning and the Geography of New Jobs

Without doubt, the overwhelmingly most important problem on the agenda of Jobs 2001 is the problem of bringing employment to the unqualified, unskilled, disaffected young inner-city resident. All else pales into relative insignificance. Yet more traditional planning concerns, the concerns of those happier times of the 1960s, have not gone away. There will be a problem of managing and guiding growth as well as a problem of encouraging growth. Many new jobs are being created, will be created, in the dynamic sectors and in the dynamic centres of the region. Exactly how they are created, above all exactly where they are created, will have profound planning consequences in terms of job match or mismatch, ease and convenience of commuting, traffic congestion, local economic multiplier effects, and a score of other aspects. Planning can profoundly affect these issues for good or ill. Too often, as shown in Chapter 1, the results have been ill. The point is how to do better.

The first question must be how location can help grapple with mismatch. That, as explained, must depend in part on helping unqualified and unskilled people move out to the growth areas. But, in so far as education and training will help *some* inner-city residents obtain jobs locally, they may be aided also by inner–city developments that provide new jobs. All that said, the new jobs – whether inner-city or growth-area ones – need to be planned in relation to transport, especially public transport. That also makes good sense for everyone else, including those who presently work in these areas.

But, in so far as education and training will better equip the unqualified inner-city population to compete for London jobs, they – and, again, everyone else – will benefit from good access to these jobs too via public transport. Some of the locations now reserved for mega-developments, such as the King's Cross goods yard, are potentially good in this regard; some, such as Spitalfields, are less so. The aim should be to identify points in the deprived inner ring of London – above all in East and South-East London – with potentially good access to public transport which are currently unexploited, and then (as explained in Chapter 5) to develop the facilities. There are four or five sites in the inner and middle rings of London where this is outstandingly true (Fig. 9).

(1) *The 'City fringe' sites*. These – Fleet Street, Smithfield, Barbican, Broadgate, Spitalfields, Hay's Wharf – offer outstanding central locations for financial services and related jobs. But, because of their fringe location, not all are equally well located. Fleet Street and Smithfield will benefit from the opening of the new Thameslink in May 1988, taking trains from Bedford and St Albans to Gatwick and Sevenoaks. Hay's Wharf (London Bridge City) is outstandingly well placed for commuters from south and south east London, less so from the west and north west; it really needs an extension of the Jubilee Line from Charing Cross to London

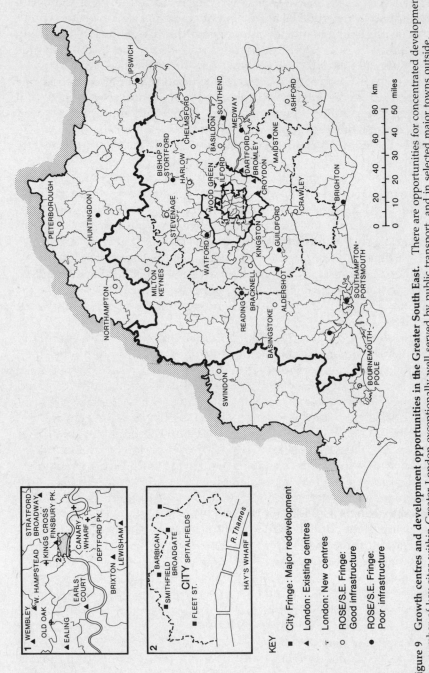

KEY

■ City Fringe: Major redevelopment

▲ London: Existing centres

✝ London: New centres

○ ROSE/S.E. Fringe:
Good infrastructure

● ROSE/S.E. Fringe:
Poor infrastructure

Figure 9 Growth centres and development opportunities in the Greater South East. There are opportunities for concentrated development at a number of key sites within Greater London exceptionally well served by public transport, and in selected major towns outside.

Bridge, as suggested in Chapter 5. Spitalfields, one of the biggest development opportunities of all, has no direct rail link and would benefit immeasurably from extension of the East London Line from Shoreditch to Liverpool Street.

(2) *Canary Wharf.* Canary Wharf is in a special category because the facilities are committed. The Docklands Light Railway will be capable, with longer trains and a rebuilt Canary Wharf station, of taking peak-hour flows of up to 22 000 passengers between there and the Bank, with a convenient connection to Fenchurch Street–Southend services at Limehouse. It can also deliver substantial flows to Stratford, there connecting with a wide range of British Rail and Central Line services fanning out across North-East London. An extension under the river to Lewisham could massively enhance access from south-east London. Therefore Canary Wharf, with its potential 45 000 office and ancillary jobs, is outstanding in terms of its accessibility to some of London's most deprived areas.

(3) *King's Cross goods yard (Belle Isle).* This 100-acre site immediately north of King's Cross station, just about to be redeveloped in late 1988, could become a mini-Canary Wharf. It is in the unusual position of being criss-crossed by railways, none of which presently serve it: the Bedford–St Pancras line, extended in summer 1988 into the Thameslink to Sevenoaks and Gatwick; the Letchworth–Stevenage–King's Cross electrics, which could and should be linked to the St Pancras lines; the North London link; and the Piccadilly Line, where York Road station has lain derelict since 1932. Potentially, therefore, this is one of the most outstandingly accessible sites in London: accessible, furthermore, to most parts of the deprived inner ring. And it offers unusual possibilities of a multiple development including offices, shopping, and leisure facilities in the restored warehouses alongside the Grand Union Canal.

(4) *Deptford Park.* This site, lost and neglected in a triangle of railways near the Millwall Football Ground, has similar characteristics to King's Cross: it is served by a host of rail lines that do not stop here. British Rail's multiple tracks from London Bridge here split three ways, to Croydon, Lewisham, and Greenwich; they are crossed by the East London lines from Whitechapel to New Cross and New Cross Gate. As suggested in Chapter 5, it would make eminently good operational sense for London Transport to extend the Bakerloo or Jubilee Line, or both, in tunnel as far as here, thence taking over British Rail lines to Greenwich and Slade Green and perhaps also, via Lewisham, to Barnehurst and Dartford. There is also the possibility of converting the East London line into a light rail system and extending it northward

to Liverpool Street and southward to Croydon, as suggested in a recent BR-LRT study (London Regional Transport and BR Network Southeast 1986). Together, combined with a new interchange station in the centre of the site, such developments would convert this derelict site into one of the most accessible in London. Further, it lies close to some of the most deprived localities of inner south-east London.

(5) *Old Oak Triangle*. This is Deptford Park's analogue in west London – strictly, since it is in Brent and Ealing, outer west London. On the edge of the great Park Royal industrial area, bordered on one side by Western Avenue, it is crossed without stopping by several lines: the Western Region main line from Reading to Paddington, which is likely soon to carry a new Heathrow service (Chapter 5); the Central Line from Ealing Broadway and Ruislip to Marble Arch and Bank; and the North London line from Richmond to North Woolwich. Again, these lines unusually offer the possibility of access from all points of the compass, including ones from deprived areas of high unemployment; and they could be linked by a single interchange station in the middle of this overgrown, almost jungle-like-site.

(6) *Existing centres*. In addition to these totally unexploited sites, there are a number of other centres which already have outstanding accessibility by public transport, and in one or two cases by road also. In inner London these include Finsbury Park, Stratford Broadway, Lewisham, Brixton, Earl's Court, and West Hampstead. In none of these cases is the potential fully exploited; in at least one – the triangle of land between Finchley Road and West Hampstead stations – it is almost totally unexploited.

In outer London the sites include Wembley, Wood Green, Ilford, Dartford, Bromley, Croydon, Kingston, and Ealing. All these are outstandingly accessible by public transport; some are on the North Circular Road, on radial motorways or trunk roads, or (Dartford) on the M25. Interestingly, several of them were designated strategic shopping centres in the ill-fated Greater London Development Plan of 1970. Some, like Croydon, are very fully developed; some, like Wembley, are in course of being developed; others are hardly exploited at all.

Outside London in the Outer Metropolitan Area, the best locations must be the ring of medium-sized towns 30-40 miles from London on the main rail and motorway corridors. Within them, the most accessible positions are the central ones, easily reached by bus (and sometimes train) from the surrounding areas. But at present, as the case of Reading so clearly shows, this advantage is being

70

squandered by the resulting congestion on the radial streets. Here, selective road construction is sorely needed: the road system in these towns is clearly inadequate to the demands now being placed on it. But equally, no amount of road construction will deal with the problem, because traffic growth will simply fill up the available space. Therefore, construction must be balanced by traffic restraint and by priority to public transport on the radials, especially approaching the centres. I return to this point where it belongs, in Chapter 5.

From this standpoint, it obviously matters whether the town already has a good-quality road system. The towns in the 30-40-mile ring differ widely in this respect. Some – New Towns like Stevenage, Harlow, Basildon, Crawley, and Gatwick, Expanded Towns like Basingstoke, and one or two older places like Chelmsford – have a reasonably good network of improved roads. Many others – Reading, Watford, Bishop's Stortford, Southend, the Medway Towns, Maidstone, Guildford, Aldershot – most definitely do not, though some have plans that are long overdue for fulfilment.

Many of these places were designated as growth areas in the 1970 Strategic Plan – some (like Reading and Basingstoke, Basildon and Southend, and Gatwick) as part of major growth areas, some (like Bishop's Stortford and Harlow, the Medway Towns and Maidstone) constituting medium-growth areas. That designation now appears to have been officially dropped, but in some cases, as already seen in Chapter 2, the reality continues. Therefore, they really demand some kind of plan to deal with the resulting pressures.

Farther out on the fringe of the South-East standard region, at about 60-80 miles from London, there exists a ring of even bigger regional cities: Southampton-Portsmouth (and, even more distant, Bournemouth-Poole), Swindon, Milton Keynes-Northampton, Peterborough-Huntingdon, Ipswich, Ashford. These, as already noted in Chapter 1, are among the fastest-growing places in all of Britain in the 1980s. They are strategically sited on the InterCity rail system and on national motorways and trunk roads. Like their counterparts in the 30-40 mile ring, some – especially those that are New and Expanded Towns – have excellent internal road networks, while others (so far) have not. And again like their nearer counterparts, many were designated as growth centres either in the 1970 Strategic Plan for the South East (SPSE) or in its predecessors, the 1964 South-East Study and the 1967 Strategy.

The need therefore is to plan the expansion of at least some of these places, but to do so in relationship with the revitalization of outworn inner-city transportation or port sites which are located along the same radial corridor, for instance Reading-Basingstoke/Old Oak Triangle; Peterborough-Huntingdon/Stevenage/King's Cross; Southend-Basildon and Ipswich/ Chelmsford/Stratford Broadway/Canary Wharf; Ashford/Medway-Maidstone/Dartford/Lewisham-Deptford Park. The reason for doing so is that planned development of large sites is likely to be more efficient in transport terms, and also more visible to investors, than smaller developments peppered across the region. They would be linked primarily by high-speed rail transport along these radial corridors, but the outer ones would be linked also by radial motorways, connected for cross-journeys by the M25 and an upgraded North Circular Road. This, recall, was also the strategy of 1970; but that in turn was only the reinterpretation of the principles of Abercrombie, Unwin, and Howard in a different socioeconomic context. We need a similar reassertion now, nearly twenty years on.

It is not possible, and not necessary, to spell out this strategy in detail; Fig. 9, which cites the possibilities, needs to be interpreted selectively. All the sites, whether inner-city or outer-fringe, are so commercially attractive that developers should fall over themselves for the right to take them over. Many, however, will need fairly massive injections of capital for the necessary transportation infrastructure, in the form of tube extensions, light rail systems, new roads and new InterCity stations. Since much or all of this will not be provided without some capital subsidy, the amount and type of such subsidy will need to be determined as part of a regional development plan. Several different providing agencies will be involved: the Department of Transport, the shire counties, the London boroughs and shire districts, British Rail, London Regional Transport, perhaps others. So a massive job of co-ordination remains to be undertaken both at the regional and subsequently at the local level, to which I will return in Chapter 6.

There are two important remaining questions about the strategy for Roseland and the Fringe. One is a macro-scale question: Can and should strategic policy be used to counteract the pronounced East/West imbalance in the region? The other is a more micro–scale question: Within the growth areas, should policy seek to develop new commercial activities right in the centres, or at the edges? We need to look at each in turn.

The East–West Imbalance

There have been two, somewhat contradictory, arguments about the pattern of economic development in Roseland. One is that the completion of the M25 in October 1986 will inexorably, despite all the contrary efforts of the planners, pull industrial and (above all) office and distributive development out from London into a ring close to it (SERPLAN 1982; Simmons 1985; Damesick *et al*. 1986). The analysis earlier in this chapter suggests that the pull is so sharply outwards that the M25 may exert only a marginal extra influence, though there is some anecdotal evidence of major planning applications in the Green Belt next to M25 interchanges, such as the proposed retail centre at Wraysbury near Egham. But there is an additional concern: that the M25 may help reinforce the traditional magnetism of London's north-west sector, observable ever since interwar years, because of the linkages here to the major radials – the M1, M40, M4 – lining London with major segments of the home market.

The other, perhaps more significant, argument is that the Channel Tunnel might help reverse this marked East–West contrast (SERPLAN 1987a, Simmons 1987). However, the impacts of the Tunnel are likely to be by no means large; and, in so far as they will occur, they may actually be disadvantageous. True, there is likely to be an overall increase in both passenger and freight traffic, with the port of Dover continuing to handle the bulk of freight; but the Channel ports are likely to suffer employment loss overall, and the pattern of through traffic means that any economic impacts are likely to be felt much closer to the centre of London. The most careful work done so far, by Robert Vickerman's group at the University of Kent, suggests fairly minimal impacts because most activity is not very sensitive to changes in transport costs; but it, too, stresses that infrastructure improvements on the French side could have a cumulative, synergistic effect. This reinforces earlier work, which suggested that the gains from increased accessibility would be small (Keeble, *et al*. 1982; Vickerman 1987, 195-6).

So Kent planners worry publicly that the main beneficiaries will be the French, who are investing huge amounts in infrastructure at the Pas-de-Calais end of the tunnel. The main UK opportunities, the Kent planners think, are likely to be in Ashford–where the freight clearance depot will be located, and perhaps along both banks of the river between the London boundary and Tilbury-Grays, in particular the north-west Kent riverside around Dartford, close to the M25. They would particularly like this, because, significantly, this area has some of the highest unemployment rates in Roseland. But it will need a lot of new infrastructure – not merely the new East London River Crossing and associated links, but also extensive investment in better riverside road and rail links. And in spring 1988 the county suffered a major blow when Nicholas Ridley rejected a big development package deal, including a northern bypass, for the Dartford area.

A few weeks later the London Planning Advisory Committee, which is the statutory successor to the GLC in respect of London-wide planning functions, published its draft strategy based on major economic growth points on the eastern side of London: Stratford–Temple Mills-Walthamstow Marshes, Rainham-Wennington, Barking Reach, Greenwich Peninsula, Thamesmead-Belvedere, and Enfield Lock (London Planning Advisory Commitee 1988, 9.11). It wanted to see the growth points in place by the mid-1990s, and to boost them by controls on the outward creep of the central business district into West London. The point is that, until Docklands is finished, only sites close to it – such as Barking Reach, or Stratford with its exceptional accessibility – are likely to have much chance of success. And the major opportunities will come only when the huge East London transport package is concluded, which means the mid-1990s at earliest.

Out-of-Town: The SEEDS Argument

The micro question concerns what will happen within the growth centres. In these places, whether 40 or 70 or 110 miles from the centre of London, much of the key commercial development will need to be right in the centre, where it will be most accessible to high-speed InterCity train services. That includes back offices, some headquarters offices, and specialized kinds of shopping. Equally, other types of development – R&D, high-tech manufacturing – will go anywhere but here. About all that, there need be little disagreement. But on one important kind of development controversy rages. That is shopping.

Until the 1980s, most retailers and consequently most shopping developers in Britain showed relatively little interest in anywhere but the High Streets. That, presumably, reflected the facts of life; not until the 1970s did a majority of British households own cars, and even then the car was not ordinarily available to the wife who still did most of the shopping. But now the facts of life have changed: car ownership nationally was 61 per cent in 1985, and over 70 per cent in the shire counties around London; here, a majority of women drive. The result is a flood of proposals for large out-of-town shopping centres, especially close to the M25 motorway (Fig. 10).

Not everyone is happy. SEEDS (the South East Economic Development Strategy, organized by a number of district authorities in the

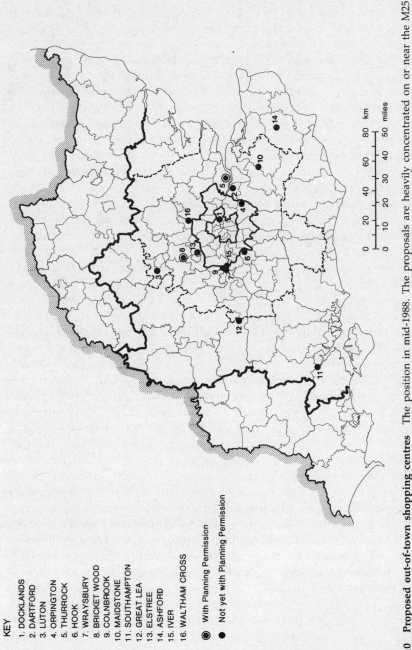

KEY

1. DOCKLANDS
2. DARTFORD
3. LUTON
4. ORPINGTON
5. THURROCK
6. HOOK
7. WRAYSBURY
8. BRICKET WOOD
9. COLNBROOK
10. SOUTHAMPTON
11. MAIDSTONE
12. GREAT LEA
13. ELSTREE
14. ASHFORD
15. IVER
16. WALTHAM CROSS

◉ With Planning Permission
● Not yet with Planning Permission

Figure 10 Proposed out-of-town shopping centres The position in mid-1988. The proposals are heavily concentrated on or near the M25 London Orbital Motorway and in some favoured growth areas of ROSE.

South-East) argues that 'we should recognize that the out-of-town movement is a major threat to the viability of existing shopping centres', which 'contributes to process of inner-city (and central area) decline'. It goes on to suggest that in the United States, where this process has gone farthest, major new downtown developments are seen as the key to the revival of inner urban areas, such as the Rouse schemes in New York and Baltimore. Hence, it argues, we should 'reconstitute town centres as just that: town centres rather than merely retail centres which simply open and close during office hours'. This requires a 'positive re-orientation' of centres to improve the quality of shopping, accepting new trends in consumerism, but also providing facilities for leisure and social intercourse, especially with a view to giving them life in the evenings. It involves four elements: structural renewal, public services (notably fast, cheap, reliable, frequent public transport), cultural initiatives, and marketing (SEEDS 1987, 125–8).

All this is unexceptionable, and indeed is what James Rouse and other successful developers are achieving in the United States. But three comments are in order. First, the SEEDS report wants it both ways: it wants to achieve Rousification, but it also wants to retain kinds of retail activity – notably, food – which now, for good reason, show the least affinity for town centres. Second, it requires a range of public spending – on public transport, for instance – which seems right out of line with current policies. (Perhaps, indeed, the report is addressed to another government than the current one; but if it is to have any prospect of early realization, it needs to be adopted to the reality of present constraints on local authority spending.) Third, it seems naive to assume that planning controls in themselves can cause retailers and developers to change their behaviour. It calls for 'planning control over the composition of shopping units' (requiring legislation), 'rental policy designed to safeguard food stores in town centre areas', 'direct provision and subsidy for local exhibitions, street theatre, cafes, advice centres and community areas', and 'a system of loans and grants to improve the physical condition of certain shops in return for agreement on employment conditions, accessibility and facilities for consumers' (SEEDS 1987, 135). If these were the free-wheeling, free-spending 1960s, such policies might have some relevance. But for the average British local authority in the late 1980s, operating in a Thatcherite world, they must seem like fantasy.

The fact is that Rouse-type leisure shopping developments, now being emulated in some schemes in Britain, are highly specialized;

there is no place in them for food or other convenience shopping. Though doubtless the High Streets will retain some such shopping, for the convenience of those who work in the centres and want to shop in their lunch hours, it is simply unrealistic to think that most of it will stay there; it is not where the people are. The aim, rather, should be to recognize that there are two different kinds of shopping centre: one based on convenience and some basic comparative shopping, which is most easily and efficiently done in purpose-designed malls accessible by car, the other based on a highly specialized shopping associated with leisure time, much of which can and should be provided through sensitive rehabilitation of historic urban cores. The two are in fact not very compatible, and the attempt to provide for the first may well inhibit the second – which would be no one's gain.

Randstad England

When thinking about jobs, therefore, we need to think about two different spatial scales. At *regional* scale we should be trying to develop several major employment nodes both within London and outside it. These would be the points of maximum accessibility from all other places. In the past, the City and West End of London have uniquely had this quality because of the pattern of the radial commuter rail system that focuses on them. In the future, with the progressive development of the motorway system and the future Regional Express Rail system, they will cease to be unique: they will share that quality with up to a dozen other places, two or three within London's built-up mass, the rest outside. Regional policy, hand in hand with the development industry, needs to build on that fact. It should not find it difficult.

The result would be a pattern of centres uncannily resembling Ebenezer Howard's famous diagram of the polycentric Social City – the 'Group of Slumless Smokeless Cities' in the first edition of his book (Howard 1898). A central city, London, would be surrounded by a ring of satellite cities, each with its own employment areas surrounded by homes, all linked by an 'Inter-municipal Railway'. It would also resemble that most celebrated actual polycentric city, Randstad Holland, the 'Ring City' that incorporates all the major cities of the Netherlands – Rotterdam, the Hague, Leiden, Haarlem, Amsterdam, Utrecht – running in a 110-mile horseshoe around the western half of that country. To turn London progressively into

77

Randstad England should be a primary aim of any strategic plan for the South East.

At *local* level, as just seen, planners will need to steer a fine balance to ensure that horses run on appropriate courses. Especially in Roseland, where existing centres are bursting at the seams, they will find that they have to recognize that these places simply cannot do everything at once. More and more, they will come to resemble central London: they will be specialized, high-intensity, high-rent centres, dedicated to performance of the region's higher-level functions. Though they will be able to house a modicum of more local shopping and other services, a large part of these – whether grocery superstores or DIY warehouses, solicitors' offices or doctors' surgeries – will inevitably need to hive themselves off to locations more convenient to the places where their clientele live and to the means of transport they use to visit them. That means not vast out-of-town centres in the midst of green fields – a solution that would be as non-viable commercially as it would be offensive in terms of planning – but well sited edge-of-town developments, convenient both for car access and for bus routes. It is not a very difficult locational problem: such sites exist around every town now, and more should become available as bypasses and orbital links are completed. And, as further new communities are developed away from the existing towns, these too can and should play their role in housing the more local functions. That, however, brings us to the matter of Chapter 4.

4

People, Houses and
Land 2001

As with jobs, so with people: the movement has been and will be
outward, from core to ring, from ring to fringe. As shown briefly
in Chapter 1, the ring of maximum population growth has moved
progressively and inexorably farther out: in the 1950s it formed a solid
belt, 15-30 miles distant, around London; in the 1960s it had moved
to the 30-50 mile limits, and had also broken into a series of growth
areas around the major towns of that belt; by the 1970s it had already
decomposed into a number of growth areas, some as near as 30-40
miles, others as distant as 70-80 miles distant; by the 1980s, it consists
of half a dozen growth areas, some still relatively near in, others as
far as 100-110 miles from the capital (Table 11 and Fig. 6).

The relationship between these two movements, of jobs and of
people, is somewhat complex. As explained in Chapter 3, traditionally many of the jobs were in the centre of London. People moved
out, away from their jobs, for housing reasons; but, having done
so, many found jobs locally. Thus, in a curious way, the outward
movement of people has helped generate the outward movement of
jobs: in some cases because these jobs cater for the local population,
in some cases because they draw on the local work-force. The
farther out the people go, the farther – after a time lag – the jobs are
likely to go too.

Table 11 South East: population change, 1961–86

	Population change						Share Greater South East		
	1961–71	1971–81	1981–86	1961–71 (%)	1971–81 (%)	1981–86 (% decennial)	1961–71 (%)	1971–81 (%)	1981–86 (%)
'Greater South East'	1 266 550	131 154	406 500	7.0	0.7	4.1	100.0	100.0	100.0
South East	937 514	−134 874	254 200	5.0	− 0.8	3.0	74.0	−102.8	62.5
Greater London	−540 097	−739 181	−30 500	− 6.8	− 9.9	−0.9	−42.6	−563.6	−7.5
Inner London	−460 944	−533 957	−38 500	−13.2	−17.6	−3.0	−36.4	−407.1	−9.5
Outer London	− 79 153	−205 224	8 000	− 1.8	− 4.6	0.4	− 6.2	−156.5	2.0
Outer Metropolitan Area	816 744	255 087	67 400	18.6	4.9	2.4	64.5	194.5	16.6
Outer South East	660 867	349 220	217 500	18.3	8.2	9.3	52.2	266.3	53.5
ROSE	1 477 611	604 307	284 900	18.5	6.4	5.6	116.7	460.8	70.1
South East Fringe	329 036	266 028	152 300	14.8	10.4	10.7	26.0	202.8	37.5
ROGSE	1 806 647	870 335	437 200	17.7	7.2	6.7	142.6	663.6	107.6

Source: Office of Population Censuses and Surveys (1984, 1987).

Table 12 Growth areas: population growth, 1961–86

	Population change						Share GSE			Share ROGSE		
	1961–71	1971–81	1981–86	1961–71 (%)	1971–81 (%)	1981–86 (%) decennial	1961–71 (%)	1971–81 (%)	1981–86 (%)	1961–71 (%)	1971–81 (%)	1981–86 (%)
Major growth areas	391 876	224 753	102 000	20.5	9.7	8.0	30.9	171.4	25.1	21.7	25.8	23.3
Reading–Wokingham–Aldershot–Basingstoke	121 203	54 142	31 900	33.8	11.3	11.8	9.6	41.3	7.8	6.7	6.2	7.3
South Hampshire	80 390	5 663	2 200	11.9	0.7	0.6	6.3	4.3	0.5	4.4	0.7	0.5
Crawley–Gatwick	53 167	39 411	11 700	26.4	15.5	7.9	4.2	30.0	2.9	2.9	4.5	2.7
South Essex	95 101	36 015	3 700	20.4	6.4	1.2	7.5	27.5	0.9	5.3	4.1	0.8
Milton Keynes–Northampton	42 015	89 522	52 500	19.6	34.9	30.1	3.3	68.3	12.9	2.3	10.3	12.0

Source: Office of Population Censuses and Surveys (1984, 1987).

Oddly, at first sight, in their headlong outward progress the people seem to have blithely ignored the strategic planning prescriptions of the 1970s. Table 12 extracts from the figures the growth areas of the 1970 *Strategic Plan*, and Table 13 compares the 1981–86 figures with the projections made by the planners in 1970. The result is chastening: the entire region attained only one-third of its 1970 projected growth; within that total, the five major growth areas achieved only 40 per cent of the total, against a planned 53 per cent; among them, two growth areas – south Hampshire and south Essex – achieved very little growth at all. But these results need to be treated with due caution: the 'failure' of the plan might just be because the planners, or their political masters, did not want it. They stopped the growth in some places, and it just rolled on to the next place down the line. In other words, the outward movement of population has been aided, even engineered, by negative planning policies nearer in.

This is totally speculative. We have no way, in the existing state of knowledge, of saying whether or to what degree this has happened. In so far as – according to media anecdote – London's commuter catchment area has been extending apparently without limit, to 80 and even 100 miles from the capital, it is plausible. Growth within these rings, however, has been by no means even. Table 14 analyses the data in a different way: by radial corridors or sectors. It brings out the sharp disproportion between the favoured sectors north

Table 13   South East: forecasts and reality, 1981–91

	Population Change ('000)	
	Forecast (South East Strategic Plan 1970)	Actual*
South East†	1400	508
Greater London	− 336	− 61
ROSE (SE less Gtr London)†	1740	570
Major growth areas	917	204
Reading–Wokingham–		
Aldershot-Basingstoke	227	64
Milton Keynes	180	105
South Hampshire	220	4
Crawley–Burgess Hill	120	23
South Essex	170	8

* 1981–6 figures, doubled
† 'Old' South East, as in the 1970 Plan: includes Bournemouth.
Source: South East Joint Plan Team (1970); Tables 11 and 12.

Table 14 Growth in radial corridors, 1961–86

	Population change			1961–71 (%)	1971–81 (%)	1981–86 (% decennial)	Share GSE			Share ROGSE		
	1961–71	1971–81	1981–86				1961–71 (%)	1971–81 (%)	1981–86 (%)	1961–71 (%)	1971–81 (%)	1981–86 (%)
Corridors	1 806 647	870 335	437 200	17.7	7.2	6.9	142.6	663.6	107.6	100.0	100.0	100.0
M1/A6	195 410	151 197	62 900	16.2	10.8	8.9	15.4	115.3	17.0	10.8	17.4	15.8
A1/M11/A11	244 398	152 296	65 800	21.4	11.0	8.4	19.3	116.1	16.2	13.5	17.5	15.1
A12/A127	261 091	138 144	54 200	20.4	9.0	6.4	20.6	105.3	13.3	14.5	15.9	12.4
A2/M2/M20	200 899	68 156	16 700	16.8	4.9	2.3	15.9	52.0	4.1	11.1	7.8	3.8
A21/A22/A23/A24	177 912	68 331	48 000	12.6	4.3	5.7	14.0	52.1	11.8	9.8	7.9	11.0
A3/M3	381 970	155 059	85 500	15.9	5.6	6.2	30.2	118.2	21.0	21.1	17.8	19.6
M4	185 882	90 166	66 500	20.1	8.1	10.9	14.7	68.7	16.4	10.3	10.4	15.2
M40	159 085	46 986	31 300	24.3	5.8	7.1	12.6	35.8	7.7	8.8	5.4	7.2

Source: Office of Population Censuses and Surveys (1984, 1987).

Table 15 England and Wales: population changes, 1971–2001

	1971–81	1981–86	1981–2001	1971–81 (%)	1981–86 (% decennial)	1981–2001 (% decennial)
England & Wales	405 112	441 100	2 536 700	0.8	1.8	3.4
Major urban areas	−1 279 426	−217 900	−436 000	−6.7	−2.4	−1.6
% England & Wales	−315.8	−49.4	−30.6			
The 'Golden Belt'	649 158	366 000	1 313 800	10.1	10.2	12.2
% England & Wales	160.2	83.0	92.2			

Source: Office of Population Censuses and Surveys (1988).

Table 16 Greater South East: major growth points, 1961–86

	Population change						Share GSE			Share ROGSE		
	1961–71	1971–81	1981–86	1961–71 (%)	1971–81 (%)	1981–86 (% decennial)	1961–71 (%)	1971–81 (%)	1981–86 (%)	1961–71 (%)	1971–81 (%)	1981–86 (%)
Major growth points	389 714	323 004	194 200	21.1	14.5	15.7	30.8	246.3	47.8	21.6	37.1	44.4
Milton Keynes–Northampton	42 015	89 522	52 500	19.6	34.9	30.1	3.3	68.3	12.9	2.3	10.3	12.0
Reading–Wokingham–Aldershot–Basingstoke	121 203	54 142	31 900	33.8	11.3	11.8	9.6	41.3	7.8	6.7	6.2	7.3
Peterborough–Huntingdon	43 448	54 770	30 700	27.3	27.0	23.7	3.4	41.8	7.6	2.4	6.3	7.0
Bournemouth–Poole–Wimborne	36 079	24 857	26 400	11.6	7.2	14.2	2.8	19.0	6.5	2.0	2.9	6.0
Swindon	28 725	20 381	15 700	14.0	8.7	12.2	2.3	15.5	3.9	1.6	2.3	3.6
Ipswich	35 087	24 036	15 100	11.6	7.1	8.3	2.8	18.3	3.7	1.9	2.8	3.5
Crawley–Gatwick	53 167	39 411	11 700	26.4	15.5	7.9	4.2	30.0	2.9	2.9	4.5	2.7
Chelmsford	29 990	15 885	10 200	32.2	12.9	14.6	2.4	12.1	2.5	1.7	1.8	2.3

Source: Office of Population Censuses and Surveys (1987, 1987).

and west of the capital, and the relatively weak growth in the east and south–east. Growth is not merely rolling outwards; it is rolling westwards and north-westwards. In the progress, it is contributing to a striking new feature of the geography of Britain. A quite disproportionate part of the population growth in the entire country, in the 1970s and early 1980s, was concentrated in a belt overlapping the boundaries of the South-East standard region, and including also the neighbouring counties in the South-West, East Midlands, and East Anglia regions: Dorset, Wiltshire, Northamptonshire, Cambridge-shire, Suffolk. This 'Golden Belt', which also incorporates South-East fringe counties like Hampshire, Berkshire and Oxfordshire, had in-creased by 1 million people between 1971 and 1986; it had some 80 per cent of national growth in the early 1980s, and is projected to con-tinue to take no less than 92 per cent down to the end of the century, adding 1.3 million people between 1981 and 2001 (Table 15 and Fig. 11(a)). And, within it, a relatively few extended city regions – Bournemouth-Poole, Swindon, Northampton-Milton Keynes, Peter-borough-Huntingdon, and Ipswich – completely dominate the picture, taking some 31 per cent of growth in the extended outer region in the 1960s, 48 per cent in the 1980s (Table 16 and Fig. 11(b)).

This pattern is likely to persist down to the century's end and beyond (Tables 15 and 17). And this has been emphasized by new 1985-based population projections published early in 1988, which have produced huge forecast increases in some of the counties of the fringe: Cambridgeshire's 2001 population has risen by 97 000–an unparalleled 14 per cent–compared with the projection made two years earlier, Hampshire's by 67 000, Kent's by 49 000, that of east Sussex by 39 000. Even more exaggeratedly than in the 1983-based projections, during the 1980s and 1990s the 'Golden Belt' will con-tinue to dominate the national picture of population growth (Table 15): with more than 1.3 million extra people, it will account for no less than 92 per cent of the net population growth in England and Wales, as against 959 000 (67 per cent) in the earlier forecast.

In consequence, within the Greater South East, growth will be concentrated at the fringe: in the 1980s just under 40 per cent of growth in the Greater South East will be there, in the 1990s over 41 per cent (Table 17). By that time, indeed, the fringe may need redefinition: it is likely to run from Dorset to Lincolnshire. Trends in the late 1980s seem to be anticipating that outcome, with a rapid growth of long-distance commuting from locations as far distant as Stamford in Lincolnshire, 105 miles from London. The critical question is whether, as in previous decades, the long-distance commuters progressively defect by finding local jobs. Lincolnshire

Table 17 South East: population projections, 1981–2001

	Popn 1986	Projected popn ('000)		change			% change			% GSE		
		1991	2001	1986–1991	1991–2001	1986–2001	1986–1991	1991–2001	1986–2001	1986–1991	1991–2001	1986–2001
Greater South East	20 266 300	20 755	21 786	488 700	1 031 000	1 519 700	4.4	5.0	7.5	100.0	100.0	100.0
South East	17 264 600	17 622	18 343	357 400	721 000	1 078 400	3.5	4.1	6.2	73.1	69.9	71.0
Greater London	6 775 200	6 806	6 916	30 800	110 000	140 800	0.0	1.6	2.1	6.3	10.7	9.3
Inner London	2 511 700	2 536	2 556	24 300	20 000	44 300	−0.6	0.8	1.8	5.0	1.9	2.9
Outer London	4 263 500	4 269	4 361	5 500	92 000	97 500	0.3	2.2	2.3	1.1	8.9	6.4
ROSE	10 489 600	10 816	11 427	326 400	611 000	937 400	5.8	5.6	8.9	66.8	59.3	61.7
South East Fringe	3 001 700	3 133	3 433	131 300	310 000	441 300	9.4	4.2	14.7	26.9	30.1	29.0
ROGSE	13 491 300	13 949	14 870	457 700	921 000	1 378 700	6.6	3.3	10.2	93.7	89.3	90.7

Source: Office of Population Censuses and Surveys (1988).

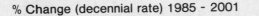

% Change (decennial rate) 1985 - 2001

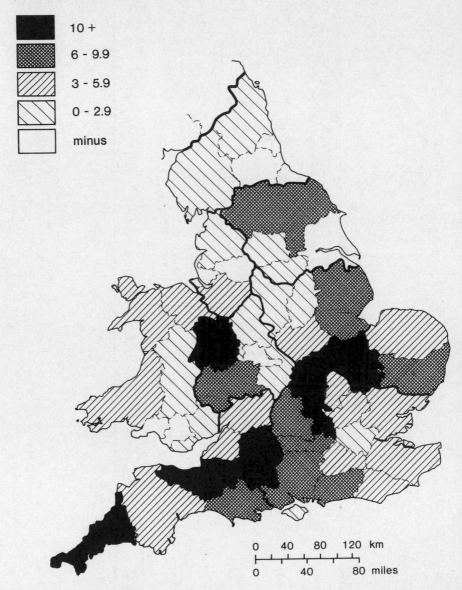

10 +

6 - 9.9

3 - 5.9

0 - 2.9

minus

0   40   80   120 km

0   40   80 miles

Fig. 11(a) The Golden Belt The official population projections for England and Wales down to the year 2001 show continued heavy growth in a belt of counties constituting the fringe of the Greater South East, from Dorset to Suffolk.

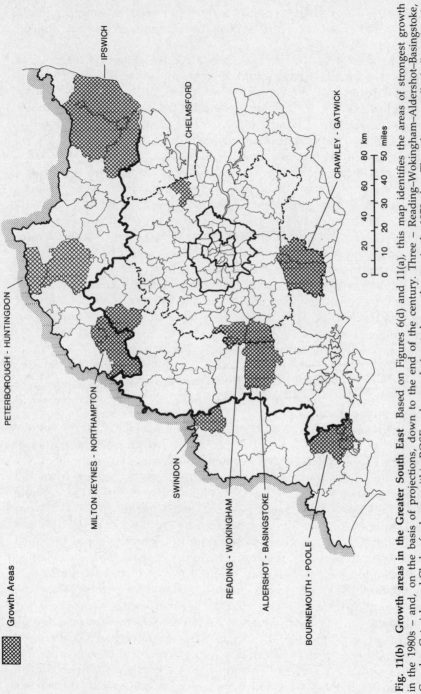

Fig. 11(b) Growth areas in the Greater South East Based on Figures 6(d) and 11(a), this map identifies the areas of strongest growth in the 1980s – and, on the basis of projections, down to the end of the century. Three – Reading–Wokingham–Aldershot–Basingstoke, Crawley–Gatwick, and Chelmsford – are within ROSE and were designated growth areas in the 1970 plan. The others are all wholly or largely in the Greater South East fringe.

Growth Areas

IPSWICH

CHELMSFORD

CRAWLEY - GATWICK

PETERBOROUGH - HUNTINGDON

MILTON KEYNES - NORTHAMPTON

SWINDON

READING - WOKINGHAM

ALDERSHOT - BASINGSTOKE

BOURNEMOUTH - POOLE

0   20   40   60   80   km
0   10   20   30   40   50   miles

in the 1980s and 1990s does not appear to have the same economic base as Berkshire had in the 1960s. But economic history is littered with surprises.

Could these forecasts be upset? Not readily. Some observers put great weight on 'reurbanization': the return to the city, spearheaded by the Yuppies and the Dinkies. They point out that in 1984 and the year following, for the first time since 1911, Greater London actually gained population (Champion 1987). The gain was concentrated in outer London, but in inner London – a more surprising reversal – the population virtually stabilized after many years of loss. That perhaps is not surprising; in both inner and outer London there has been a strong natural increase of the population, a product mainly of large numbers of young adults among the ethnic groups who immigrated in the 1960s and 1970s, and especially concentrated in certain boroughs. Net out-migration, in contrast, continues at a rapid rate. The projections, which show a very modest gain of 110 000 for the 1990s – a product of a 20 000 gain in inner London and over 90 000 in outer London – reflect these demographic realities, and also the end of the once-for-all housing bonus obtained by the redevelopment of London Docklands. They do however have an important implication for housing policies in London.

So the outward move is unlikely to be stemmed, and Table 17 reflects this. The question now is whether planning policies adequately provide for it. On that there is no agreement at all; in fact, there is fierce controversy. We turn now to lay out the main lines of the debate.

The first essential is to translate population projections into household projections. For it is not *people* who need houses and flats, but *people grouped in households*. Almost simultaneously with the new 1988 population projections came household projections from the Department of the Environment (Table 18). These showed that, while the population of the South East was expected to grow by 3.4 per cent, and that of the Greater South East by 6.6 per cent, between 1986 and 2001, the increase in separate households would be much more spectacular: 13.9 per cent in the South East, 15.2 per cent in the extended region. The reason is not a growth in the numbers of conventional married-couple households: the very reverse. In the entire region these are projected to decline marginally, by 0.9 per cent in the Greater South East, by 2.4 per cent in the standard region; in Greater London their shrinkage is more spectacular: 9.8 per cent in both inner and outer London. Compensating for this, however, is a huge projected growth in single parents – by over 30 per cent in the Greater South East – and in one–person households, which are

Table 18 Households: projected numbers, 1986–2001

	1986	1991 ('000)	2001	1986–2001 ('000)	(%)	1991–2001 ('000)	(%)	Ave. size of household		
Greater South East	7785	8254	8965	1180	15.2	711	8.6	2.56	2.47	2.39
South East	6649	7023	7572	923	13.9	549	7.8	2.55	2.47	2.38
Greater London	2707	2808	2932	225	8.3	124	4.4	2.46	2.38	2.32
Inner London	1058	1108	1153	95	9.0	45	4.1	2.32	2.23	2.16
Outer London	1649	1700	1779	130	7.9	79	4.7	2.55	2.48	2.42
ROSE	3942	4214	4641	699	17.7	427	10.1	2.62	2.52	2.42
South East Fringe	1136	1231	1393	257	22.6	162	13.2	2.59	2.51	2.44
ROGSE	5078	5445	6034	956	18.8	589	10.8	2.61	2.52	2.42

Source: Department of the Environment (1988).

expected to grow by over 40 per cent. Other kinds of households, including unrelated people living together, are projected to grow by just under 30 per cent (Table 19).

The significance of these figures, of course, is that they spell a greatly increased need for small, separate dwellings. And much of this need will be felt outside London, in and around the embattled towns of the home counties. During the 1990s, household numbers in the South-East region would rise by 549 000 – 90 000 more than the figures used by SERPLAN in their most recent statements (SERPLAN 1985b, 10–11; 1986f, 13). And, worse, less of this would be in London: only 124 000, against the 150 000 assumed by SERPLAN.

There is a further complication in all this, which is the allowance that ought to be made for existing shortages of housing in London. Now this is like the old question of the length of a piece of string: it depends on what you mean. London council waiting lists in 1985 totalled more than 240 000, a total that had been steady since 1980. But no one thinks that the lists are very reliable, since some people on them may have found housing, while some people who need it may not have joined (Conway 1985, 41-3). Jean Conway's own careful

Table 19 Households: projected changes in composition, 1986–2001

	Married couple	Lone parent	One person	Other
		Changes ('000), 1986–2001		
Greater South East	− 39	222	809	185
South East	− 90	184	669	160
Greater London	−132	77	202	78
Inner London	− 41	40	63	33
Outer London	− 91	37	139	45
ROSE	42	107	467	87
South East Fringe	51	38	140	25
ROGSE	93	145	607	112
		Changes (%) 1986–2001		
Greater South East	−0.9	31.3	41.6	29.7
South East	−2.4	29.8	39.9	28.9
Greater London	−9.9	25.8	26.3	25.0
Inner London	−9.8	28.2	18.0	22.9
Outer London	−9.8	23.7	33.3	30.4
ROSE	1.7	33.4	51.3	33.3
South East Fringe	7.2	41.8	52.2	35.7
ROGSE	2.9	35.3	51.6	33.8

Source: Department of the Environment (1988).

Table 20   An estimate of London housing need, 1985

1981:	*Census households*	*2 658 000*
	plus: Concealed households	+ 81 000
	minus: 'Voluntary' sharers	− 22 000
	Total households needing separate accommodation	2 717 000
	Total dwellings	*2 713 000*
	minus: Non-available	− 61 000
	2% mobility allowance	− 54 000
	Net available dwellings	*2 598 000*
	Shortage	*119 000*
1995:	*1981 shortage*	*119,000*
	minus: Net additions 1981–84	− 52 000
	plus: Demolitions 1985–95	+ 50 000
	Estimated new households 1985–95	+ 230 000
	minus: Net gain from conversions	− 30 000
	Additional net build required 1985–95	*200 000*

Source: Conway (1985).

estimate is that the total shortage was at least 119 000 in 1981 and had perhaps shrunk to 99 000 by 1984; additionally, to keep pace with needs, 200 000 more units might be needed between 1985 and 1995 (pp. 14–15, 65) (Table 20). But these estimates were based on older projections of household formation in London, now reduced.

It is difficult to know the policy implications of these figures. Particularly, it is difficult to say where the resulting houses should be provided. Given current government policies, the councils will not provide them; private landlords and housing associations will. And they will provide them where they can find land, which in turn will depend on the price of land. The likelihood is that not many dwellings to meet need will be provided in London itself, unless the cost of land can be artificially written down. To that question, I return in Chapter 6.

Meanwhile, on the broader regional scale, the numbers for supply and demand no longer agreed. And this gave renewed fire to the great housing land debate of the 1980s, which has so regularly made the headlines.

The Great Housing Land Debate

In a sense, this debate has been continuing ever since the passage of the 1947 Planning Act – or, at least, since the private builder became enmeshed with the planning system in his return to the scene in the early 1950s. It seems to have waxed and waned. In the 1980s it has very much waxed, in the form of a sometimes-acrimonious debate between the big housebuilders – represented by the House Builders Federation and Consortium Developments – on the one side and SERPLAN (the Standing Conference of South East Planning Authorities) on the other. And, squeezed uncomfortably in the middle, have been successive Secretaries of State for the Environment.

The debate effectively began in May 1985, when Consortium Developments, formed in August 1983 by ten (later reduced to nine) of the country's largest housebuilders, announced a plan to build the first of a series of new communities in the South East, at Tillingham Hall in south Essex. Such new communities were necessary, the consortium said (and still says), because local planning authorities were not allocating enough land for building; by the end of the 1980s, they argued, there would be a shortage of 250 000 new houses. In support, they quoted a Department of the Environment forecast of March 1985, indicating that there could be 720 000 additional households in the South East between 1981 and 1991, 180 000 more than the 540 000 on which SERPLAN was then basing its plans (SERPLAN 1985b, 10–11). On top of that, there was a need to cover existing shortages in London (68 000), to allow a margin for mobility (36 000), and to replace obsolescent dwellings (60 000). Altogether, the consortium claimed, this gave a minimum need for 884 000 extra homes – against which the planners were providing for only 600 000. In the 1990s this would get worse, since the planners were providing for a mere 460 000 homes.

The Tillingham proposal was predictably rejected by the local planning authority, went to appeal and to public inquiry, and was finally lost. That perhaps was also predictable: the site, halfway between Upminster and Basildon, sits in the middle of the metropolitan Green Belt at a particularly narrow and sensitive point. But, in his letter of February 1987 to the Secretary of State, the inquiry inspector also rejected Consortium Developments' arguments about housing land need: he concluded that there was no apparent shortfall in the supply of land for the region during 1981–91. Nevertheless, while subsequently confirming rejection of the appeal, the Secretary of State emphasized that this was based largely on the Green Belt status of the site: in general, he said, properly sited new communities could help meet the demand for new homes. So the debate rumbled on.

As it did so, adding fuel to the consortium's fires, house prices in the South East have continued to escalate in dizzying fashion. A much-quoted estimate of mid-1987 was that in London they were rising by £53 a day. In 1987 overall, according to the Halifax Building Society, they rose 23 per cent in London, 25 per cent in the South East and no less than 30 per cent in East Anglia, against 16 per cent nationally. Figures from the Nationwide Anglia Building Society were a little more modest: 25 per cent in Greater London, 21 per cent in the OMA, 20 per cent in the Outer South East, and 25 per cent in East Anglia, against 16 per cent nationally. For 1988 Nationwide Anglia predicted a lower rate of increase – but only because buyers could no longer keep up. Figures issued by the Halifax Building Society in October 1987, showed that every county in the South East, save the Isle of Wight, recorded an average house price of £55 000 or more; no other county in the country did so, but significantly, four out of the next five highest-priced counties were found in the South-East fringe (Fig. 12). But, said the Tillingham inspector, such trends were not the result of a shortage of building land.

Shortly before the inquiry inspector issued his recommendation, in May 1986, SERPLAN had published a report by an independent consultant, W. S. Grigson, on house prices in the South East. Perhaps predictably, it concluded that 'The region has been pulling its weight on new building' (SERPLAN 1986c, 8): it had 36 per cent of new starts in the whole of Britain in 1984, higher than its share of national population, and between 1981 and 1984 it had seen a 41 per cent increase in new private housebuilding, higher than the national increase of 35 per cent (p. 4). There was, Grigson found, no evidence of a divergence between house prices and growth of incomes in the region: no confirmation of a differential between the South East and the rest; no exceptional rise in regional house prices; and no evidence that the land share in house prices was any faster than in Britain as a whole (Fig. 13(a)). The planners, he concluded from SERPLAN's annual reports, were making plenty of land available: in 1985 it was 23 per cent above the requirements of structure plans approved by the Secretary of State. Since Grigson reported, two more such monitoring exercises have appeared; the latest, dated June 1987, indicated that provision was as much as 32 per cent above the planned five-year provision in the Structure Plans (SERPLAN 1987d, 2).

Needless to say, the housebuilders did not believe it. They commissioned Professor Alan Evans of the University of Reading to make an independent study. He showed that the Department of the Environment's index of housing land prices had risen by some 1000 per cent between 1969 and 1985, against only a 400 per cent increase in the general Retail Price Index (Evans 1987, 4). It was difficult to say why this should be, he concluded, unless it was due to a fixed

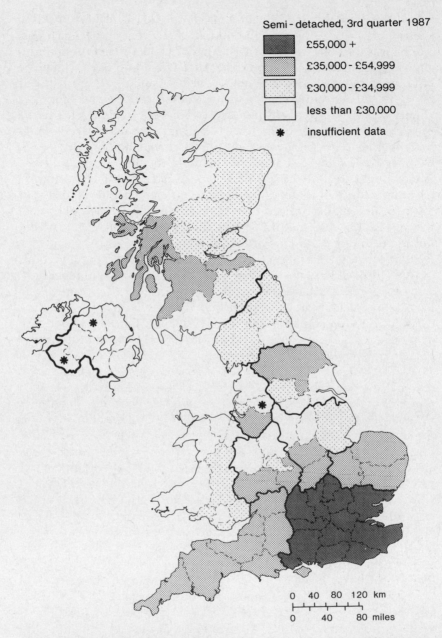

Figure 12 House prices, regions, and counties The position in late 1987, according to Halifax Building Society figures. Huge variations now exist between the prosperous South East and the peripheral northern regions of the country. The Greater South East fringe counties, forming part of an intermediate zone, have recorded dramatic increases in the six months since this map was prepared.

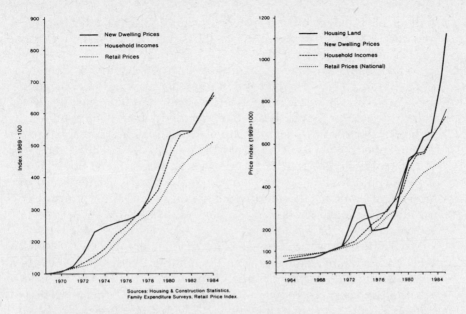

Figures 13(a) and 13(b) Land prices, earnings, and the retail price index W. S. Grigson's analysis for SERPLAN (Figure 13(a)) shows that new house prices have kept in line with average incomes. Professor Alan Evans's analysis for the House Builders Federation (Figure 13(b)) indicates that, though this may be true, land prices have raced ahead of the Retail Price Index.

supply (Fig. 13(b)). Similarly, the land proportion of the house price had indeed risen, though only in line with national trends: in ROSE from 22 to 27 per cent, in the whole country from 13 to 20 per cent over a somewhat longer period (p. 4). The reason, he argued, must be land famine – as evidenced by the fact that, over the same period, terraced housing rose from 12 to 20 per cent of the total mix of new housing, and flats from 3 to 12 per cent (pp. 7-8). In fact, the evidence was that the supply of building land, as measured by sites sold with permission for four and more dwellings, had fallen (p. 10).

Meanwhile, some further light on the problem had come from a study by independent consultants, Roger Tym & Partners, jointly commissioned by the Department of the Environment (DOE) and SERPLAN. They concluded that the majority of new building was by the likes of Consortium Developments, though the majority of starts came from smaller builders who worked with relatively small land banks, much of them without planning permission (Roger Tym & Partners 1987, 4). Most importantly, perhaps, limited housing land supplies were considered by housebuilders to be the most important constraint in their ability to achieve planned programmes: 80 per cent of all builders quoted availability and price as chief factors, and this rose from 71 per cent for the small developers to 94 per cent of the large ones (p. 11).

So there is no agreement – except on one point, which is a matter of fact. SERPLAN's 1987 housing monitor for the first time included an (admittedly, imperfect) estimate of where the new housing was being provided: 52 per cent, it concluded, was within built-up areas, 46 per cent in sites peripheral to settlements, and precisely 1 per cent on other rural sites (SERPLAN 1987d, 5). This compares with Tym's estimate that 12 per cent of all starts in the South East were on 'old urban', 43 per cent on 'new urban', 34 per cent on 'greenfield', and 11 per cent on 'other non-urban' sites; 'greenfield' on this categorization could be 'urban' on SERPLAN's (Roger Tym & Partners 1987, 6).

Down through 1986, the SERPLAN planners resolutely stuck with their regional figure of 460 000 for the 1990s. They thought it important that, by then, much of the demand would come from what in the jargon is known as household fission, rather than from migration into the region; this, they say, must be catered for where it is, not where planners would like it to be. This means a much more even level of provision across the region, rather than the growth-area approach of the 1970s. All that said, in 1986 they reiterated their 1985 statement that they planned to put 150 000 extra dwellings, one-third of the regional total, in the GLC area (SERPLAN 1986b, 4-5).

That last point is very important. For it has been accepted by the Secretary of State in a critical regional guidance letter of June 1986. The letter stated three major strategic objectives: fostering economic growth, revitalizing the older urban areas, and accommodating new development while conserving the countryside. On this last, it mainly dealt in generalities. But the Secretary of State did emphasize that he expected a significant proportion of the region's new housing need to be met in urban areas, including the metropolitan area; and that he accepted SERPLAN's point that there was no need to concentrate a large part of development in major growth areas (SERPLAN 1986f, 11). So he accepted the SERPLAN proposal to put fully 150 000 of the total of 460 000 dwellings into Greater London. And, in the former growth areas, he allocated a mere 25 500 dwellings to Berkshire, 27 500 to Buckinghamshire, and 18 500 to West Sussex (p. 13).

In mid-1987, the SERPLAN planners reiterated their earlier housing estimates. For 1991–2001, they repeated, they thought that there would be a total need for 460 000 dwellings: 150 000 of these could be provided in Greater London, leaving 310 000 dwellings to be provided in ROSE; against this, Structure Plan proposals already provided around 190 000 for the period 1991–6 alone, about 60 per cent of the projected demand (SERPLAN 1987c, 4). So down to the mid-1990s, they concluded, there would be no problem – though later, there might be shortages in the west of the region.

Would it work? The indications were not encouraging. London made a significant contribution to the region's housebuilding in the early 1980s because of development in London Docklands. But even so, this contribution declined steadily: from 19 161 in 1981 to 10 305 in 1984. (Starts, more encouragingly, rose from 9131 in 1981 to 13 692 in 1982, but then declined also, to 11266 in 1984: SERPLAN 1987b, 47-8.) There is no evidence here that London could produce anything like the projected 150 000 houses without a massive drive. But the SERPLAN team in 1987, working from DOE estimates of changes in dwelling stock, have produced an estimate of 17 000–19 000 extra dwellings per year during each of the years 1981-85 – which, if projected, would be comfortably in excess of the 150 000 figure. So the question now must be which SERPLAN figure to believe.

Meanwhile, Consortium Developments and their competitors were pressing ahead with their programmes. The 1987 SERPLAN *Monitor* listed 12; since then, there have been some half-dozen other proposals, including two by Consortium Developments, one at Stone Bassett east of Oxford, the other outside the region but in its fringe, at Wilburton north of Cambridge (Fig. 14). Four of the proposals, interestingly, were in the Reading–Wokingham–Aldershot–Basingstoke major growth area of the 1970 plan. Two others were in the Crawley–Burgess Hill major growth zone, and two more (one of which was Tillingham Hall) were close to the south Essex area. Others were close to Harlow–Bishop's Stortford and Maidstone, medium growth areas in the 1970 Plan. The volume builders, it might be said, seemed to be the last believers in the principles of strategic regional planning left in the South East. Of the proposals, two (effectively, new neighbourhoods for Crawley and Harlow New Towns) had received approval by end-1987; one (Tillingham) had been rejected; one (Wilburton) was a site approved by the county council (though there were about a dozen different proposals for the same area). Yet another – Foxley Wood north of Hook in the Reading–Basingstoke area – went to public inquiry in June 1988. Many thought that this would prove to be the critical test case; for, unlike Tillingham, Foxley Wood, a town of 11 500 people with associated commercial and social development, is not on Green Belt land and is reasonably well sited in relation to the M3 and the Waterloo–Southampton commuter line.

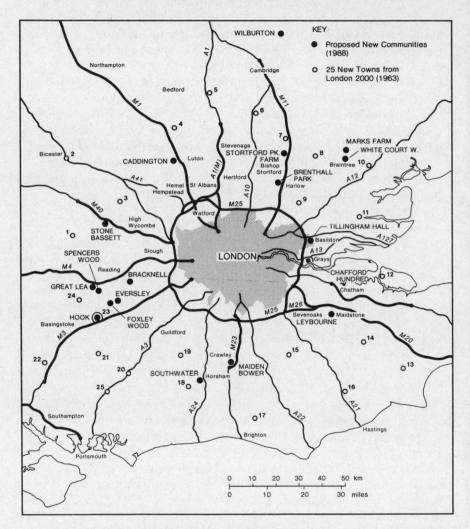

Figure 14 Proposed new communities in the South East The position in mid-1988. There are nearly 20 proposals for major privately developed new communities from different developers, among whom Consortium Developments is heavily represented. Many are clustered in the growth areas suggested in the 1970 Strategic Plan, especially in the Reading–Wokingham–Aldershot–Basingstoke quadrilateral. The map also shows the 25 proposed new towns from the original *London 2000* (Hall 1963).

Some indication of the likely response to all these proposals came from the Environment Secretary, Nicholas Ridley, in a speech to the House Builders Federation in December 1987. Mr Ridley warned that the revised population projections, which eventually appeared in February 1988 (Table 17), would outstrip land allocations, and said that these would have to be raised. Further, he specifically said that social and economic changes would lead more people to want to live outside existing urban areas. He did not go all the way to meet the pressures of the builders, but the speech seemed to represent a major shift in policy.

In May 1988, it came. He told SERPLAN that the new household projections would raise demand from 460 000 to 610 000 new homes in the 1990s. He was insistent that people in the South-East shires, who had acquired a comfortable house and a comfortable life-style to fit, should not be allowed unilaterally to declare NIMBY: Not In My Back Yard. But, with a huge row just then blazing over his addition of 7000 houses to the Berkshire Structure Plan, he was at the same time placatory: the target, he said, could be met just by maintaining the recent rate of building in the region.

Yet, given that SERPLAN was still planning for a total of only 310 000 outside London, it did not add up. To make confusion worse, as the row continued unabated, a month later Ridley contradicted his statement, reducing the scale of the extra demand from 150 000 to between 100 000 and 120 000. There were new factors, he said: more deregulated rental units for sale as a result of the government's 1987 Housing Bill, more housing being built than he had thought, and successful urban regeneration which would attract business and people away from the South East. Some wondered that all these factors could have intervened so rapidly, and surmised that the reversal represented political pressures above all else.

It seemed, in fact, to mark another turn in an apparently endless political circle. The May statement marked a return to the liberal spirit of 1984, when the DOE Circular 15/84, *Land for Housing*, had stressed the need for the planning system to make available an adequate supply of land for housing developments, taking account of market demand and other housing requirements. And, by the same token, it was a move away from the restrictive spirit represented in the 1986 response to SERPLAN. Clearly, as Ridley told the House Builders Federation in 1985, he had to balance the views of local constituents with those of the builders and their customers. Just how much encouragement he gave to each, in such a delicate political situation, appeared to turn on the electoral cycle: cool just before the hustings, hot immediately after, lukewarm a little after that.

Where Now?

We come back to the rhetorical questions posed at the end of Chapter 2. We can add to them: Shall London and the South East grow? By how much? And how?

The answer to the first is, simply, yes. To the second it is, by as much as it is going to grow anyway. Whatever attempts have been made, the region has grown. Probably, planning has made little or no impact on the fact of growth, or on its overall amount. Regional policy at its strongest, in periods like the 1960s, had at best a marginal impact in steering factory jobs to the Development Areas; it had no impact on other kinds of jobs, which happened to be the ones that were growing fastest; now, in any case, regional policy barely exists.

Where planning has had an impact, and where it could continue to have one, is on the local shape of growth: whether it happens to take place in and around existing towns, in villages, in new communities, in the open countryside. And more than this, by making development land scarce and expensive, it can affect the geography of growth in a larger sense, pushing market demand farther out in search of lower values. There is evidence - partial and anecdotal, to be sure, but accumulating – that this larger effect has been occurring. Otherwise it is difficult to understand why people should be willing to commute 100 miles each way each day from locations like Grantham and Norwich; difficult to explain why, in 1987, house prices rose even faster in East Anglia than in the South East. Life in small East Anglian towns may be very agreeable, but at least some commuters are there because they found no option.

The best judgement – and it has to be a judgement – is that planning restrictions have indeed driven up house prices in the South East, contributing to the North–South gap. The planners may protest that they carefully estimated the demand, and tried to provide for it; the fact, as seen, is that their calculations are based on a quite extraordinary set of assumptions about London's capacity for new homes. If this proves right, then the escalation of house prices observable in 1987 could be far worse by 1990 or 1991, and the electoral consequences could be considerable. Hence, perhaps, Ridley's speech to the House Builders.

The extraordinary irony is that we have been here before. In the 1950s, too, we had a minimalist approach to planning coupled with vigorous urban containment policies. Then, because the birth rate rose, the resulting pressures caused a hasty reappraisal in the South East Study of 1964. This time round, we need not posit an upsurge in births; household fissioning may produce much the same effects. We shall need more land for houses, and it cannot and should not all be found within the urban envelopes. As at the time of *London 2000*, we need a new generation of new towns for the South East.

The difference, of course, is that we are no longer talking about New Towns of the traditional kind: towns produced by public agency, in the form of housing for rent, designed for people who cannot afford to buy their own. That was the model of the unaffluent 1940s. In the affluent 1980s – as Milton Keynes shows – the new towns are going to consist principally of houses built by commercial developers for sale. Hence that subtle marketing distinction, new *communities*.

Nevertheless, they are going to need public intervention. First, only planning – in one form or another – is going to allow them to happen. Second, they are going to need a lot of public provision in the form of roads, sewers, schools, hospitals, and other things, even if the private developer is persuaded to foot much of the bill. It only makes sense, therefore, that the private and the public sector should be involved as equal and co-operative partners.

That suggests new mechanisms for public–private co-operation, which I will develop in detail in Chapter 6. We have such mechanisms in the inner cities, exemplified in their different ways by the London Docklands Development Corporation and the Scottish Development Agency's Glasgow Eastern Area Renewal (GEAR) scheme. But we refuse to emulate their success in developing greenfield communities. It is strangely inconsequential. The objective should be to follow the logic.

Meanwhile, assuming that Chapter 6 will get it right, the immediate question must be, How many, how big, and where? In *London 2000* I spent many pages on elaborate calculations of need. I am older and more sceptical now. We need a figure that will ease the log jam, and that may mean trial and error. My arbitrary suggestion would be more than halfway from the SERPLAN estimates to the House Builders Federation's: say, 700 000 new homes for the 1980s, and at least 600 000 for the 1990s, a total of some 1.3 million for the last two decades of the century. That is equivalent to a total additional population of 4 million, though – as seen – much of the demand does not reflect population growth at all, but rather household fission and replacement of obsolescent stock. It does not take any account of demand in the so-called South-East fringe, just outside the boundaries of the region, for which neither SERPLAN nor the House Builders have made estimates, and for which at least another 200 000 would be in order: a total, minimally, of 1.5 million homes or 4.5 million people. It compares interestingly with *London 2000*'s estimate of 3.75 million for the entire 40-year period 1961-2000, which referred only to the GLC plus Outer Metropolitan Area.

New communities cannot and should not cater for all this demand, of course. *London 2000* suggested that half the regional growth should go into existing towns, as is now the preferred SERPLAN philosophy. In the circumstances of the early 1960s, it looked to expansions that were invariably large, sometimes huge: 145 000 extra people at Northampton, 138 000 at Peterborough, 130 000 at Norwich, 133 000 at Ipswich, 108 000 at Swindon. That was reasonably prophetic: Northampton and Peterborough became New Towns, Swindon a major town expansion, while Ipswich was rejected for expansion only after a major inquiry. All that, now, is water under the bridge. The point is that growth is still happening in these places: 'substantial towns farther out, between sixty and one hundred and ten miles from London, as far as the hypothetical "Solent–Wash line"' (Hall 1963, 136). As Chapter 1 showed, these are the fastest-growing places in Britain in the 1980s. The aim should be to recognize that fact, and plan for it to continue to happen. Much of the remaining planned growth will take place in and around these towns and cities. Some will also happen around towns closer to London, in the 30 to 60-mile ring, like Reading and Luton, Chelmsford and Maidstone and Guildford. But here the pressures to limit growth, physical and still more political, are greater.

Suppose now that, of the 1.5 million homes, as many as 250 000 can be provided in London: the most that can be expected, on the basis of trends. That leaves some 1.25 million to go into Roseland and the South-East fringe. We might suggest that more than half should be provided in expansions of existing towns, some of them large expansions. Of this growth, up to one-third may occur in the fringe; and up to one-half will occur in and around the major growth points, both in Roseland and the fringe, as shown in Tables 16 and 17. Notice the curious relationship: we may need 1.25 million new dwellings, to cater for a projected population increase in the Roseland and fringe of only 1.3 million. That is a direct result of the phenomenon stressed in Tables 18 and 19: that the region's population will grow far less rapidly than its total of separate households.

A Pattern of Development

Table 21 tries to bring together these projections and suppositions in terms of needed dwellings. It assumes – a fairly heroic assumption,

Table 21   A pattern of urban growth, 1981–2001

	Total dwellings
Greater South East	1 500 000
Greater London	250 000
ROSE	850 000
Existing settlements	650 000
New communities:	200 000
Major growth areas*	100 000
Medium growth areas	50 000
Elsewhere	50 000
South East Fringe:	400 000
Major growth centres*	300 000
Other	100 000

* In these estimates, the Milton Keynes–Northampton–Wellingborough growth area is regarded as partly within ROSE, partly within the South East Fringe.

this – that one-third of these 1.2 million dwellings, 400 000, will go into the fringe, the great majority of them into expansions of the growth points of the fringe (Bournemouth–Poole, Swindon, Milton Keynes–Northampton, Peterborough–Huntingdon and Ipswich). About a half, 650 000, may go into expansions of existing settlements in Roseland; this figure is close to the revised expectations of the SERPLAN planners. But that would still leave us with a need for some 200 000 homes, for the equivalent of 600 000 people, in new communities: say, 30 communities of 20 000 each, or 10 of 60 000 each. It is a fairly awe-inspiring figure.

Where should they be? Oddly, our philosophy on location seems to have come full circle. *London 2000* pepperpotted its 25 new towns, for 100 000 people each on average, fairly evenly across Roseland. The 1970 *Strategic Plan* wanted concentration in five major growth areas and a half-dozen medium ones. Now, SERPLAN argues again for pepperpotting, while the builders seem to be putting most of their proposals into the old growth areas. Some combination of the two might prove right. We could aim to house about one-half of the growth, 300 000 people (100 000 dwellings), in new communities within the five major growth areas, another 150 000 in the seven so-called medium growth areas, and the other 150 000 close to existing centres across the region. And, especially for those last, we might go back to the *London 2000* list, which was designed to provide for a much bigger total of people: some 3 million in all (see Fig. 14 and the Appendix to this chapter).

Here then is a tentative list:

(a)   *Reading–Wokingham–Aldershot–Basingstoke.* One of the two really successful growth areas, which has expanded despite restrictive planning policies. There are four new community proposals, two effectively satellites of Reading, and two (Foxley Wood and Hook) freestanding in the green heart between Reading, Aldershot, and Basingstoke. *London 2000* also proposed Hook, plus a new town at another site in this open area, Silchester. At least three of these proposals, perhaps all five, should go ahead, to provide for a total population of about 100 000.

(b)   *Milton Keynes–Northampton.* This is the other truly successful growth area, in part because it encompassed two of the three Mark II new towns of the 1960s. The logical step would be to expand both towns further towards their original target populations by means of new neighbourhoods, to be built and financed by private enterprise; 50 000 might go into each.

(c)   *Crawley–Burgess Hill.* One new community proposal, at Maidenbower – an additional neighbourhood for Crawley – has been approved. Another, for Southwater south of Horsham, is close to the Billingshurst site proposed in *London 2000*. There should be one such additional development, which together with Maidenbower should provide for an additional 25 000 people.

(d)   *South Essex.* This has been the most conspicuously unsuccessful of all the 1970 growth areas, partly because it was posited on massive airport development (at Maplin Sands) which failed to happen. It would take a major boost to regenerate it, but there is room for modest development in the Basildon–Southend corridor. *London 2000* proposed a new town at Woodham Ferrers, which in the event was developed by the Essex County Council. This might be further extended. The aim should be to house another 20 000 people here.

(e)   *South Hampshire.* This has been perhaps the most surprising failure of the 1970 Plan. Intended as the largest of all the growth areas, it experienced minimal growth during the 1970s, partly because of economic contraction in Southampton and Portsmouth. Nevertheless, it has a strong economic base in high–tech industries based in part on defence orders. Much of the growth expected here appears to have been diverted into the Bournemouth–Poole area some 30 miles distant, suggesting that planning policies may have had some impact. There is a strong case for a satellite community between Southampton and Portsmouth, capable of serving London commuters as well as local workers, with a target population of 50 000.

(f) *The medium growth areas.* The *Strategic Plan* proposed Aylesbury, the Stort Valley, Chelmsford, the Medway Towns, Maidstone, Ashford, and Hastings. *London 2000* had earlier proposed new towns close to these locations: at Princes Risborough and Bicester; at Quendon and Great Dunmow and Kelvedon; at Queenborough on the Isle of Sheppey; at Ashurst near Tunbridge Wells and at Headcorn between Maidstone and Ashford; at Hamstreet south of Ashford; and at Plumpton north of Hastings. Some of the Consortium Development proposals for new communities are in similar locations, e.g Stone Bassett east of Oxford, Bishops Park near Bishop's Stortford, and Leybourne near Maidstone; a site near Ashford is rumoured to be yet another (Fig. 13). The aim should be to build at least one new community in each of these seven areas, providing for a total of 100 000– 150 000 people by the century's end.

(g) *The remainder of the region.* For the rest, the aim should be to identify sites well placed for commuter transport by road and rail, on land not of top quality, and with no other major constraints. The *London 2000* list (Fig. 13) can provide a suitable starting point; the 25 sites (some, as already seen, in or close to the growth areas) are well distributed around the outer parts of the region, with no special spatial bias. The aim should be to provide at least one new community, for say 15 000–25 000 people, in each of eight major sectors outside the growth areas.

Figures 9 and 14 give apossible picture of the resulting pattern of development in the region down to the year 2001. It is a picture that evolves naturally out of the region's present-day settlement structure. The pattern of relative outward movement has continued, bringing big expansions to the major urban complexes at the region's fringe. The two outstandingly successful growth areas – one, Milton Keynes–Northampton, actually straddling the fringe, and the other, Reading–Wokingham–Aldershot–Basingstoke, well within the South-East – have continued to grow, in the latter case mainly through new communities in the area's green heart, as originally intended

107

by the authors of the 1970 Plan. Crawley–Gatwick has also expanded through new community developments. Likewise, the medium growth centres of that plan have also grown, some of them through new communities a short distance from the core towns (Bishops Park and Quendon for the Stort Valley, Dunmow and Kelvedon for Chelmsford, Leybourne and Headcorn for Maidstone, Hamstreet for Ashford). A series of new communities in other parts of the region, some representing the growth of existing smaller towns – places like Liphook or Petersfield in the south west, Princes Risborough in the north west, Sandy in the north – helps cater for demands occurring outside these growth centres.

The Coming Surplus of Farmland

The point is that the extended region can readily absorb these developments. Indeed, it can absorb them very easily, for two reasons. The first is that, contrary to myth, the South East is not a very heavily urbanized region. Robin Best's comparison of different estimates of urban cover, made some years ago, suggested that in 1969–70 between 17 and 19 per cent of the region was thus urbanized – and much of that, of course, consisted of gardens and parks and playing fields. A more recent estimate, from Margaret Anderson of Wye College, suggests even more conservatively that between 1954 and 1981 the built-on area extended from 11.9 to 15.7 per cent, and that by 2001 this might grow to 17 per cent (Best 1981, 65; House Builders Federation 1987, 32). For the extended region, of course, these figures would be considerably lower.

The second reason is that during the remaining years of the century we are likely to see a remarkable amount of surplus agricultural land appearing in the region – and, indeed, in the nation as a whole. The very real possibility, in fact, is that, as Table 22 shows, by the year 2000 up to one-quarter of the United Kingdom's agricultural land will no longer be needed for food production (Countryside Commission 1987). Estimates like these provided the basis for the government's highly controversial proposals on rural land use, which were published in early February 1987 and were substantially modified in May of the same year. The EEC, the Minister for Agriculture said in February, was now producing surpluses in many of the main agricultural commodities; so it no longer made sense simply to maintain and expand UK food production. He went on to argue:

a new balance of policies has to be struck, with less support for expanding production; more attention to the demands of the

Table 22 Surplus agricultural land, year 2000

Annual rate of productivity growth	1.5%				2.0%				2.5%			
Level of self-sufficiency	75%	80%	85%	90%	75%	80%	85%	90%	75%	80%	85%	90%
					% of land available for all other uses							
Demand (1985 = 100)												
103.0	22.7	17.6	12.4	7.2	28.4	23.7	18.9	14.1	33.4	29.0	24.5	20.1
103.5	22.3	17.2	12.0	6.9	28.1	23.3	18.5	13.8	33.0	28.6	24.1	19.7
104.0	22.0	16.8	11.6	6.4	27.8	23.0	18.1	13.3	32.7	28.3	23.8	19.3
104.5	21.6	16.4	11.1	5.9	27.4	22.6	17.7	12.9	32.4	27.9	23.4	18.9
105.0	21.2	16.0	10.7	5.5	27.0	22.2	17.3	12.5	32.1	27.6	23.0	18.6
105.5	20.8	15.6	10.3	5.0	26.7	21.9	17.0	12.1	31.7	27.2	22.6	18.1

Source: Countryside Commission (1987).

market; more encouragement for alternative uses of land; more response to the claims of the environment; and more diversity on farms and in the rural economy. (*Hansard*, 9 February 1987)

Among these, there would be a scheme to encourage the planting of woodlands to take land out of agricultural production; the release of better-quality lowland to forestry; the designation of Environmentally Sensitive Areas; and the diversification of farm enterprise by grant-aided ancillary businesses, including the provision of recreational and amenity features. All this was in line with the subsequent proposals of the Countryside Commission inquiry, chaired by former President of the Country Landowners' Association John Quicke, which proposed government spending of £320 million to create 150 000 full-time rural jobs, thus more than offsetting a projected loss of some 117 000 farm jobs (Countryside Commission 1987). And this in turn was in line with an earlier report from the National Economic Development Office, which called for a diversion into profitable non-agricultural uses for land, especially those that would enhance the enjoyment of the countryside by everyone – but which, doubtless correctly, saw planning difficulties ahead (NEDO 1986).

The controversial part of this package was the parallel Department of the Environment proposal to relax the controls over development of rural land, which removed the need to consult the Department of Agriculture over proposed developments on the 83 per cent of agricultural land that is not of Grade 1 or 2 quality, which were attacked by the Royal Town Planning Institute, the National Farmers' Union, and the Council for the Protection of Rural England. The sudden policy reversal, coming as it did a month before the general election, doubtless reflects shrewd political appreciation of the combined strength of the farming lobbies and, still more, of district councils in the rural areas faced with pressure from the House Builders' Federation. But the facts remain. If much farmland is to go out of use, then either it has to go to other rural uses – such as woodland and recreation – or it has to go to urban development. The third option, to leave as much as a quarter of the present agricultural area in wasteland, is not likely to be a politically viable option. And nowhere will the implications be felt more than in South-East England.

Appendix: Twenty-five New Towns for London

Explanatory Note

This appendix was published in the original *London 2000* in 1963. The basic details have been updated, as far as possible.

Population is from 1981 Census, where stated; otherwise, estimated.

Rail access is time by best morning commuter train to relevant London terminus; 15–20 minutes should be added for door-to-door access to the office.

Agricultural land is grading according to Ministry of Agriculture and Food 1:63,360 Land Classification maps. There are five grades, 1 (highest) to 5 (lowest). Grade 2 is very predominant north of London; south of London, soils are more mixed.

V-land (land of special landscape, scientific, agricultural, and related value) is from current approved County Structure Plans. Many counties in the South East have now designated the great majority of their area in one or another of these categories, sometimes using designations special to themselves.

Water shows area of the relevant water authority. Department of Environment figures for 1977, apparently the last available, show the following picture (Department of the Environment Water Data Unit 1978):

Authority	Reliable yield (ml/day)	Home population	Yield (ml/day) per '000 pop.
Anglian	2000	4778	0.42
Southern	1360	3770	0.36
Thames	3690	11597	0.32

The 25 Proposed Towns

SITE 1.   WALLINGFORD (Berks.)

Location: 47 miles London. 13 miles Oxford.

Present population: Approx. 6300.

Rail access: Cholsey Station, 60 min. central London.

Road access: Excellent. A423 (Trunk) to Henley and M4. Close A34 for access Oxford, Midlands.

Agricultural land: Grades 2 and 4. Possible difficult drainage on latter.

V-land: Clear.

Water: Probably difficult (Thames).

SITE 2.   BICESTER (Oxfords.)
Location: 57 miles London. 13 miles Oxford.
Present population: Approx. 14 400.
Rail access: 74 min. central London. Frequency fair.
Road access: Good. On line of M40 extension, under construction, to London and Birmingham, connecting near Oxford with A34 to Southampton.
Agricultural land: Border of Grades 3 and 4.
V-land: Clear.
Water: Near Thames–Ouse watershed; therefore, on boundary of Thames and Anglian water authorities.

SITE 3.   PRINCES RISBOROUGH (Bucks.)
Location: 40 miles London. 9 miles High Wycombe.
Present population: About 8000.
Rail access: 51 min. central London. Service excellent.
Road access: Excellent. A4010, thence M40 to London.
Agricultural land: Grades 2 and 3; the town would be developed on the latter.
V-land: Chilterns Area of Outstanding Natural Beauty to the south; clear to the north.
Water: Difficult (Thames Basin).

SITE 4.   FLITWICK (Beds.)
Location: 43 miles London. 8 miles Bedford.
Present population: About 8800.
Rail access: 42 min. central London. Service excellent.
Road access: Excellent. A5120 connects with M1, 5 miles to south.
Agricultural land: Grades 1 (which would be avoided) and 3.
V-land: Green Belt to the west; Agricultural Priority Area to the east; clear to the south-east.
Water: In water surplus stretch of the Great Ouse basin.

SITE 5.   SANDY (Beds.–Hunts.)
Location: 49 miles London (new town site 2 miles north of old town, 51 miles from London). 4 miles Biggleswade. 8 miles Bedford.
Present population: About 8300.
Rail access: 44–46 min. central London. Service excellent.
Road access: Excellent. On A1. A603 to Bedford, thence via Newport Pagnell to M1.
Agricultural land: Adjacent to the old town is Grade 1 land. The new town would stand on Grades 3 and 4 land to the north-east.

112

V-land: Agricultural Priority Area. (This is a special category in the Bedfordshire Plan.)
Water: Anglian Water Authority.

SITE 6.   ROYSTON (Herts.–Cambs.)
Location: 41 miles London. 14 miles Cambridge.
Present population: About 11 800.
Rail access: 47-51 min. central London. Service excellent.
Road access: On A10, in course of comprehensive improvement; 9 miles from A1 (proposed Baldock bypass). M11, 8 miles E, gives alternative access to London, also West Midlands and north-west.
Agricultural land: The new town would be built on Grade 2 land to the north of the present town, in the county of Cambridgeshire.
V-land: Green Belt and Landscape Conservation Area to the south. Clear to north-east (in Cambridgeshire).
Water: On boundary of Thames and Anglian areas.

SITE 7.   QUENDON (Essex)
Location: 38 miles London. 8 miles Bishops Stortford.
Present population: About 2000.
Rail access: 51 min. central London; but new station needed. Service good.
Road access. Excellent. M11 and extensions to London; via A604 A1–M1 link, starting shortly, to M6 and Midlands.
Agricultural land: Grades 2 and 3; the town would be built on the former.
V-land: Part a Special Landscape Area, part clear.
Water: In Upper Lea catchment area of Thames authority, deficient; but Anglian authority immediately to the north.
Note: Access to Stansted, third airport for London. There are three separate private proposals for major new developments immediately to the south between Bishop's Stortford and Harlow; one is approved.

SITE 8.   GREAT DUNMOW (Essex)
Location: 39 miles London. 10 miles Bishops Stortford. 13 miles Chelmsford.
Present population: About 5000.
Rail access: Line at present closed to passenger traffic. If re-opened, London would be within 55 min. (via Bishop's Stortford).
Road Access: M11 to London, bypasses Stortford on the Dunmow side. M11/A604 to Midlands.
Agricultural land: Grades 2 and 3; town would be built on the latter.

V-land: Special Landscape Area in part.
Water: On Thames/Anglian boundary; generally a deficient area.
Note: Access to Stansted Airport.

SITE 9.   ONGAR (Essex)
Location: 24 miles London. 7 miles Epping. Within the original metropolitan Green Belt.
Present population: About 1800.
Rail access: Central Line, 60 min. central London.
Road access: A113, not a heavily trafficked road, to London. M11, 6 miles W, Midlands, Channel ports.
Agricultural land: Expansion would take place on Grade 3 land: heavy London clay and stony glacial till.
V-land: Special Landscape Area to the west.
Water: Thames/Anglian boundary.
Note: Two proposals for privately financed new communities have been made for nearby Braintree.

SITE 10.   KELVEDON (Essex)
Location: 44 miles London. 13 miles Chelmsford. 10 miles Colchester.
Present population: 2400.
Rail access: 50 min. central London. Good service; probably improved if new town built.
Road access: On A12 to London, comprehensively improved inward to M25; improvement of A120 cross-route, programmed, necessary for access to M11, Midlands.
Agricultural land: Grades 2 and 3.
V-land: Special Landscape Area to the south.
Water: Anglian area, though outside main catchment area.

SITE 11.   WOODHAM FERRERS (Essex)
Location: 35 miles London.
Present population: About 4000.
Rail access: 50-56 min. central London. Single-track, but service good.
Road access: B1012 leads south to Southend arterial road (A127) for London; Midlands link (via Chelmsford and link to M11, undergoing improvement.
Agricultural land: Grade 3, heavy London clay grassland.
V-land: Clear to the north.
Water: Anglian area.

Plate 1 Old Oak Triangle Intersecting railways – the Paddington main line with future Heathrow link, the Central Line and the North London link – confer unique accessibility on this large west London site, so far completely unexploited. The Brunel Line, proposed in the text, would be based on the new Heathrow link.

Plate 2(a) Canary Wharf in 1988 The huge linear site astride the Isle of Dogs, heart of the London Docklands development area, three miles east of the Bank of England, on which work began in spring 1988.

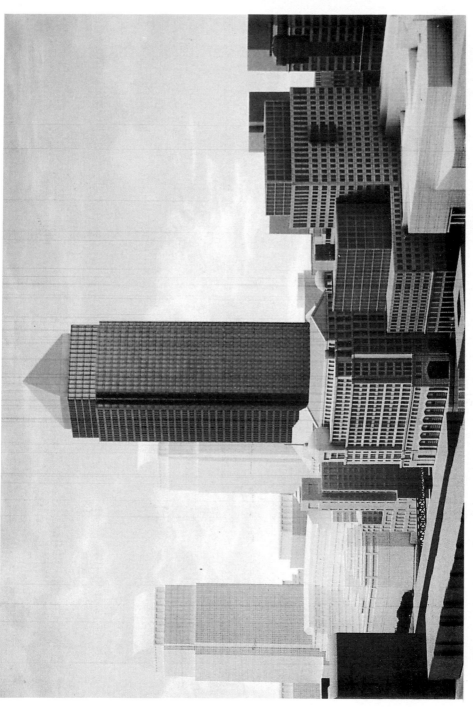

Plate 2(b) Canary Wharf in 1993 An artist's impression of the finished project, London's biggest-ever office development, where 46000 will work. The massive architectural style, necessary for the information technology inside, recalls Chicago before Louis Sullivan invented the skyscraper.

Plate 3 Luxury housing at Wapping Housing like this, whether new or in converted riverside warehouses, is transforming the face of Docklands – but is attacked by community groups for promoting the area's Yuppification.

Plate 4 The 'New Town' at Beckton The London Docklands Development Corporation's answer to the Yuppification charge: a complete new town of affordable housing at Beckton, close to the eastern end of the LDDC area and eventual terminus of the Docklands Light Railway.

Plate 5(a) King's Cross goods yard in 1988   The vast 100-acre site immediately north of King's Cross and St Pancras Stations, which will constitute the largest redevelopment, apart from Docklands, during the next decade.

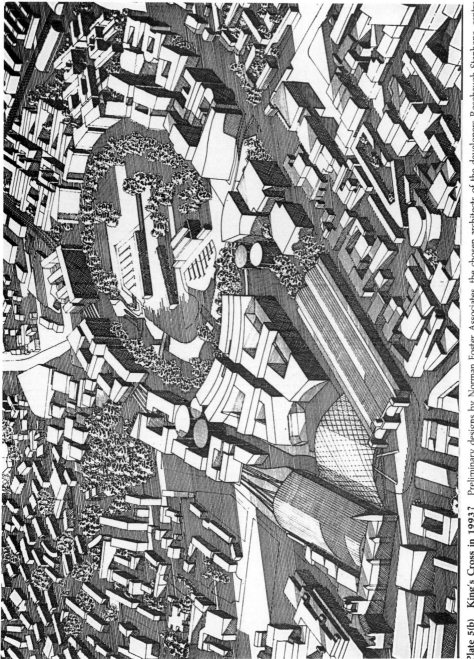

Plate 5(b) King's Cross in 1993? Preliminary designs by Norman Foster Associates, the chosen architects of the developers Rosehaugh Stanhope, centre on a large oval park incorporating the Regent's Canal and the area's nineteenth-century warehouse buildings.

Plate 6 Thameslink The new north–south express rail link under central London, opened in May 1988, connects Bedford with Sevenoaks, Orpington, Gatwick and Brighton. It connects here at Farringdon with the Metropolitan Line (left), which could provide the basis of a similar east–west link, the Brunel Line.

Plate 7 Gridlock on the M25 Morning congestion on the northbound London Orbital Motorway, photographed only months after its completion. Already, there are proposals for a parallel toll facility and for an outer orbital connecting important centres like Reading, Luton, Chelmsford, Maidstone and Guildford.

Plate 8 **'Heseltown' north of Bracknell** The site of the bitterly contested proposed urban development north of the Berkshire r
town, which is glimpsed top left. During 1988, controversy over developments like these became a major national news item.

Plate 9 Lower Earley The huge privately built suburb south of Reading, bordered by the M4, which was developed as part of the proposals for major urban growth in this area in the 1970 Strategic Plan for the South-East.

Plate 10(a) Foxley Wood in 1988 The abandoned gravel pit at Bramshill Plantation south of Reading, which Consortium Developments have proposed for one of their new communities; inevitably controversial locally, it went to public inquiry in spring 1988.

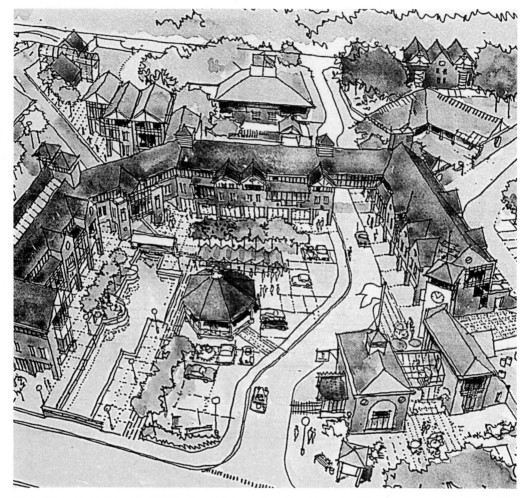

Plate 10(b) Foxley Wood in 1993? An artist's impression of how the centre of the new community might look if the inquiry gives it the go-ahead. Many planners in the South-East regard this as the test case of the government's intentions.

Plate 11(a) The Channel Tunnel terminal in 1988   The huge site at Cheriton west of Folkestone, English end of the tunnel, six months after start of construction.

Plate 11(b) The Channel Tunnel terminal in 1993   An artist's impression of the completed facility, with the terminal for the shuttle trains which will take cars and trucks through the tunnel, plus the through rail tracks for high-speed trains from London to Paris and Brussels.

Plate 12 Central Reading   One of the most dynamic growth points in the entire Greater South-East, Reading owes it
prosperity especially to its high-technology manufacturing and to back offices established here by London firms, drawn her
by the town's accessibility and by local labour supplies.

Comment: Since this proposal was made in 1963, Essex County Council has constructed a small new town here; it could be expanded.

SITE 12. QUEENBOROUGH-MINSTER (SHEPPEY) (Kent)
Location: 49 miles London. 4 miles Sheerness.
Present population: 3500.
Rail access: 87 min. central London. Service fair (involves change).
Road access: A249 via new Queenborough Bridge to M2 for London, Dartford–Purfleet tunnel, eventually Channel ports. The port at Sheerness could be developed.
Agricultural land: Grades 3 and 4.
V-land: Clear.
Water: Southern Water Authority area.

SITE 13. HAMSTREET (Kent)
Location: 61 miles London. 7 miles Ashford.
Present population: Negligible.
Rail access: 85-104 min. central London. Present service (Ashford-Hastings line) barely adequate, but presumably could be improved.
Road access: M20 to London and Channel Tunnel; will require bypass east of Ashford (firmly programmed for 1993, as part of the plan).
Agricultural land: Grade 3.
V-land: Clear. Area of Special Significance for Countryside Conservation to the south.
Water: Southern area.
Note: Exceptional potentiality for Channel Tunnel. For this reason, Ward Holdings have proposed a private enterprise new village close by at Appledore.

SITE 14. HEADCORN (Kent)
Location: 45 miles London. 11 miles Ashford.
Present population: 2000.
Rail access: 61–64 min. central London. Service adequate; could be greatly improved if a Channel-Tunnel-dedicated route built, freeing existing tracks for commuter traffic.
Road access: A274 to M20 Maidstone bypass, M25 and London; and to Channel Tunnel.
Agricultural land: Grade 3.
V-land: Clear.
Water: Southern area.

SITE 15.   ASHURST (Kent)
Location: 32 miles London. 8 miles Tunbridge Wells.
Present population: Negligible.
Rail access: About 55 min. central London. Service good.
Road access: Link needed to A21. Thence M25 connects to London,
M26 to Channel Tunnel.
Agricultural land: Grade 3.
V-land: Area of Special Significance for Countryside Conservation.
Water: Believed good.

SITE 16.   ROBERTSBRIDGE (Sussex)
Location: 52 miles London. 12 miles Hastings.
Present population: Negligible.
Rail access: About 72-80 min. central London. Service excellent.
Road access: A21 to M25, London.
Agricultural land: Grades 3 and 4. Very varied soils.
V-land: High Weald Area of Outstanding Natural Beauty.
Water: Good (big collecting area).

SITE 17.   PLUMPTON (Sussex)
Location: 44 miles London. 8 miles Lewes.
Present Population: Negligible.
Rail access: 56-57 min. central London. Service good except late
night.
Road access: B2126 (needs upgrading) to A23, shortly to be compre-
hensively improved.
Agricultural land: Grade 3.
V-land: Clear. South Downs Area of Outstanding Natural Beauty
immediately to the south of the town.
Water: Presumed good.

SITE 18. BILLINGSHURST (Sussex)
Location: 43 miles London. 7 miles Horsham.
Present population: 5400.
Rail access: 61 minutes Central London. Service excellent.
Road access: A29 to London, connects with M25. Or A272 to im-
proved A24. Good access to Midlands.
Agricultural land: Grade 3; Weald clay, mainly grass.
V–Land: Clear.
Water: Southern area.
Note: A consortium have proposed a new development nearby at
Maidenbower, south of Horsham.

SITE 19. CRANLEIGH (Surrey)
Location: 37 miles London. 9 miles Guildford.
Present population: About 11 100.
Rail access: No direct service; line closed. Bus to Guildford in 25–30 min. thence 38 min. central London.
Road access: A281 to Guildford, thence to Midlands (but improvements necessary); A29 to London.
Agricultural land: Grade 3.
V-land: Area of Outstanding Natural Beauty and Great Landscape Value.
Water: Southern area.

SITE 20. LIPHOOK (Hants.)
Location: 46 miles London.
Present population: Negligible.
Rail access: 57–66 min. central London. Service excellent.
Road access: On A3, programmed for improvement (with Liphook bypass). Access to Midlands via B roads to A32 and A332 at Alton.
Agricultural land: Grade 3.
V-land: Area of Particular Landscape Importance.
Water: Southern area.
Note: Longmoor military camp 1 mile distant.

SITE 21. ALTON (Hants.)
Location: 49 miles London. 12 miles Basingstoke.
Present population: 14 600.
Rail access: 64 min. central London.
Road access: A31, bypassing Alton, to improved A3, thence M25 and London.
Agricultural land: Grade 3, chalk downland.
V-land: Area of Particular Landscape Importance.
Water: On boundary of Southern and Thames areas.

SITE 22. MICHELDELVER (Hants.)
Location: 59 miles London. 7 miles Winchester.
Present population: 1300.
Rail access: 84 min. central London. Service adequate.
Road access: M3 to London. A34 to Midlands.
Agricultural land: Grade 3 chalk downland.
V-land: Area of Particular Landscape Importance, together with *all* chalklands west of Basingstoke.
Water: On boundary of Southern and Thames areas.

SITE 23. HOOK (Hants.)

Location: 41 miles London. 6 miles Basingstoke.

Present population: 2900.

Rail access: 61–64 min. central London. Service good.

Road access: M3 to London. Easy access northwards to A34 and Midlands.

Agricultural land: Grades 3 and 4.

V-land: Clear.

Water: Southern area.

Note: This is the LCC site of the late 1950s, abandoned in favour of a series of Town Expansions. There is now a proposal by Charles Church for a development here, another from Consortium Developments for a new community at Foxley Wood to the north, and a third from Charles Church for a development at Eversley.

SITE 24. SILCHESTER (Hants.)

Location: 47 miles London. 9 miles Reading. 10 miles Basingstoke.

Present population: 500.

Rail access: Mortimer Station, 59 min. central London. Service adequate.

Road access: About 3 miles from M4. To north, a new link would lead to this, also giving access via M4 to A34 Oxford and Midlands.

Agricultural land: Grade 3.

V-land: Clear.

Water: Thames area.

Note: The Roman remains give exceptional opportunity for an imaginative town design. There are two separate proposals for major new developments close by at Spencers Wood and at Great Lea.

SITE 25. PETERSFIELD (Hants.)

Location: 54 miles London. 17 miles Portsmouth.

Present population: 10 000.

Rail access: 68 min. central London. Service excellent.

Road access: Excellent. A3 to London (bypass programmed). Via A272 to A34 at Winchester.

Agricultural land: Grades 3-4.

V-land: Area of Particular Landscape Importance (together with most of western Hampshire).

Water: Southern area.

5

Transport 2001

Transport, as Colin Clark put it many years ago in a memorable phrase, is the Maker and Breaker of Cities (Clark 1957). It is the key to their efficient and convenient operation, and if it is not right, then the city will work badly and its quality of life will suffer. So in an important sense it is the key to almost everything else – which is why it must get extended attention here.

The fact is that in London, as in any great city at any time in history, there is some kind of relationship between the development of the city – the way it is shaped, the way it works – and the development of its transport system. But in London this relationship has always been distorted, and over the past forty years this distortion has if anything got worse: the city and its transport system are increasingly out of synchronization. And this is due to muddle and plain wilful misunderstanding of the relationships. If we continue thus to fail, the penalty may be severe: London may increasingly lose out to its non-muddled, highly rational neighbours, who are doing the things we should have done and are doing them extremely well.

Some History

To understand why, we need to go back to the history in Chapter 2, and fill in some gaps. Modern London is largely a creation of its

119

transport system, and that system in turn is the result of several key events and non-events.

The first is a non-event: the fact that London never had a Haussmann, or anyone resembling him. Haussmann rebuilt central Paris between 1855 and 1870, according to a grand plan. In certain details it was not a very good plan, but it was a plan, and it gave that city a coherent ring and radial network of streets. In contrast, no one has ever planned London's streets, with two minor exceptions. There was the unknown Roman officer who laid out Cheapside, Bishopsgate, Oxford Street, Piccadilly, Edgware Road, Clapham Road and several of London's other main thoroughfares, about AD. 50. And there was the Metropolitan Board of Works (MBW), which between 1855 and 1888 performed a kind of mini-Haussmann on central London.

The MBW might almost be called a Victorian urban development corporation. The government decided that London local government was hopelessly inefficient and corrupt, so it substituted a body that would get things done, tearing down slums and building badly needed new roads. It did not quite work out like that. The MBW was abolished in 1888 after a series of epic financial scandals, to be replaced by the first democratically elected London-wide body, the LCC. Compared with Haussmann, the MBW did not achieve all that much. But it did build a few major central London streets – Charing Cross Road, Shaftesbury Avenue, Rosebery Avenue – and it planned Kingsway, which the LCC later completed. And, for the record, it did something that no successor ever seems to have equalled: by putting all services in conduits underground, it solved the roadworks problem. So these are the only London streets you never see dug up.

The second key agency was the Victorian Parliament, which in 1846 determined that the main-line railways should not enter or cross the central area. (There was an exception: the Snow Hill tunnel connecting Blackfriars and Farringdon, which consequently has a special significance in the London railway pattern.) This ruled out a giant *Hauptbahnhof* on the German model. It did more: it ensured that over succeeding decades, as London's suburbs spread, commuters would be dumped some way from their offices. For the next seventy years, Victorian and Edwardian entrepreneurs found ingenious ways around this ban, by building underground railways: first the sub-surface Metropolitan and District Lines of the 1860s, tied together into the Circle Line in the 1880s; then the deep–level tubes of the era 1890-1907, many of them built by American capital. The sub-surface lines could be tied into the main-line railways, and were indeed originally extensions of them; the deep-level tubes, with their restricted loading gauges, could not. So the commuters could be delivered to their offices, but only via a change of train.

The third major set of actors consisted of Ashfield and Pick, those great managers in charge of the underground during its heroic era from 1907 to 1940; and Herbert Walker, their opposite number on the Southern Railway during that same period. As seen in Chapter 2, by extending convenient electric commuter services into open countryside, these were the true creators of modern London.

North of the Thames, Pick ran the numbers to discover the gaps in London's railway system. They occurred in the interstices between the main-line railways, particularly in the North London highlands. Here he could extend Yerkes's railways above ground into virgin country, creating instant development land. In west London, once Stanley had effectively taken over the rest of the system (except for the stubborn Metropolitan Line) in 1912, Pick could hook his extensions on to existing District Line tracks. Because his empire also included the General buses, he could use these as feeder services, exploiting the new arterial roads being built as part of an employment programme in the 1920s; hence, as recorded in Chapter 2, that vast world of semi-detached housing that spread in all directions around their stations in the 1920s and 1930s.

As Pick repeatedly told professional and technical audiences during the 1930s, there was a limit beyond which he could not go: the sixpenny (2 ½p.) ride, the 45-minute journey. In his last great enterprise, the New Works programme of 1935–40, he reached an historic concordat with the main-line railways to take over their white elephants and incorporate them into his system. The biggest involved large chunks of the suburban system of the former London and North Eastern Railway (LNER), which was going bankrupt and had no means of modernizing itself. Its Barnet and Edgware branches from King's Cross became part of the Northern Line; its Ongar branch out of Liverpool Street was hooked into the Central; a whole branch of the Great Western, out to Ruislip, went into the Central in the same way. When the programme was finally completed in 1947, delayed by the Second World War and severely truncated by Green Belt restrictions, the tube extended in almost all directions up to 12–14 miles from the centre: the limit, according to Pick, of commercially successful operation.

The one place Ashfield and Pick hardly dared venture was south of the river. There, the companies had sedulously encouraged commuter traffic and had even begun tentatively to electrify. After the railway grouping of 1921, the new Southern Railway, headed by an energetic and imaginative manager, Sir Herbert Walker, embarked on wholesale electrification – first of the shorter-distance lines, then, after 1933, of the longer-distance routes also. The pattern was however different from that north of the river, in two important ways. First, it was operationally much more complex, with lines that branched and rejoined in bewildering ways. Second, all the lines terminated at the edge of the central area – and, in two critically important cases (Waterloo, London Bridge), south of the river. So most of the Southern's passengers either had to walk on to work – that famous trek across London Bridge – or to make difficult and time-consuming transfers to the tube. They still do. And so do the rest of the old LNER passengers on the dense suburban routes into Liverpool Street, which were electrified after the war – another legacy of the 1935 plan.

By that time, Pick had joined the chorus of voices calling for limits on London's further growth. He was totally rational in that: beyond the critical 14-mile limit, the traffic would go to the main-line trains, not to London Transport. Ironically, after his death in 1941, the resultant Green Belt spelt commercial death for some of his last works: the Northern Line extension to Bushey Heath, the Central to Denham. Bits of the earthworks survive as industrial archaeology in the middle of the fields. That was the end of that particular era of London's growth.

This was certainly not a car-based city. Nationally, only a fortunate one in ten of families owned one in the 1930s, perhaps double that proportion in the affluent London suburbs. But, because there was huge congestion along the old inadequate radials stretching out from London, along which ribbon development stretched for miles, the governments of the time embarked on a huge arterial roadbuilding programme. It consisted of bypasses connecting these radials, plus two rings north of London, the North Circular, about 6 miles from the centre, and the partially completed North Orbital, 15–20 miles out. Both of these were built fairly cheaply along the lines of river valleys, tributaries of the Thames, which happened to represent old courses of the river when it was being pushed about during the Ice Age. Unfortunately, the ice stopped at Finchley (a fact that originators of political legends should be able to exploit). There are no such easy lines for new roads south of the river; apart from a mile south of Greenwich, the South Circular did not get built. Thus, all because of the ice, from the 1920s onwards a huge imbalance developed between north London's road facilities and south London's. It has never been righted.

The new roads were not remotely as good as they ought to have been, because they were immediately lined by spec-built houses:

Osbert Lancaster's bypass variegated. There were no powers to stop such building until 1935, when, too late, Parliament passed the Restriction of Ribbon Development Act. Even that was farcically inadequate; its main effect was the minuscule service roads that can still be seen along the bypasses. There was no attempt at all, anywhere in Britain, until the Winchester Bypass of 1939, to build anything resembling a proper segregated, grade-separated highway. A Royal Commission of 1930s determined that Britain did not need such fancy continental notions as motorways. When in the 1960s and 1970s the motorways got built, to bypass the bypasses of the 1920s, the full bill for this folly came in for payment.

After the war, as recorded in Chapter 2, the planning system stopped London's growth; but in fact London went on growing, in new ways. Instead of what Frank Pick had called the 'confluent pox', there was the Green Belt. Outside it, the planning system worked to keep the towns small and separate. So London grew, effectively, as a series of blobs across the face of the home counties. But people were either unwilling or unable to buy houses next door to their work; so commuting increased. It all looked like what the planners intended; but it failed to work like that. Instead, there was the layering that Pick feared; but it was now a layering separated by wide strips of green.

Inevitably, this was – as before – part cause and part consequence of changes in the transport system. Pick, as usual, had been dead right in his 1938 evidence to the Barlow Commission: the two agents of change were the main-line railways, now BR, which carried new commuters from distant homes in the Outer Metropolitan Area to central London offices, and the private car, which performed the overwhelming majority of non-central trips, meaning the overwhelming majority of all trips. London during the 1950s and 1960s thus became a different kind of city again.

Since no one really foresaw all this, no one planned for it. BR adapted piecemeal by developing longer-distance suburban services from up to 40 and 50 miles distant, partly by electrifying stretches of main line: Kent coast in the 1950s, Waterloo to Southampton in the early 1960s, Euston to Rugby in the mid-1960s, King's Cross and Moorgate to Letchworth in the mid-1970s, St Pancras and Moorgate to Bedford in the late 1970s. The inter-city motorways of the era 1959–1975, built for quite different purposes, attracted large numbers of radial commuters; so, later, did the orbital M25, which they used to dog-leg from bad radials to better ones, quite disconcerting the forecasters who had never apparently thought of the possibility. The whole system grew like Topsy, without benefit of plan.

To that, of course, there were two shining – and closely related – exceptions: the great Abercrombie plans of 1943-4, and the Greater London Development Plan of 1966–9. Both produced massive plans for new road and rail systems. And essentially, the road system is the same in both plans, for the Greater London planners simply dusted down Abercrombie's grand design. There was to be a series of ringways, some built – in Abercrombie's parlance – as arterials, or urban motorways, some built as sub-arterials, meaning high-quality dual carriageways segregated from frontage development and with occasional light-controlled intersections. There were to be radials, on the same lines. The 1960s plan simply upgraded most of Abercrombie's sub-arterials into arterials. Abercrombie the planner also had a purpose that the 1960s engineers lacked: his roads were planned not only to cure congestion and cut accidents, but to define London's neighbourhoods and thus give them a sense of community.

But in retrospect, quite apart from the politics that finally killed the 1960s plan, we can see that both plans were fatally flawed. Both failed to evaluate roads and public transport investments as part of a coherent package. And both were hopelessly grandiose and expensive, even in relation to the mood of the swinging sixties, let alone that of the sombre eighties. Before the Greater London Development Plan was finally abandoned by the incoming GLC Labour administration on that fateful morning in 1973, the Layfield inquiry – one of the longest and most dispassionate in our entire planning history – had given its magisterial verdict: financially and environmentally, London could afford not four ringways, but only two, one outer, one inner, plus the connecting radials.

As a matter of historical record, contrary to what most people think, the London highway plan was not killed on that fatal day in April 1973. What disappeared were the bits for which the GLC was responsible, meaning the bits in inner London for which the old LCC had been responsible. The rest remained firmly in the hands of the Department of Transport as part of the trunk roads network, and simply went ahead. It did so at glacially slow speed, but for that we can blame mainly the lack of funds and the top priority given to completing the M25, which has meant all too little remaining for improvements within London itself.

However, if we believe the Department's forward roads programme – and, it must be said, the London parts of it have shown a remarkable tendency to slippage for as long as anyone can remember — what we can deduce is shown in Figure 15. As confirmed in 1986 by Mr Bottomley, by the mid-1990s – at a guess, 1994 – the North

Circular Road will have been comprehensively rebuilt, effectively to urban motorway standard, all the way from at least Hangar Lane in the west to the Thames in the east, and – according to the outcome of a certain highly contentious inquiry – across the river to the A2 in South-East London. The major radials north of the river will all have been reconstructed to urban motorway standard at least inwards to the North Circular, and in some cases - the A40 in the west, the M11/A11 in the east - virtually to the edge of central London. What London will then have is about three-quarters of the Layfield recommended network of 1972: one continuous outer motorway, and half an inner one. (Pedantry forces me to say that Layfield recommended that the inner ringway should be Ringway 1, while – thanks to the GLC's 1973 withdrawal from the fray – we are getting Ringway 2 instead.) Still missing will be Ringway 2 South: the South Circular Road. Long before 1994, it is hoped, we will also have a government decision on the corridor studies, one of which – significantly – covers the line of the South Circular.

There was also a subsequent rail plan, produced by a committee under Sir David Barran in 1974 (Greater London Council and Department of the Environment 1974). Many of its recommendations have in fact been implemented, after a fashion: Thameslink, opened in 1988, a modified version of the London Ringrail proposal (the North London Line from Richmond to Woolwich); and the Docklands Light Railway, representing a modified version of the so-called River Line North. By the early 1990s, as a result, there will have been significant improvements in public transport: BR's Thameslink via Snow Hill, with through trains from Bedford to Gatwick and Brighton; the Docklands Light Railway (LDR) from Bank to Island Gardens and Stratford, and very probably to Beckton; through electrics from Liverpool Street to Stansted and to Cambridge; and, most probably, a modernized Waterloo and City tube with an intermediate station at Blackfriars.

There is, however, one obvious remaining anomaly: the gap in the original River Line proposal between the present Jubilee terminus at Charing Cross and the DLR city terminal at the Bank (actually, Monument). This is exacerbated by the fact that DLR is built on a completely different system from either the LRT tubes or BR's suburban services: it is an automated light rail system with special trains, operating on much tighter curves than conventional trains, but requiring conventional-size tunnels bigger than tube standards. Thus, short of expensive reconstruction, there is no chance of hooking DLR up directly with either the Jubilee Line or BR's Waterloo and City Line. The best that could be done, given the likely scale of commercial redevelopment at Blackfriars, would be to extend DLR from Bank to Blackfriars, there to connect at a new interchange with the District, Thameslink, the reconstructed Waterloo and City and an extended Jubilee Line. This would become one of the major interchanges of central London, comparable with Chatelet–Les Halles on the Parisian RER system. It is a key feature of the proposed RER system for London, described below.

The Gaps in the System

It sounds fine. But of course, as in the past, it all represents the art of muddling through. And, in comparison with Europe's other major cities, it still represents a pathetically inadequate response to the evident deficiencies in the system.

First, the highway system will give glaringly unequal access to different parts of London and the South East. In general, the Outer Metropolitan Area will be much better served than London itself, though with glaring local pinch-points arising from the failure of construction to keep up with traffic demands in an area where most commuters are car-dependent (as in Reading). Within London there will be at least two kinds of inequity. Outer London will be much better served than inner London; north London, especially North-East London, will be much better served than south London, which – lacking a South Circular – will become England's uniquely inaccessible, transport-deprived area. And deprived in more than access: for, as the unemployment figures in Chapter 3 have shown, inner south London is at least as economically depressed as any of the great northern cities: an exclave of Britain's North, in the heart of the South (Fig. 15).

Second, the public transport investments will do nothing to remedy the two most obvious historic deficiencies of the system, which have been well underlined in a number of reports from Martin Mogridge (Mogridge 1986, 1987). These are the failure of the outer commuter services – and of the inner commuter services south of the Thames – directly to serve central London destinations; and the lack of adequate circumferential or orbital services, especially in middle and outer London.

Third, there is still no apparent attempt to integrate the different elements of the system into a coherent whole. Most strikingly, there is no real plan for linking highway and rail investments through the development of park-and-ride stations at points well located both from the point of view of highway access and from that of rail

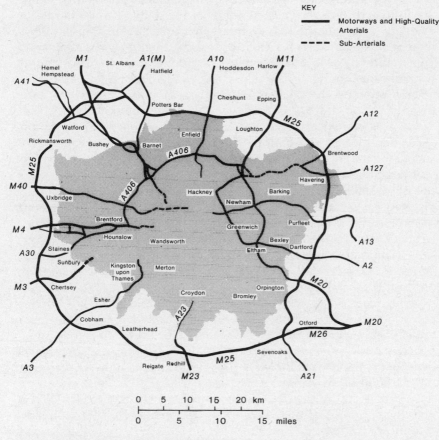

KEY

━━━━━ Motorways and High-Quality Arterials

╌╌╌╌ Sub-Arterials

Figure 15 London's road network in the mid-1990s If current plans go ahead, the result will be a series of imbalances: outer London will be better served than inner London, north and (above all) east London will be much better served than south London, which will be the least accessible part of the metropolis.

access to the centre. One perverse result of this, coupled with the other deficiencies, is that there is all too little incentive for long-distance car commuters, once in their cars, to transfer to public transport in outer London. They either continue all the way, or transfer at inadequate sites in the middle ring, causing needless rush-hour congestion and environmental nuisance at no real gain to themselves; everyone loses.

This is all the more lamentable when we consider that the GLC was created in 1965 specifically as an authority to produce integrated strategic plans for transport and land use. If there was one overwhelmingly good reason why the GLC should have been abolished, it was not – as government ministers said – that there was no need for a strategic function of this kind: it was that there evidently was, yet the GLC was failing to provide it. And this is all the more lamentable when we look to cities on the European mainland, which – in one case after another – are doing just what in London we have failed to do.

Paris provides the outstanding example. To appreciate how, we need to understand that its history was quite different. Though its Metro was started at about the same time as the tube – between 1900 and 1910 – it was built by the city. And the city was intensely jealous of the big railways, so it made sure to build the Metro so that main-line trains could not run on it. (The trains even drive on the right, while the main-line trains, following the British practice, drive on the left: a fact that now causes confusion on the RER.) So the Metro has many more lines, but much shorter ones, than the tube, with stations closer together: the system is very convenient, though slow. The main difference is that the system stops at the historic *Portes* of Paris: it made no attempt to serve the spreading suburbs of the 1920s and 1930s, which were left right out in the cold.

Thus, when Paris came to draw up a completely new regional plan in the mid-1960s, it virtually had to create a new public transport system from scratch. The Metro lines could be extended a short way, but they could never hope to serve the more distant new towns that were an integral part of the plan. Progressively, the Parisian planners hit on the idea of a *Reseau Express Regional*, or RER. There would be new tunnels under the city, carrying express trains that would link with the existing Metro at every fifth or sixth Metro station. Outside the city centre (and, on one line, even inside it) they could link with existing suburban tracks of the SNCF, the French railways. This had the additional merit, for SNCF, that it freed their termini for their new *'Trains à Grande Vitesse'*, or commercial redevelopment, or both. Part of the system would be operated by RATP, the Parisian equivalent of London Transport; part by SNCF. But to the customer, it would all appear to be a single system.

The result of the 1965 Paris plan, and of the investment bonanza that followed, is spectacular: three ring highways connecting the railways, with special provision for public transport on them, plus a completely new express rail system which brings outer suburban commuters directly into the centre, all integrated with construction of five vast new cities. What we should be asking is how such a system could be replicated here in London.

Given our traditions, I suppose that it would all have to be done on the cheap, with string and sealing wax, Heath Robinson fashion.

Strange to say, I think that it might actually be done that way. It would have five main elements.

First, there would be an RER-type network for London. This would have two elements: short-distance lines within London, created by joining BR suburban services across the centre; and longer-distance operations, created in the same way.

Second, it would entail completion of a minimal good-quality highway network. This would consist of motorway-standard orbital and circular highways, with motorway-standard connecting radials, and arterial tangents skirting the central area.

Third, it would call for the development of a local transport system for orbital and other non-central journeys within the middle ring, based on express buses and light rail, utilizing the new highway system, and focusing on the main commercial activity centres of this ring, there connecting with radial (underground and RER) services.

Fourth, it would require intensive and effective management of street and parking space, including both existing streets and the new highway system, to ensure the effective use of such space, with high priority for public transport and other high occupancy vehicles (HOVs).

Fifth, there would be a plan for movement in Roseland, which would start from the Regional Express Rail Network but would recognize that, here, most people would continue to travel by road; and which, in consequence, would work through trying to use the existing system more effectively and by upgrading it to the same end.

An RER for London

The easiest part, in some ways, would be to build an RER for London. London's RER would represent the biggest single change in the London rail network since the construction of the central London tubes in the decade 1900–10 and their extension into the countryside in the period 1924–47. Nevertheless, it could be built quite parsimoniously, without large-scale new construction, because most of the network is already there; all that would be necessary would be to link it up, via short stretches of new or reconstructed tunnel under the centre (Fig. 16).

It would serve three purposes, and in doing so would correct three huge historic deficiencies of the present system. First, it would do at last what the old Southern Electric failed to do in the 1920s and 1930s: it would connect many of the shorter-distance suburban

129

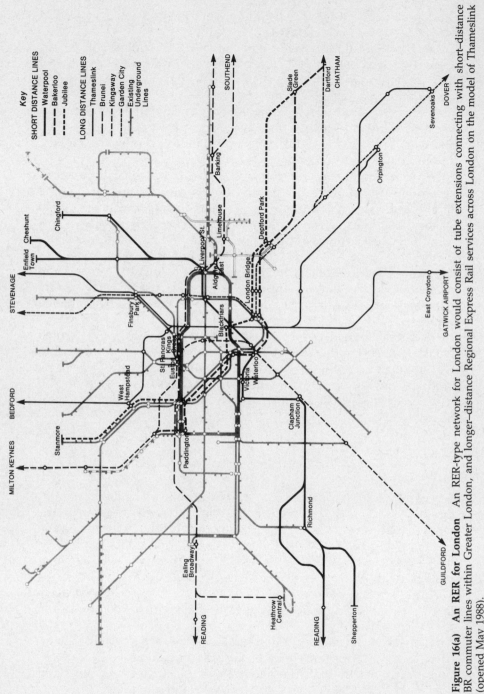

Figure 16(a) An RER for London An RER-type network for London would consist of tube extensions connecting with short-distance BR commuter lines within Greater London, and longer-distance Regional Express Rail services across London on the model of Thameslink (opened May 1988).

Key

SHORT DISTANCE LINES
— Waterpool
— Bakerloo
····· Jubilee

LONG DISTANCE LINES
— Thameslink
– – Brunel
–·– Kingsway
–··– Garden City
— Existing Underground Lines

MILTON KEYNES

BEDFORD

STEVENAGE

Stanmore

Enfield Town Cheshunt

Chingford

West Hampstead

St Pancras Kings

Euston

Finsbury Park

Liverpool St.

Limehouse

Barking

SOUTHEND

Paddington

Blackfriars

London Bridge

Aldgate East

Deptford Park

Slade Green

CHATHAM

Dartford

Victoria

Waterloo

Ealing Broadway

Heathrow Central

READING

READING

Shepperton

Richmond

Clapham Junction

GUILDFORD

East Croydon

GATWICK AIRPORT

Orpington

Sevenoaks

DOVER

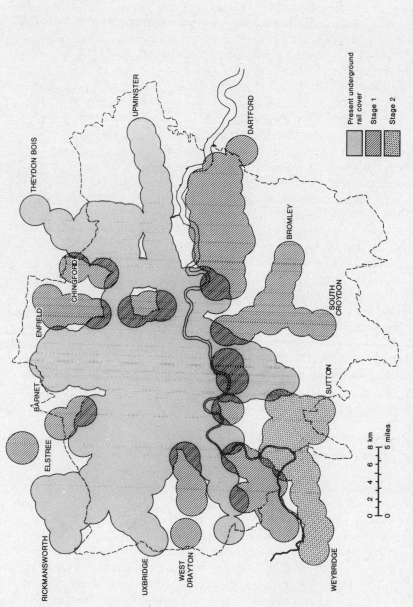

Figure 16(b) Impact of the RER This network would offer direct access to central London from wide areas in south-west, south-east, and north-east, London now lacking it. The map shows how this would be achieved in two stages: stage 2 is the more difficult and expensive.

Present underground rail cover

Stage 1

Stage 2

THEYDON BOIS

UPMINSTER

DARTFORD

BROMLEY

SOUTH CROYDON

CHINGFORD

ENFIELD

SUTTON

BARNET

ELSTREE

RICKMANSWORTH

UXBRIDGE

WEST DRAYTON

WEYBRIDGE

0 2 4 6 8 km
0   5 miles

routes south of the Thames (the old Southern Electric) and north-east London, via new tubes under central London. These lines would thus effectively become part of the tube system; some would be operated by LRT, some by BR. This part of the plan would extend and complete the 1935–40 New Works Programme. One result would be to extend tube-type service to large areas in west, south-east and north-east London that presently lack it, and are (in the case of the south-east and north-east) very deprived areas. There is extra point to it today, because it would help clear capacity in the central termini for the longer-distance traffic that has grown so much since 1945.

Second, and more ambitiously, it would similarly connect some of these longer-distance outer suburban routes to destinations up to 40–60 miles from the centre, via new routes under central London. This part would truly be equivalent to the Parisian RER system. It would give at least some longer-distance commuters direct access to the centre for the first time. Again, some of these routes would be worked by BR; some by BR and LRT in co-operation.

Third, as a by-product, it would produce new and convenient direct connections within the central area itself. It would give enhanced accessibility, in particular, to those areas identified in Chapter 3 as ripe for massive commercial development, particularly at the fringe of the City of London (Fleet Street, Smithfield, Spitalfields) and in certain other locations at the fringe of the central area, including Docklands north and south of the Thames, and the King's Cross goods yard. It would also serve major existing office developments now poorly connected to the commuter system, such as Millbank.

In achieving these purposes, in contradistinction to earlier plans, an RER would specifically not duplicate existing services. To do so would be a nonsense, both in narrow financial accounting and even in cost–benefit terms. It was what condemned LT's over-ambitious River Line South, and what would condemn its equally ambitious Chelsea–Hackney Line. Line 1 of the system outlined below would secure many of the same benefits for north-east London passengers as the Chelsea Line, for a fraction of the cost.

Like its Parisian equivalent, London's RER would be built in co–operation by BR and LRT. Some lines would be transferred from LRT to BR, some the other way round; some would be operated jointly (for which there are existing precedents). In the process, there would need to be considerable restructuring of timetables and even of routes. In particular, some of BR's shorter-distance services would need to be simplified and regularized on a fixed-interval basis, giving them the characteristics of tube services. This element of the scheme is crucial: the evidence so far is that London Underground and British Rail have continued to plan their improvements separately, almost in rivalry, rather than co-operating to build a new system that would be greater than the sum of the parts. This barrier, so far as it exists, needs breaking down.

The Short-Distance Lines

In the network now described, Lines 1–3 are short-distance lines running within the Greater London boundaries, and providing extensions of the existing tube system south and north east of the river to take in relatively self-contained parts of the old Southern Electric and LNER systems. Effectively, they would complete the unfinished job of the 1935 New Works Programme. Because of the complexity of these systems, it is essential to identify – as Ashfield and Pick did in 1935 – sections that can be physically detached from the rest, with traffic loadings that would allow them to be slotted into intensive underground-type operations across the central area. And, since these would be tube systems, it is also essential that they be fairly short lines suitable for frequent-stop rapid-transit type operation.

Further details of the lines are found in the Appendix that follows this chapter.

Line 1, the Waterpool Line, would hook up BR's shorter-distance Windsor Line services (including the Hounslow loop, Shepperton and Windsor Lines, and Kingston loop), via Richmond and Putney, to a short new tube link under Chelsea, thence via a reconstructed Waterloo and City Line to pick up BR Network SouthEast services from Liverpool Street to Enfield Town, Cheshunt, Chingford, and Stratford.

Line 2, the Bakerloo Line, would be extended from its present terminus at Elephant and Castle to Bricklayer's Arms, where it would connect with the New Cross branch of the East London Line to connect with the southern arm of BR's Dartford loop to Barnehurst and on to a terminus at Dartford, with a branch at Lewisham to take in the existing Addiscombe/Hayes Line to a terminus at Beckenham Junction.

Line 3, the Jubilee Line, would be extended from Charing Cross to London Bridge, thence emerging to surface to take in the existing BR services on the northern arm of the Dartford loop via Greenwich, Woolwich, and Thamesmead to Slade Green.

The effect of Lines 2 and 3, together with Line 7, would be to free much of the existing BR track capacity into London Bridge for longer-distance services, and in particular to ease the notorious pinch-point between London Bridge and Waterloo East, which would otherwise involve costly remedial work. They would also give a greatly enhanced service to this relatively transport-deprived part of London, including Thamesmead New Town, which would have direct connection to the West End for the first time. Through the connection at Deptford Park with the East London Line, and possibly at Lewisham or St John's with an extension of the DLR, they would also open up the southern Docklands.

The Long-Distance Lines

Lines 4–7, now to be described, specifically serve the long-distance function; they are the true equivalents of the Parisian RER, or the *S-Bahn* systems recently created in and around leading German cities.

Line 4, the Thameslink Line, was opened in May 1988. The electrification of the short Snow Hill Tunnel, between Farringdon and Holborn Viaduct, allows BR trains to operate under central London from Bedford in the north to Gatwick/Brighton, Orpington and Sevenoaks in the south. A new underground station, to replace Holborn Viaduct, will shortly start construction. The line could and should be improved by connecting the Great Northern electrics at King's Cross.

Line 5, the Brunel Line, would be the east–west equivalent of the Thameslink Line. Like it, it needs minimal new construction, which would take the form of new connecting junctions. A new direct service from Heathrow to Paddington, eventually incorporating suburban electric services from Reading and beyond, would connect via the northern half of the Circle Line between Paddington and Aldgate to the Fenchurch Street–Tilbury–Southend Lines, with a possible branch via Stratford to Stansted. It would require reorientation of existing LRT Metropolitan and District services.

Line 6, the Kingsway Line, would connect BR outer suburban service from Basingstoke, Reading, Bromley and Sevenoaks, via a new tunnel from Waterloo to Euston, with those to Milton Keynes and Northampton. Charing Cross Station would be freed for redevelopment with shopping below and offices above; Hungerford Railway Bridge would be converted into a pedestrian footbridge lined with shops, providing a major new shopping precinct which would link the West End with the South Bank. As well as providing new RER-type services across central London, this line would fill an important gap in the central London tube map.

Line 7, the Garden City Line, would connect BR's existing Welwyn Garden City–Moorgate services, via a short connection under the heart of the City between Moorgate and London Bridge, with stopping services to Bromley and Sevenoaks and to Dartford via Sidcup. It would allow complete redevelopment of Cannon Street and part of London Bridge stations.

Lines 6 and 7, which are relatively ambitious and expensive, are suggested as a second-priority investment.

The entire package, minimal-cost as it may be, would involve big investment both in tunnels and track, and in new stock (much of it built, like BR's Great Northern electrics and the new Crosstown stock, on dual-standard pickup). But part of the cost, at least, could be paid by closure and redevelopment of existing main-line stations such as Fenchurch Street, Cannon Street, and Charing Cross. Further, by developing new interchange stations between these new lines and BR's own North London link, as well as with the underground, it should be possible to exploit huge development possibilities on BR-owned land, particularly on two sites which are, after Docklands, among London's prime potential office sites: the King's Cross goods yard (Belle Isle), and the Old Oak Triangle in Acton.

A Modest Proposal for New London Roads

The roads will be far less easy, for the reasons everyone in London too well knows. First, they will be expensive; second and even more importantly, they will be politically unpopular. We all want new roads – until they come past our front door, when we turn passionately against them; the resulting coalition almost inevitably blocks the scheme. The problem then is to create a new force that will minimize the opposition, even in a sense co-opt it, and make roadbuilding acceptable to Londoners. And the job has to concentrate on south London, because that is the location of the major problem. It is also, let it be said, the location of some of the most difficult local politics.

The heart of the scheme would be a new South Circular Road. As part of a concordat with LT and the Department of Transport, which would provide investment funds for the RER, BR would close certain of its lesser-used commuter lines and non-commuter lines: the Wimbledon–Mitcham–Croydon Line, the West London Line, the Addiscombe and Woodside Lines south of Beckenham Junction. These lines would be replaced either by new express bus services or by light rail services using surface right-of-way (as proposed for lines in the Croydon area in a recent LRT–BR study (London Regional Transport and British Rail Network Southeast 1986). Together with the already-closed Woodside Line, these would be transferred to a new company in which BR Property Board had a substantial interest, the London Expressway Company. This company, which would raise money commercially (and would sell shares, TSB-wise, to the general London public), would then build a limited-access expressway, partly on these rail rights-of-way, partly through public open space, from the M4 at Chiswick via Croydon and Catford to the A2 at Falconwood in east London. It would run at about the same distance from central London as the North Circular, about six miles; and, like it, it would pass close to the major commercial centres of outer London: Kingston, Croydon, Bromley. It could be called Southway.

From the terminus of the existing North Circular at Chiswick flyover, Southway would run underground to the river, whence it would be immersed in tube on the south bank as far as Barnes. Thence it would turn south to run across Richmond Park and Wimbledon Common, going into deep bored tunnel under Wimbledon and emerging on viaduct to cross the Southern Region mainline tracks south of Wimbledon Station. It would then take over the right-of-way of the Wimbledon–Croydon Line as far as West Croydon, from where it would use an elevated structure to skirt the Croydon central business district as far as Addiscombe station. Here it would take over the existing rail right-of-way north to Beckenham Junction. At this point it would turn east and then north, using open land to connect with Sidcup Road at the London end of the Sidcup Bypass.

Southway would have several unusual key features. First, it would be built almost wholly underground, using the cut-and-cover method already successfully employed for two sections of the M25 and for the A1(M) at Hatfield. Because of the narrowness of the right-of-way, however, much of Southway would have to be built double-deck: a method commonplace in America for motorways above ground, but rarely used here, and rarely used anywhere for underground construction. (It was however used on some early tube lines, as at South Kensington and Chancery Lane.) Underground construction would minimize environmental damage (especially in Richmond Park and Wimbledon Common, across which Southway would run for about two miles) and permit the creation of an attractive landscape feature along the former rail rights of-way. There might be linear parks, light rail lines, extensions to existing back gardens (which would provide part-compensation for the environmental impacts during construction), and, closer to commercial centres, redevelopment for shops or offices.

Second, the new road would be a tollway, recovering its cost from user charges. Third, it would have relatively few access points for ordinary traffic, mostly with major radials like the M4, A3, and M23, and with some other roads where environmental impact would be minimal, such as the proposed new relief roads in the Mitcham area which are described below. It would link with special park-and-ride carparks next to stations on the RER network and with new wholesale–retail complexes which would themselves pay the cost of construction and connection. Fourth, it would have special preferential access points for public transport, thus helping to remedy the chronic deficiencies of circumferential bus transport in south London, and providing a superior alternative to the lost rail services. The vehicles operating these systems would most likely not be conventional buses, certainly not the traditional double-deckers, but more likely midi-buses of the kind now widely used in provincial towns and just being introduced in London. They would run express services via Southway but would fan out to penetrate residential areas, thus giving as close an approximation as possible to a door-to-door service.

Southway would deliberately cater for the longer through journeys of five miles or more, which would not divert to the M25 but would otherwise continue to clog south London's inadequate streets. It would do so in a way that meets most if not all of the criticisms traditionally levied against road construction in London. And it would be built at no net cost to the public purse, in such a way as to enhance the revenues of BR – both directly, and through increased patronage on the new RER services.

Southway would have one deficiency, which is that it would not approach close to the major areas of deprivation and economic decay in inner south London. To remedy this, there is need also for an inner link. Its function would be analogous to that performed in the north-west sector of London by Westway, which provides motorway access to the corner of the central area, feeding into a sub-arterial, high-capacity inner ring road (Marylebone–Euston Road). If the proposed Western Environmental Route is built along the line of the West London Railway, it could be extended across the river, thence to a submerged tube along the south bank to the Battersea Leisure Centre and Nine Elms, where it would connect with the existing inner ring at Vauxhall Cross. This, also, could be a tollway. At the south-east corner of this ring, Bricklayer's Arms, another spur would give off via rail right-of-way to a duplicated Rotherhithe Tunnel connecting to the projected Docklands Northern Relief Road, which at this point would also run underground (Fig. 17). A convenient connection between this system and Southway could be based on the very extensive system of relief roads under construction by the London Borough of Merton, which could be extended down the Wandle Valley to connect with the southern approach to the Wandsworth Bridge.

There would thus be a rough symmetry, at last, between the road system north of the Thames and that south of it. Completed by the proposed tangent along the line of the Hackney Road, central

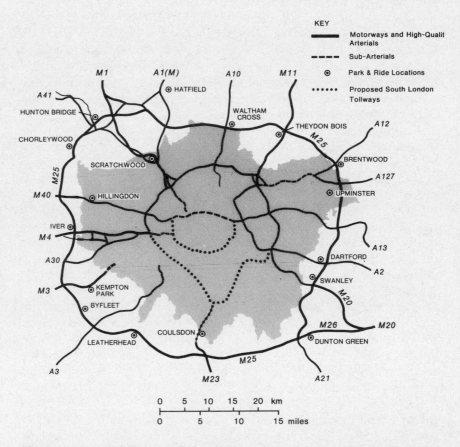

Figure 17 New Tollways and Park-and-Ride Lots A new Southway, built as a toll facility and mainly underground, would provide the missing complement to the North Circular Road and would be supplemented by an inner southern ring closer to the Thames. Park-and-ride lots could be provided at selected rail stations close to the M25, drawing commuter traffic off before it reaches the congested streets of London.

London would be bounded by four tangents linked to the main radials. The outer parts of these tangents (the East Cross Route, the Western Environmental Route) would be built to near–motor-way standards; the inner parts (Euston and Marylebone Roads; Kennington Lane and New Cross Road) would be sub-arterials controlled by traffic lights or gyratories.

There is one final element in the total infrastructure package. This is to develop additional large new park-and-ride complexes on the M25, and on the major radials and trunk roads at the edge of London, linked to the new RER services. Obvious sites include Chertsey on the M25, Kempton Park on the M3, Iver on the M25/M4, Scratchwood on the M1, Dartford on the A2/M25, and Coulsdon on the M23 (Figs 16a and 17). Construction of these facilities, fully justified in terms of the relief of congestion and the improvement of the environment on London streets, should again help BR's revenues. They might therefore be built by the Expressway Corporation.

In no sense can this represent a fully worked-out plan. I present it as a way out of our present transport discontents in London, which may deserve examination. If it proved viable, it might well be the first stage in a new development, allowing BR's South East Network to develop into a diversified transport corporation which would provide an integrated package of services for commuters and other travellers. But one thing at a time: in England, we like to proceed incrementally, not by a grand French-style design. At least, let us stop muddling along.

Transit for the Middle Ring

A neglected part of London's entire public transport system is the part serving those Londoners – an actual majority – who work outside the central area. For more than a century, the main obsession of those who plan and maintain the system has been the huge radial flows converging on the centre. Perhaps because they are more modest, the myriad of criss-cross, non-central journeys tends to be ignored. Little specific provision is ever made for it. Most of it travels by bus. The routes, often inherited from the old tram networks of the London United Tramways and the Metropolitan Electric Tramways, traverse densely built-up, very congested streets. There are relatively few non-radial rail routes – the North London link from Richmond to North Woolwich, some stretches converging on Croydon – and these do not connect well with the underground network, or (Croydon apart) with the main activity centres of the middle ring.

139

There are two main alternative ways of improving the service. One, canvassed by Martin Mogridge in a typically intelligent and perceptive contribution (Mogridge 1987), is to develop light rail networks to serve these orbital and cross-town demands. But pursued in detail, this runs into a problem: the necessary rights-of-way, which could only be on abandoned or lightly used rail rights-of-way or old tramway reservations, are not there. An intensive study of light rail possibilities in London, commissioned by LRT and BR (London Regional Transport and British Rail Network Southeast 1986), shows that the best possibilities of all are in the south:

(a)   A *Croydon Light Rail* in which a whole series of lightly used BR network branches – from Wimbledon, Sutton, Tattenham Corner, and New Cross – and a new route from New Addington could be converted into a light rail network converging on the streets of central Croydon: the most highly developed of all the major commercial centres of the middle ring. This makes good sense, save that two of these routes would also be necessary for Southway; light rail might be put back on top.

In south London, apart from the Croydon case, the BR Network SouthEast system is so well developed and well used that there is little case for developing an alternative. North of the Thames, there are thin pickings:

(b)   An *Ealing–Brent Cross Light Rail* with two branches, one from Ruislip Gardens via a lightly trafficked part of the Central Line, linking with a truncated Central at Greenford, thence via a little-used BR branch to West Ealing; the other from Southall via an old tram reservation on the Uxbridge Road, joining to converge on Central Ealing (District, Central, and the proposed Brunel Lines), continuing via a freight line to Harlesden (Bakerloo), Neasden (Jubilee), and Brent Cross (Northern Line).

(c)   A *Wood Green Light Rail*, based on the abandoned line from Finsbury Park to Alexandra Palace and on the BR Seven Sisters–Palace Gates branch, which would neatly connect with the Piccadilly at Finsbury Park and Wood Green, the Northern at Highgate, and the Victoria at Seven Sisters.

(d)   An *Ilford Light Rail* from Newbury Park on the Central Line, via the streets of central Ilford, to Leytonstone (Central) and Walthamstow (Victoria).

If these proved feasible on further study, they could provide useful skeletal routes; but it would be idle to suppose that they could cater for more than a small fraction of the total demand. Buses, then, would have to provide the main basis of such a system. The aim would be to combine an intensive pick-up service in suburban areas and in central commercial areas with express line haul on arterial highways, using special bus lanes which might be segregated from general traffic. There is a special case for priority for high-occupancy vehicles on the existing North Circular and on the proposed Southway, in the form of both bus lanes and preferential access (ramp metering), as is widely and successfully used on Californian freeways. Here, again, Paris provides another model; such a system is being developed there for precisely this kind of journey, using reserved *rocades* on the circumferential motorways of the middle and outer rings. The precise kind of vehicle would need to be determined through study: the conventional double-decker may well not be the answer, while the midi-bus Hopper may prove more flexible and more suited to traffic conditions.

Regulating the System

Meanwhile, we come back to a major theme of the transport chapter of *London 2000*: that investment in new transport facilities would be more or less wasted, unless the pricing and regulation of the system were also got right. That argument has lost not one iota of its force in the intervening 25 years. It has not been heeded, and that is one of the saddest facts about the history. It is one principal reason why we still have the muddle and the inefficiency that we had then.

The argument has two elements, both in essence simple but in application somewhat sophisticated. The first part says that there is no such thing as a free lunch. If you provide large quantities of a scarce and desirable good free of charge, you will soon attract a crowd and before long a riot. Applied to transport, the argument runs thus. Roadspace in cities, whether to drive on or park on, is extremely scarce and is in effect a valuable resource. But we provide it free to anyone who can afford a tax disc and a gallon of petrol (and, in some places, 20p for a meter). Small wonder that many more people try to take advantage of the bargain than can comfortably be housed; very soon, we have something resembling Day 1 of Harrods sale. In the economist's jargon, there is a divergence between marginal private cost and marginal social cost. Each person, wondering whether to bring his/her car to join the party, considers only the balance of cost and benefit to him or her. But in doing so, each imposes additional costs on all the others. And all impose environmental costs on the hapless pedestrian and on the residents of the streets along which they drive. The result, again in jargon, is sub-optimal: we get an outcome no one would wish, but no one could prevent, a modern equivalent of the medieval tragedy of the commons.

The next part of the argument says that you can seek to remedy this by price or by regulation, or by some combination of the two. You can provide few parking spaces on a first-come, first-served basis; or you can make them expensive enough that few people will ask for them. Most places, including London, attempt some rough and ready combination of these two. You can go further, and charge people a toll to come into the central area at peak times. (Singapore has been doing this successfully since 1975, using a scheme originally devised by Greater London Council traffic planners but abandoned after our politicians got cold feet.) You can even charge people on a pay-as-you-go basis, using meters; the technology is there, and Hong Kong has successfully experimented with it. And, combined with these, you can make special provision for buses and other so-called high-occupancy vehicles (taxis, minibuses, car pools), on the basis that they use roadspace much more efficiently than the average one-person-in-a-car commuter. You can manage traffic to keep it out of some areas altogether (pedestrianization) or to keep extraneous traffic out (precinctual planning, or Buchananization), or to quieten all traffic (the Dutch *Woonerven*, 'living yards', and the German techniques of traffic calming) (Hass-Klau 1986, Roberts 1988). I return to this point in Chapter 6.

London has done some of these, though less enthusiastically and less effectively than many other cities; in particular, it has funked full pricing of roadspace on at least two occasions in the 1970s. It has metered a large central and inner area. It has pedestrianized a few streets (though far fewer than many British provincial and continental cities), and has used traffic management to keep extraneous traffic out of residential areas. It has given buses and taxis priority through bus lanes and exemptions from other traffic regulations.

The major problem is first, that it has not done so very consistently; second, and much more importantly, it has woefully failed to enforce its own regulations. It has been inconsistent, because it has tried to work mainly through parking regulation, but it has largely stopped after metering the central and inner areas. There is now a very large area of middle London, the so-called gluepot ring, where traffic congestion is endemic but where regulation of on-street parking is quite inadequate. And, more seriously, it has proved very difficult to control off-street parking: there is a great deal of private non–residential space that is used by all-day commuters, and much of the public space is similarly let to contract parkers rather than short-term casuals, who ought to have first priority. Further, since the costs of metered parking seldom reflect its true scarcity, for long periods far too many drivers are pursuing far too few meters, further congesting the streets in consequence. There are bus lanes, but they have not been extended – as they should be – to cover other kinds of high-occupancy vehicles, like car pools.

The major problem, however, is enforcement. Here, London is woefully poor compared with almost any other similar city. The traffic wardens are too few in number: 1800, against the Metropolitan Police's own estimate of 4000 needed to do a proper job (Greater London Group 1985, 36). They are also poorly managed. In particular, they fail to concentrate on the crucial task of keeping the main traffic arteries cleared. The result is farcical: so-called clearways and bus lanes packed with hundreds of parked cars, which no one ever makes any apparent attempt to remove, while wardens concentrate on issuing tickets to cars overparked in meter bays.

The problem of enforcement really comes in three parts. First, penalties should be greatly increased to the point where they have an impact. Second and most crucially, they should be effectively enforced to the point where there is a very high probability that an infraction will result in penalty. Third, the collection of the penalty should be made quick and certain. At present, not one of these elements is remotely effective.

First, penalties should reflect reality. A £10 parking fine is trivial to an office worker earning £500 a week, let alone a company director earning £5000 a week. It should be increased to at least £50 (in 1988 values), and to £250 fine and tow charge for certain offences (clearway and bus lane regulations). Second, the likelihood of a ticket should be increased by a massive expansion of the warden force, made possible by income from fines. The easiest way to achieve this would be by legislation to contract out the warden service, coupled with payment by results (a percentage of the penalty). And third, collection should be eased by adopting a variety of the American system: all tickets would become a keeper responsibility, and the licence could be annually renewed only on payment of all outstanding fines.

The objective of all this would be to achieve what is done every day in well run cities abroad, where serious offences against parking regulations are virtually unknown. If it came to be understood that, at 4.30 in the afternoon, every parked vehicle on a clearway would be summarily removed to a distant pound, with a £250 recovery charge, there would very soon be no parked vehicles on clearways. There are none in Paris, Frankfurt, San Francisco, and scores of other places. The psychology is no different there. It is a matter of will.

Such a system would have one interesting side-effect: it would increase the incentive to build off-street parking space. If this went too far, of course, it could reverberate on the performance of the whole system: traffic congestion would again rise, not through standing vehicles, but through too many moving ones. This is why, beyond a point, parking regulations in themselves are not a very effective regulator. Control of the moving vehicle, through a pricing system, is.

It may be argued, indeed has been argued, that such a system is inequitable: the rich person can afford to pay and will pay, the poor person is driven off the road. To this there are several answers. The first is that no one who can afford to drive in London is truly poor in an absolute sense. The second is that the system would be applied in places and at times when there is a perfectly satisfactory alternative to the use of the car, in the form of a well developed public transport system. The third is that, if there really is a group of 'merit drivers', such as performers of essential public services, no doubt special permits and concessions can be issued to them. So, though it has been used before and will doubtless be trundled out again, this does not really amount to a serious counter-argument.

Transport in Roseland

Out beyond the edge of London, the nature of the transport problem changes. History and postwar planning policies have produced a different pattern of living and working here: no longer a sprawl, but a series of discrete towns and villages. As seen in Chapter 1, beyond 25 or 30 miles from London most of the larger towns have a considerable degree of self-containment, each with its own relatively compact commuter catchment. Yet there is also a huge volume of commuting between one place and another, both radially and orbitally. Though some of the radial flows travel by rail, most travel by private car on increasingly congested roads. Thus, though physically these places appear separate, they are connected by what is effectively an urban road system, running through green fields. And, increasingly, the problem is the same as that identified by Robert Cervero in the United States: suburban gridlock (Cervero 1986). A highway-based system of travel, once capable of carrying the demands placed upon it, now increasingly buckles under the strain.

Public transport can at best provide a supplemental and minority role here. On the radials into the bigger towns, where congestion is most acute, buses may carry an actual majority of peak-hour commuters; and it should be the aim of policy to increase this proportion, by a combination of parking policies, park-and-ride services, and bus priority schemes. Elsewhere, it is a question of increasing the efficiency of the network through management, and of providing extra roadspace. There will be no escaping the latter. Roadbuilding in Roseland has been underfunded for a long time in comparison with other more favoured parts of the country, and the system is simply not up to the job of accommodating the highest car ownership levels in the country. Nor will it be possible, as it will in London, to divert substantial demand on to public transport.

The aim of policy therefore ought to be to develop a skeletal high-quality system, of motorway or near-motorway quality, connecting the main centres. Much of the construction will be between the cities and so not particularly difficult or expensive; but it will involve some radial links into the hearts of the towns, which would be managed for public transport priority at congested periods. This network would consist essentially of a spider's web of radials and orbitals. The M25 would form the heart of the web, at an average 15-20 miles from central London. Complementing it at the outer limit would be another motorway box, already almost complete, consisting of the A34, A43, A604–A45, and A27 highways, running at distances between 50 and 70 miles from London and open on its eastern side. Between them, the first priority will be an intermediate ring on average 40 miles from the centre, connecting the major towns of the Outer Metropolitan Area: Reading, Aylesbury, Luton, Stevenage, Chelmsford, Medway, Maidstone, Crawley, Guildford. As suggested by the British Roads Federation, this could be built piecemeal, much of it by improvement of existing roads like the A329 in Berkshire, the A418 in Buckinghamshire, the A414 in Essex, and the A264 in Sussex. This complete, it should be possible to develop progressively a series of short feeders to serve most of the important places.

Such a grid would achieve a number of desirable objectives. It would relieve the already congested M25 (though that will almost certainly require additional measures, such as a supplemental express tollway using the present right of way). It would help channel traffic which will otherwise cause intolerable congestion and nuisance on the roads of the Outer Metropolitan Area. In particular, it

145

will massively aid environmental conditions in the congested towns of this ring. It should be an early candidate for completion as part of the Department of Transport's national roads programme.

The Elements in Concert

These different bits of transport policy have been presented separately. But they need to be considered as a coherent, logically consistent package. Here is how they would work.

First, the aim would be to effect a significant further shift of radial, suburb-to-centre commuting from the private car to public transport, mainly rail-based. This would be achieved by a combination of more effective enforcement of restrictions, introduction of supplementary charges to enter the central area, and greatly improved rail access directly into and across the centre.

Second, though this is more difficult, an attempt would be made to effect a similar shift of orbital suburb-to-suburb commuting from the private car to public transport. The main element in this would be a new kind of bus service combining suburban pickup and deposit with express line haul. Light rail might provide an alternative basis in some parts of London, particularly south London, where a suitable infrastructure base existed. Both these kinds of service would interchange with the regular heavy-rail based radial system at key interchanges in the middle suburbs, which also happen to be major concentrations of commercial activity.

Third, enhanced orbital highway capacity should be provided in the middle ring. The objective should be a modified version of what Abercrombie aimed to achieve in 1944 and the GLDP planners in 1969: two orbital routes of motorway standard (the outer orbital or M25, the inner circular or A406), two arterial tangents serving the central area, with connecting radials built to motorway standard inward to the circular, and to arterial standard inward from that to the tangents. This entire system should be managed to achieve priority for buses and other high-occupancy vehicles.

This is not a visionary or utopian plan. On the contrary: it is designed to recognize both the fiscal and the political constraints on action. Much of the necessary infrastructure is already in place, or in an advanced stage of planning. The necessary additions are in many cases marginal. Much of the funding could and should be provided by the private sector for profit. The entire package could and should be achieved comfortably within ten to fifteen years.

Appendix: An RER Network for London

The Short-distance Lines

In the network now described, Lines 1–3 are short-distance lines running within the Greater London boundaries, and providing in effect extensions of the existing tube system south and north east of the river to take in relatively self-contained parts of the old Southern Electric and LNER systems.

Line 1, the Waterpool Line, would hook up BR's shorter-distance Windsor Line services (including the Hounslow loop, Shepperton and Windsor Lines, and Kingston loop), via Richmond and Putney, with the Waterloo and City Line. Via a new transition north-east of Clapham Junction, trains would descend into tube via stations at Battersea, Chelsea (King's Road), Sloane Square, Victoria, and Millbank (Lambeth Bridge), to Waterloo. Thence the Waterloo and City Line would be reconstructed – as already planned by BR – with a new interchange station at Blackfriars. From Bank the line would be extended to a sub-service station under Liverpool Street.

Thence it would divide. The main branch would take in all the stopping services of the Hackney Downs Line to Enfield Town, Cheshunt, and Chingford. (Direct services via the Lea Valley route to Broxbourne and beyond would continue to terminate at Liverpool Street.) The other branch would take in the old Broad Street Line to Dalston Junction, thence joining the North London link tracks eastward via Hackney Central to Stratford (and possibly to North Woolwich).

The Waterpool Line would achieve almost all the objectives of LRT's proposed Chelsea–Hackney Line. It would provide tube service for the first time to the important business area of King's Road, Chelsea, and the surrounding residential area, as well as to Battersea. It would give virtually blanket tube coverage to inner north-east London, including the very deprived borough of Hackney, providing fast access to the job opportunities of the central area. But, in addition, it would free tracks on the congested approaches to Waterloo and Liverpool Street stations – a very important consideration, because of the Channel Tunnel traffic into Waterloo and the growth of longer-distance commuting from East Anglia into Liverpool Street.

In combination, the BR services at each end of this line should provide sufficient traffic to feed through the central area. It might be possible to consider incorporating the Wimbledon branch of the District Line in the west (as LT intended for its Chelsea Line) and the East London Line in the east, but only by greatly complicating operations. Generally, it seems better to convert the East London line to become part of the Docklands Light Railway and to extend it to Liverpool Street via the Spitalfields redevelopment area, as suggested in the joint LRT–BR study of light rail in London (London Regional Transport and British Rail Network Southeast 1986). This could be structured to provide convenient interchange with the Waterpool, Central, and Circle lines and also the proposed Brunel Line (Line 4).

Line 2, the Bakerloo Line, is a relatively simple matter: it involves the extension of the Bakerloo from its present terminus at Elephant and Castle to Bricklayer's Arms, where it would emerge to surface to connect with Line 1 and the East London Line at a new interchange at Deptford Park. Thence it would use the New Cross branch of the East London Line to connect with the southern arm of BR's Dartford loop to Barnehurst and on to a terminus at Dartford, with a branch at Lewisham to take in the existing Addiscombe/Hayes Line to a terminus at Beckenham Junction.

The CILT (Campaign to Improve London's Transport) report also suggests a western extension of the Bakerloo Line from Paddington to Hammersmith. This is discussed separately below, under the Brunel Line (Line 4).

Line 3, the Jubilee Line, would entail the extension of the Jubilee from Charing Cross to Aldwych, Blackfriars, and London Bridge, thence emerging to surface to take in the existing BR services on the northern arm of the Dartford loop via Greenwich, Woolwich, and Thamesmead to Slade Green. It would connect at Deptford Park with Lines 1 and 2. At Deptford Park or at Greenwich it could interchange with a short extension of the Docklands Light Railway under the river, thus providing enhanced access to Canary Wharf.

Lines 2 and 3, together with Line 7 (see below), would free much of the existing BR track capacity into London Bridge for longer-distance services, and in particular would ease the notorious pinch-point between London Bridge and Waterloo East, which would otherwise involve costly remedial work. They would also give a greatly enhanced service to this relatively transport-deprived part of London, including Thamesmead New Town, which would have direct connection to the West End for the first time. Through the connection at Deptford Park with the East London Line, and possibly at Lewisham or St John's with an extension of the DLR, they would also open up the southern Docklands.

The Long-Distance Lines

Lines 4–7, specifically serve the long-distance function; they are the true equivalents of the Parisian RER, or the *S-Bahn* systems recently created in and around leading German cities.

Line 4, the Thameslink Line, was opened in May 1988. It involved the electrification of the short Snow Hill Tunnel between Farringdon and Holborn Viaduct stations, allowing BR trains to operate under central London from Bedford in the north to Gatwick/Brighton, Orpington, and Sevenoaks in the south. (Trains operate on the overhead pickup system north of Farringdon, on the old Southern third-rail system south of it.) As well as allowing through outer-suburban trains to operate across the centre of London for the first time, thus providing the city's London's first RER-type service, this line has particular value in serving the zone of commercial redevelopment that stretches from Smithfield to Fleet Street and across the river to Bankside. Eventually it should be completed by the construction of a new underground station at Holborn Viaduct, allowing closure and redevelopment of the existing station.

Thameslink could and should be further improved by linking in King's Cross suburban services from Stevenage, Letchworth, and beyond. This is currently impossible because of the tightness of the nineteenth-century curves at King's Cross. They might be eased; or an alternative link could be provided across the King's Cross goods yard to the St Pancras tracks. This has the further advantage that it would permit the development of a major interchange with the North London link (on which the long-abandoned Maiden Lane station would be reopened) and with the Piccadilly Line (on which York Road station, closed since 1932, would be likewise restored). And this, in turn, would enhance the value of this enormously important redevelopment site, second only in significance to Docklands (Chapter 3).

A major uncertainty, as this book is finalized, is whether Thameslink will be used by BR as the main link from the Channel Tunnel to the huge new InterCity interchange which is planned under the King's Cross site. If so, the entire link from Blackfriars, including the Snow Hill Tunnel, will need to be duplicated. This would still be much cheaper than the alternative, which is to build a new tunnel from Waterloo following the line of Line 6 below. And it would provide a much more direct link to any future dedicated Channel Tunnel link south of London, whatever the route that might follow, than the latter.

Line 5, the Brunel Line, would be the east–west equivalent of the Thameslink Line. Like it, it entails relatively little new construction. The basic system presupposes the development of a new direct service from Heathrow to Paddington, via a spur line from the Western Region main line near Hayes, as suggested in the 1987 Heathrow Surface Access Study, and – just announced as this book went to press – to be undertaken by private finance (Howard Humphreys & Partners 1987). A later stage would involve the electrification of the suburban services from Paddington to Slough and Reading as the first stage in the projected electrification of the old Great Western main line. These would be fed into the northern half of the Circle Line between Paddington and Aldgate, thus restoring the original purpose of this, the world's first underground line, and thus via a new link to the Fenchurch Street–Southend tracks.

From Heathrow Central, trains would run north to join the Western Region Line near Hayes. Thence they would use the slow pair of tracks, currently underused, through Ealing. At Old Oak Triangle in North Acton a new interchange with the Central Line and the North London link would permit the commercial development of this potentially valuable but unused site (Chapter 3). At Royal Oak, trains would parallel the existing Hammersmith–City services of LT; at Paddington they would take these tracks over, with a new flying junction to replace the existing at-grade junction west of Edgware Road, and an additional pair of tracks into that station. Trains would then alternate with Circle Line services as far as Liverpool Street, where a new flying junction would lead to an interchange with the District Line at Aldgate East. Thence a transition structure, using a spur into a long-derelict goods yard, would connect with the Fenchurch Street tracks close to Shadwell station on the Docklands Light Railway. The existing Fenchurch Street tracks west of this point, and the station itself, would be freed for redevelopment. Trains would run direct to Southend and Shoeburyness, and to Tilbury. Additionally, by use of an existing spur at Bow Road to the Liverpool Street line, it would be possible to operate a service via Stratford to Stansted Airport.

The Brunel Line is the most logistically difficult of the proposals, because of the intense peaking and very high peak-hour frequency of the Fenchurch Street services. It would also require reorientation of existing LRT Metropolitan and District services. Either the existing Hammersmith–Whitechapel service would be replaced by a Hammersmith–Edgware Road shuttle which might be extended into a continuous loop back via Circle tracks to Edgware Road; or it could be diverted at Paddington to become a branch of the Bakerloo, as suggested by the Campaign to Improve London's Transport (CILT 1987), perhaps thence connecting at Hammersmith to incorporate the District Line's Richmond branch. Many existing travellers on the Aldgate East–Barking line would transfer to the new express service. For this purpose an additional stop at West Ham, interchanging with the District and with the North London link, might be desirable.

150

So would a new station for the District Line at Campbell Road, between Bromley-by-Bow and Bow Road, interchanging with the DLR. Fenchurch Street station and its approach tracks would be freed for commercial redevelopment. The line would also encourage major commercial development in the Old Oak Triangle and in the Barking Reach area, forming the next logical extension of the Docklands redevelopment, as proposed by the London Planning Advisory Committee.

Line 6, the Kingsway Line, is a more ambitious and expensive enterprise. It would connect BR outer suburban services to Basingstoke, Reading, Bromley, and Sevenoaks with those to Milton Keynes and Northampton. A new transition structure south of Waterloo, built jointly with that required for Line 1, would take these tracks to a new underground station under Waterloo, with cross-platform interchange to Line 1. Another transition, from BR's Charing Cross tracks, would bring in these services under the South Bank. Thence the line would run under the Thames to LRT's anomalous Piccadilly Line spur from Aldwych to Holborn, which would need to be opened up to 16ft gauge. New tunnels would connect onward to a sub-surface station at Euston and thence to a transition north of Hampstead Road with the main-line tracks. This line could also branch to link with BR's King's Cross InterCity services at the King's Cross goods yard, including the possibility of through running for Channel Tunnel trains. There would be stations at Waterloo, Aldwych, Holborn, and Euston. Charing Cross Station would be freed for redevelopment with shopping below and offices above; Hungerford Railway Bridge would be converted into a pedestrian footbridge lined with shops, providing a major new shopping precinct which would link the West End with the South Bank. As well as providing new RER-type services across central London, this line would fill an important gap in the central London tube map.

Line 7, the Garden City Line, would connect BR's existing Welwyn Garden City–Moorgate services with the South Eastern stopping services from Cannon Street and London Bridge to Bromley and Sevenoaks and to Dartford via Sidcup. From Moorgate southwards, it would first use an existing but never completed extension to Lothbury. This would extend to a new interchange at the Bank. Thence the tube would connect under Arthur Street with the long-disused City and South London Tunnels under the Thames. These, constructed to an archaic 10ft 2in. bore (smaller than the present tube dimensions), would need to be opened out to the BR 16ft standard (Pennick 1983). Under London Bridge station a new transition (constructed jointly with that needed for Line 3) would

bring the tracks up to join the present lines to New Cross ar
Bromley. Alternatively, both this and Line 3 could be diverted
Bricklayer's Arms to share a joint transition structure with Lir
2. Construction of the Garden City Line would allow comple
redevelopment of Cannon Street and part of London Bridge station
Additionally, this line might incorporate some BR outer-suburbे
services from Cambridge, Chelmsford, and Southend Victoria in
Liverpool Street, allowing partial redevelopment of that station as ề
extension of the Broadgate scheme. This also would be a relative
ambitious and expensive scheme. Like Line 6, it is suggested as
second–priority investment.

6

Building 2001

In no one area of planning has there been quite such a drastic sea-change, over the quarter-century since *London 2000*, as in the area of urban design. Ask any self-respecting planner of 1963 how to renew London's outworn fabric, and the answer would come straight back: bring in the bulldozers. Tear it all down. Rebuild from the ground up. Segregate the traffic from the people, preferably on different levels: put the pedestrians on decks, put the flats in the air above them. Elsewhere, leave the people on the ground, but segregate different kinds of traffic: put fast through traffic on to new urban motorways; distribute local traffic via appropriate local streets to parking spaces between or below flats and offices and shops; leave pedestrians in full charge of busy shopping streets.

London 2000 reflected the spirit of that time. It was full of suggestions for simultaneous multi-level reconstructions of huge areas of inner London, based on vertical segregation of people and traffic (V-segregation for short), and for creation of traffic-free precincts (precinctual or P-segregation) in others; for urban motorways slashing boldly through the fabric; for developing new institutions and financial mechanisms to ensure that this happened more quickly and more comprehensively.

London 2000 was not alone in this. The far more influential Buchanan report on *Traffic in Towns*, appearing some four months later, suggested identical notions and applied them to an area that *London 2000* called Fitzrovia, west of Tottenham Court Road and north of Oxford Street (Minister of Transport 1963, 290–371). To be fair to Buchanan and his colleagues, he did not specifically suggest tearing London down; he did say that the first need was to establish standards for taming and civilizing the car in the cities and towns of Britain, whereupon there was a choice: more cars with more reconstruction and more money, or fewer (perhaps many fewer), with less rebuilding and less cash. But the hapless journalists and public saw none of that; what they seized upon were the imaginative drawings of a future multi-level London. Buchanan, who had intended no such thing, became identified with the razing of London, and every other British city to boot.

In that spirit, the newly born GLC in 1965 unveiled its plan for what was then called the Motorway Box, later Ringway 1, an urban motorway snaking its way through the inner Victorian suburbs; in the same spirit, two years later, the same authority produced the full plan for a spider's web of rings and radials. And in exactly the same style, a joint GLC–Westminster–Camden team in 1971 proudly displayed their concept of a new Covent Garden, rebuilt on different levels, with a dual-carriageway Strand that carved ruthlessly though landmarks like Rule's restaurant and the network of small streets south of the market. The reaction that these plans provoked is instructive: to the first, euphoria; to the second, more muted adulation; to the third, execration. There had been, as one bemused member of the Covent Garden team put it at the time, something like a complete reversal of attitudes within a period of some six months. If their report had appeared just that much earlier, it would have been lauded to the skies; now, nothing was too bad to say about it. The fact was that everything that had been in was now out; everything that had been good was now bad. Big was now beastly, small was beautiful. Comprehensive was now castigated, piecemeal was pleasing. The Covent Garden plan was routed; after huge protests, the then Minister (Geoffrey Ripon) approved it with so many holes that it was effectively stone dead.

That was a great turning point in the history of planning in London, indeed in Britain. It was followed by the abandonment of the ringway network by an incoming Labour GLC, in April 1973. For the rest of that decade, no one had a word to say in favour of rebuilding, or comprehensive redevelopment, or motorways. It has taken the best part of another decade to restore even a partial equilibrium. We now at last see large-scale redevelopment again, in Broadgate, in the London Docklands, soon in Spitalfields; we may see it in a host of other schemes, as at King's Cross. But – as already mentioned – most of these are still controversial, some bitterly so, on the grounds that they do not respect either the local urban fabric or the local community. And the battle, already fought in Docklands and at Coin Street, is likely to be fought time and time again.

Were the 1960s all Wrong?

The history so far might suggest that the 1960s – including all its products, such as *London 2000* – were totally misconceived. But that needs to be critically considered; in our anxiety to chase the *Zeitgeist*, we might just be in danger of jumping over the cliff.

The dilemma is that during the 1970s, in rejecting the bulldozer, we almost arrived at the conviction that *all* change should be stopped; that it would be best to set London in aspic at a particular point in time. In a profound sense, that is a rejection of the spirit of town planning, which is that we can create places that look and feel and work better than places do now. And it happened to be associated in time with the emergence of a philosophical viewpoint that essentially said: in reality, all planning only serves the needs of capitalists; all planning values are relative. If you believe that, then good luck to you. I am proceeding here on the basis that, though planning admittedly can hurt some people while helping others, it may nevertheless make things better for the great majority; and that is why it is worth having.

If we start from there, then we do have to use a kind of felicific calculus, distasteful as that may be. We have to say: we can move a great deal of traffic from this neighbourhood, but at the expense of knocking down the houses of Mr Jones and Mrs Bloggs. How much do we care about their pain, grief, and suffering as against the psychological gains to all the others? Now, as part of the great attitudinal change of 1967–74, there was a tremendous revulsion against this approach, and in particular against cost–benefit analysis, which was said to embody it. Peter Self pilloried it in a book called *Econocrats and the Policy Process*; John Adams parodied it in a paper called '...and how much for your Grandmother?' (Self 1975; Adams 1974). They objected to a whole number of things: to the process of adding up gains and losses into one big number, called a 'rate of return'; and to the barbarism (as they saw it) of putting money values on priceless things, like a Norman church.

To meet those justifiable criticisms, there were in time reasoned suggestions. In the Leitch report on Trunk Road Assessment, published in 1977 (Advisory Committee on Trunk Road Assessment

1977), a group of us put forward a kind of felicific calculus, derived from Nathaniel Lichfield's Planning Balance Sheet, which did not try to aggregate the unaggregatable or to quantify the unquantifiable. It said in essence: let us do the best we can. Let us cost the things that can be costed (time savings, for instance). Let us quantify the things that can be quantified but not costed (noise levels, for instance). And let us write down in words the things that cannot be quantified (a fine landscape or fine building, for instance). It was far from perfect, but it was an improvement, and it has been used with some success in judging major motorway and trunk road schemes ever since.

It has also been used, increasingly, in urban road schemes. I am now arguing that something like it should be used much more for any planning proposal that benefits some people and disbenefits others – which means virtually every planning scheme. It will not supplant the political process, or remove political cowardice, as a basis for reaching decisions. But it will help produce some kind of rational counterweight. The main case for it is that it provides a basis for reasoned disputation. I may care desperately about that church, you about that dangerous street crossing. We can express what we feel, and try to resolve how much other people care about these and other aspects, and how that weighs (not in a precise sense, but judgementally) against the things that can be counted, like the number of worshippers or visitors to the church, or the number of recorded accidents. That will help lead to a better decision that more people can go along with. And it might result in some things actually happening.

Alternative Communities, Alternative Fabrics

We can usefully start by applying that kind of approach to some contemporary London planning controversies. Take what is undoubtedly the biggest: Docklands. As earlier said, there are two different but closely related questions, here and in all similar cases: What kind of human community do we want? and What kind of physical fabric do we want? The question about the local community essentially is, Which community? The relatively small community that was here before, or the much bigger one that is being wrapped around it (or, some would say, smothering it)? The question about the fabric is, What kind of fabric? There was an old fabric, the fabric of the slums, but that was swept away, partly by rebuilding in the 1930s, partly in much more fundamental rebuilding in the 1960s. What took its place is drearily institutional: five-storey walkups in the 1930s, now relapsed in turn into slumdom and ironically rehabilitated by private developers for yuppie buyers; towers and slabs in the 1960s, with sad fly-blown shops and a few residual Victorian pubs. The pubs apart, no one would shed a tear for the loss of much of that.

So, what is the question? It is what kind of urban structure we should now be building. If we go away from the areas of large–scale redevelopment, and into those vast areas of Victorian London where the bulldozer has cleared little – areas like Barnsbury, Holland Park, Shepherd's Bush – we still find a distinctive, traditional kind of London urban texture. We can call it small-scale, cheek-by-jowl. There is no large-scale segregation of land uses, though there is some at the smaller scale: houses are found close to shops, to small workshops, to schools, to odd bits of open space, though they are not mixed higgledy-piggledy with them, either. Despite gentrification, all kinds of people still live next door to each other: old and young, rich and poor, tenth-generation English and new immigrant.

This texture is quite old: it goes back before the automobile revolution of this century, even before the public transport revolution of the last one. Dickens certainly knew it well; so did Defoe. Though it has some inconveniences, it offers a great deal to those who live in it and with it: shops and all kinds of useful services within easy reach, a capacity to adapt to changing needs and standards, an interest and a variety of life, a satisfactory compromise between community and privacy. It seems to prove satisfactory to all sorts and conditions of people, and it has something to do with that unique quality of liveability which so many people from other great cities of the world profess to find in London. It is the essence, surely, of the London Planning Advisory Committee's vision of 'London as a City of Stable and Secure Residential Communities and Neighbourhoods' (London Planning Advisory Commitee 1988, 9.1).

The texture we are creating in places like Docklands, in contrast, is quite different. It is marked by homogeneity and uniformity. Rich people live in one kind of area, middle-income people in another, poor in yet another. There are vast areas that are all housing, with no shops and few pubs. In the middle of the Isle of Dogs is one huge hypermarket; the assumption is that everyone will get everything they need there, but they will certainly need a car to get to it. Apart from this, there are very few shops, very few of the kind of small-scale services that are so useful and even essential in a city (from shoe repairers upwards), and very little sense of variety. Even by the standards of the yuppies who are archetypally supposed to inhabit the place, Docklands is extraordinarily lacking in the trappings of yuppiedom: there are few restaurants, next to no wine bars.

Why should this be? The basic reason seems to be that Docklands now consists of two layers, two periods, of institutionalized rebuilding: one public, the other private, both with pernicious effects for the sense of community. The private developers of the 1980s have repeated the mistakes of the public developers of the 1960s. Neither set of developers cared at all for real urban variety, the first because it was untidy, the second because it did not pay (and, perhaps, because the developers, who had been used to building suburbs, simply did not know how). It might just happen over time: the pubs might turn into wine bars (to the fury of the old inhabitants, of course), the shops might be let to new entrepreneurs (though their public landlords will do their best to stop it). So the real threat is that Docklands will remain what it now is: a boring outpost of suburbia in the middle of London. The only thing that might change this is that the developers themselves will see the need.

Some will say that this is pure sentimentality. And I know of no survey that asks people what kind of London they want. (That, given all the fancy sociological work commissioned with public money, is in itself remarkable.) But if it is, then why does the market signal otherwise? Why do people with money pay increasingly crazy prices to live in the parts of London that offer the old qualities, the old style of London life? And why, now that the first euphoric flush is over, do prices in Docklands appear to be steadying, even weakening? These questions bear pondering, the next time round.

Making Worse Better

At the same time, people show by their actions that there are some features of inner-city life that they do not like at all. They form Neighbourhood Watch associations to battle crime in general and street crime in particular. They join civic societies to try to remove rat-running traffic from their local streets. They try, often without success, to stop redevelopment schemes that reduce the variety of their local shops and services. Their actions offer clear pointers to the kind of urban environment that people appreciate and value. It is, unsurprisingly, the environment they have now, with some of the rougher edges removed.

All this might suggest an ultimately conservative attitude to urban change: do as little as possible. And certainly, it now seems clear that it would have been far better never to have made many of the changes that were made to the fabric of London in the 1960s. But that would be too facile. The fact is that changes have come from outside, and they cannot, Canute-like, simply be bidden to go away again. We cannot and will not return to the traffic levels of the 1950s, though some environmentalists would have us do so; as the Buchanan report introduction said in 1963, the car is 'a monster of great potential destructiveness. And yet we love him dearly' (Minister of Transport 1963, para. 55). We cannot find a solution to the alienation and violence of a substantial section of the young, sickening as most of us find it. So we have to find the best ways we can to minimize these problems and to reduce their impact on us.

Traffic

Consider, first, traffic. Back in 1963, Buchanan gave us formulae: establish standards of good urban environment, and then trade off between costs and traffic levels. We dodged the issue he set, and environmental standards have gone steadily down everywhere. Some might argue in addition that some of his solutions were simplistic: multi-level solutions invite muggers, ground-level solutions too readily remove traffic from your front door to someone else's. That only means that we have to reconsider our objectives, and find new and ingenious and better ways of achieving them: the essence of good planning through the ages. First in the Netherlands, and now on an even larger scale in the Federal Republic of Germany, since the mid-1970s they have developed new concepts of traffic management the Dutch call *Woonerven* (living yards) and the Germans term *Verhkehrsberuhigung* (traffic-calming) (Hass-Klau 1986, Roberts 1988). These involve reducing the speed and the noise of traffic by creating barriers to its movement: humps in the road, sudden changes in direction, cars parked at right angles across the street, narrow places where only one car can pass, very low speed limits. Their essence is that, unlike Buchanan, they do not involve pushing the traffic from one street, one place, to another; they involve quietening it in every place. They seem to have proved very successful, yet they have been relatively little applied in this country until now.

At the same time, it needs to be recognized that – as in 1963, so in 1988 – there is a lot of London traffic that is quite simply doing the wrong thing in the wrong place. Because the main traffic streets are so hopelessly inadequate for their purpose – too narrow, trying to do too many things at once, far too inadequately policed and wardened – they are too often gridlocked; the inevitable result is that through traffic takes to the residential back streets where it has no real business. Calming it down there would not be the right solution; the traffic should not be there at all. So something like a Buchanan solution – based on environmental areas, or urban rooms, or precincts – is still the right basis, as it was in 1963 and was in 1938 when a Scotland Yard policeman, Alker Tripp, first urged it (Tripp 1938, 1942).

The problem, as Tripp already saw, is that it involves rebuilding. The main roads have to be cleared of the commercial functions that line them, which generate the local traffic and the parking and the loading that bring the through traffic to a halt. Abercrombie, with acknowledgement, borrowed Tripp's solution in his County of London Plan in 1943, and in a very few places – in the inner East End for instance – you can see it working. The trouble was, it was hopelessly expensive to compensate all the existing businesses; so very little got done, even there. *London 2000* argued therefore that we must turn Tripp inside out: the through traffic roads should be routed through the back areas, leaving the old main roads as quiet pedestrian areas in the hearts of the urban precincts. That made eminent sense then, but when the GLC sought to do it with their ringways, the residents objected; for them, it seemed a case of operation successful, patient dead. The fact is that to achieve a real and lasting improvement in London's traffic environment, someone has to be sacrificial victim; there is no way around it. When it came to the crunch, the politicians' nerves failed them, again and again. Thus does local democracy lead to a state of stalemate, where all suffer because no one may ever lose.

I must confess that, much older and, I think, wiser, I have no easy solution to this dilemma; it seems to lie at the heart of many of our petty urban discontents. Political scientists and welfare economists have analysed it intensively, and one, James Buchanan, has deservedly won a Nobel Prize for so doing (Buchanan & Tullock 1962; Buchanan & Tollison 1972; cf. Tullock 1976). To remedy it would need a rather fundamental change in the way we conduct our democratic business, and in particular less local democracy. Perhaps that is what we are getting, especially in areas like Docklands, and more generally across the nation. But if there is a way out, it must lie in a return to rational discourse, fortified by techniques of analysis such as I described earlier.

Crime

Consider, again, crime. Oscar Newman in the United States was the first to show, in the early 1970s, that much of our so-called urban design simply produced indefensible space, which isolated the potential victim and invited crime. In the 1980s, Alice Coleman has demonstrated the same for British cities by means of controlled comparisons, which lead to very concrete recommendations for remedying some of the worst design excesses of the 1960s and early 1970s: the removal, for instance, of the high-level decks which allow robbers and muggers to roam at will and to escape the scene of their crimes with minimal risk of capture (Newman 1972, 1980; Coleman 1985). No one will suggest that such measures will reverse the depressing rise in recorded crime in London; but they will help contain it, and to give ordinary Londoners an enhanced sense of security.

What such measures do suggest, interestingly, is a return to traditional kinds of design that worked well for centuries: old-fashioned streets with plenty of eyes looking out of windows at the scene outside, doorways that clearly define the boundaries between public and private space and that protect access to the latter, small groups of dwellings where everyone knows his or her neighbours at least by sight and can immediately sense a stranger.

Partly, the rules for safe design can thus be learned by rote; but they have to be applied, and developed, by trial and error. What is needed here is much more exchange between planners and designers about the lessons of experience. An extraordinary and melancholy fact about our social sciences, and their practitioners, is that, as they have steadily ascended into ever more stratospheric analyses of the global crisis of urban industrial civilization, they seem to have lost all interest in learning about small-scale solutions. We need a more prosaic, nose-to-the-grindstone, learn-by-mistakes approach to planning once again.

Shells and Functions

Supposing we painfully learned it, there is another level of problem: in creating (or recreating) the new, it may be impossible merely to replicate a desired past. That old London of the streets and squares did not spring up instantaneously; on the contrary, it represents a long and subtle process of adaptation, over one or two centuries, of people to their buildings and their buildings to them. We might reproduce the built structures, but unless the economic and social circumstances were right, it would not come out the same. There would be no friendly local newsagent and sub-postmaster unless someone were willing and able to fill the role; no picture framer or upholsterer unless training schemes had produced new ones to step into the shoes of those retiring or dying; no interesting neighbourhood restaurant unless entrepreneurial wit had allied with venture capital to produce one.

These people, these qualities, do not fall off the London plane trees: they have to be grown. The fact that, often, they still spring up in the right place and at the right time is a tribute to the continuing vibrant adaptability of the London economy; the fact that, often, they fail to do so is witness to the huge problem of mismatch, already addressed in Chapter 3. But built forms are very relevant in this process: unless the right spaces are available at the right rents, which generally means old cheap space, even the most aspiring entrepreneur will fail, and everyone will be poorer in consequence.

This argument, too, has a conservative implication. Contrary to the argument of *London 2000*, it may be desirable actually to slow the pace of physical change; to try to guarantee the largest possible stock of old, cheap premises in which new entrepreneurial ideas, as well as old traditional crafts, can flourish. And such places should be well distributed among the localities of London, so that talents can everywhere flourish, and so that they can find appreciative local markets from which larger markets can later spring. The conclusion is that, though some redevelopment may be desirable and necessary, the balance of old and new, of cheap and dear, should be maintained as far as possible in each locality. This will of course be a necessary but not a sufficient condition: all kinds of other policies will simultaneously be needed, especially in the fields of education and training.

The Role of Community Design and the Role of Land

There is of course something else. In 1988 we can hardly forget it, for it is the new urban design orthodoxy. It is community design: the people have to be brought in to design their own environment, whether that means the creation of an entirely new neighbourhood from scratch, or the reconstruction of an old one to make it work better and feel better for those living in it. Prince Charles has blessed it and those who practise it. Rod Hackney, 1987's elected President of the RIBA, has based his sensational rise to fame on it. It is the received planning wisdom of the 1980s (Wates & Knevitt 1987).

But what exactly is it? In fact, it can cover a multitude of rather different things. At one extreme, it can really mean the people creating the environment with their own hands. That is what has been done on a vast scale in the Third World following the path-breaking work of the British planner John Turner, in Peru, a quarter-century ago. It is also what was achieved by the now-famous group in the Lightmoor area of Telford New Town in Shropshire, under the genial guidance of Tony Gibson, in their award-winning work. Or, more loosely, it can mean a local community using an architect to discover what they want for themselves. That, as notable examples in Liverpool and elsewhere have shown, can also be an immensely rewarding experience for community and architect alike. But it does not mean the same immediate involvement: finally, not only does someone else do the building, but someone else draws the plans.

Our policy, surely, should be to do the best we can. Best of all, of course, is to do it yourself – but that needs enormous guts, enormous energy, and a lot of time that not many people have got, unless they are unemployed. Even then, it will also need the skills of the professional. Failing that, as second best, is to get involved in the design.

There is, though, a critical related question: money. The government is all for housing associations or co-operatives: on this point, it ironically appears, right-wing free marketeers make common cause with left-wing anarchists. It wants existing council tenancies taken out of local authority control and given to new forms of management, including tenant management. It particularly wants new agencies, called Housing Action Trusts, to take over the most-run-down council estates, renovate them, and turn them over to new forms of management, perhaps a housing association, perhaps a private company. Under new management, tenants will cease to be 'secure'; they will become 'assured' tenants, liable to rent rises that could be big, albeit cushioned by housing allowances. The same will go for private tenants. The clear hope and intention is that many renters will get the message, and will choose to buy instead.

The difficult question, though, is about the future. It will not be a simple once-for-all question of putting the poor in control of their own housing. For, unless the economic millennium arrives much sooner than we think, there will be new generations of poor; or, at very least, new generations of Londoners who cannot afford the going price for new housing, perhaps any housing at all. Jean Conway has pointed out that the average male income in London in 1985, £11 000 a year, would pay for only a £28 000 house – and less than one-quarter of first-time London buyers found a house for under £30 000 at that time (Conway 1985, 20). With council housing starts cut by nearly 80 per cent between the mid-1970s and the mid-1980s, and now seemingly destined to stop altogether, the responsibility must pass to housing associations – who housed only 4.4 per cent of Londoners in 1985 (Conway 1985, 27, 29, 36). The question then is how to devise policies that will allow them both to play a role in designing and providing their own shelter, and to do it at a cost that they can afford. The government itself thinks that its proposals will yield perhaps 25 000 additional rented dwellings a year – a fraction of what local authorities have been producing, even under the severe restrictions of the 1980s.

Third World experience – always relevant in questions of affordable housing – teaches two lessons: first and foremost, provide free or cheap land; second, as a useful ancillary, provide cheap building materials. Now it is a matter of common experience that, in London as elsewhere, there are huge tracts of urban wasteland. Alice Coleman first drew them to our attention in the 1970s; the government has since documented their extent; research by Michael Chisholm and Philip Kivell has usefully summarized the results (Coleman 1976; Chisholm & Kivell 1987). Table 23 gives the Chisholm-Kivell picture of just how much there is. As they stress, there are problems with the data: the official Land Register lists only publicly owned wasteland, and the figures for all derelict land are out of date.

Table 23(a) demonstrates the startling difference between London and other urban areas. London authorities had managed to dispose of half their vacant land between 1984 and 1987, and one-third of this was already under development. In London, evidently, inner urban land is marketable – perhaps because so much of it is in Docklands; elsewhere, it is not. Table 23(b), based on the older figures, covers all derelict land, public and private: it shows dramatic increases, in London as in other major urban areas, between 1974 and 1982, much of it directly attributable to deindustrialization and the parallel closure of port or railway facilities. And restoration was not keeping pace – though since then, of course, there may have been a dramatic change.

We can at least accept that there is a lot of vacant land in London. We might go on to conclude – though this is a matter not of objective enquiry, but of value judgement – that some of this land ought to be released on to the market at full market price, but that if we want to help poor people, then some land ought to be written down to a price they might afford. In Chapter 8, I propose a simple mechanism to take account of the fact that market value reflects the planning permission that is put on a piece of land. But here we are dealing with a very special problem: the poor need cheap land but they cannot get it. Yet if they did, their 'sweat equity' – expressive American term – would surely produce a massive increase in the value.

Table 23 Vacant and derelict urban land, 1982–87

(a) Vacant land on the Public Register, 1987

	Area vacant, 1987	Disposed of, 1984–87	Brought into use, 1984–87
Greater London	1 896	947	394
Greater Manchester	2 173	461	200
Merseyside	1 399	64	33
South Yorkshire	1 543	63	13
Tyne & Wear	1 657	263	130
West Midlands	960	328	91
West Yorkshire	2 002	113	20
Total	*11 630*	*2239*	*881*

(b) Derelict land, major urban areas, 1982

	Area derelict		Area restored, 1974–82			
	1974	1982	Total	By local authority		By other agencies
				With grant	Without grant	
Greater London	324	1 954	422	79	277	66
Greater Manchester	3 405	4 035	1727	1482	99	146
Merseyside	529	1 716	390	259	11	120
South Yorkshire	1 565	1 110	871	666	89	116
Tyne & Wear	1 314	1 458	834	697	22	115
West Midlands	1 535	1 833	1000	692	111	197
West Yorkshire	2 857	2 640	1104	820	62	222
Total	*11 529*	*14 746*	*6348*	*4695*	*671*	*982*

Source: Chisholm & Kivell (1987).

Third World planners know this paradox well enough. It occurs with almost every spontaneous squatter settlement, once it is settled down and officially tolerated. World Bank economists write papers on how to realize some of the resulting value. At least, here in Britain – a country with a surviving and reasonably incorruptible bureaucracy – it should be possible to collect the value.

The solution, therefore, would look like this. Written-down land would be given to self-build housing co-operatives. The money might come in part from the auctioning of commercial planning permissions, which I propose in Chapter 8. If then a member of the co-op sold his or her home, the proceeds would be divided: so much to the seller, for the sweat equity; so much to the co-op, for the land. The latter share would go into the pool, boosting the co-op's funds, and allowing it to buy more written-down land. For co-ops that did not practise self-build, the member's share would logically be much smaller.

What Kind of London? A Tentative Blueprint

What kind of London might we achieve with this bundle of policies? A London not conspicuously different from the one we have, that is for sure. For one thing, there is not the money to do other; for another, there is not the will. The worst slums are gone. People do not seem to care that much about the inconveniences; they accept them as part of London life. But some things could be done better. Here is a priority list.

(a) *A better traffic environment*. We could start, as argued in Chapter 5, by putting a much more realistic price on the use of roadspace in most of London. Then we would ensure that people paid that price, either through parking or road-use charges; the relatively modest cost would be fully recouped by the charges themselves, including fines for delinquent behaviour. Then we would invest as the pattern of behaviour indicated: much more off-street parking around shopping centres, for instance. At the same time, we would progressively introduce traffic-calming schemes throughout the residential areas of London, including precinctual solutions to ensure that rat-running traffic did not penetrate back streets. Where this puts severe burdens on the main road system, in terms of either congestion or environmental quality, we would seek to mitigate it by selective road construction. We would seek to challenge the biggest traffic flows on to a relatively skeletal high-quality system, some of which would take the form of new tollways, built depressed beneath the surface and even tunnelled in order to minimize environmental damage.

(b) *Better-quality streetscape*. We would provide the relatively small amounts of money necessary to produce high-quality streetscapes. These would entail both investment and enhanced maintenance. Investment would improve the quality of the pedestrian environment, especially in places (such as shopping streets) where large numbers of pedestrians congregated, by such well-known techniques as wider pavements, seating, flowers, shelters, and good-quality paving. Maintenance would ensure a high quality of upkeep, including repair of damage and removal of graffiti, which are particularly important in retaining a good feel to the streets. Some of this programme would contribute to the better traffic environment just outlined.

(c) *Better, safer residential areas*. There is an urgent need to improve the quality of many of London's inner residential areas, particularly those in more deprived neighbourhoods. Ever since the inner-city reports of 1977, we have been conscious that better physical environments are a key to the general restoration of confidence and thus to the revitalization of these areas. Yet, if anything, the problem is worse now. In particular, Londoners in many areas face something they never thought possible: the streets are no longer safe. We have to face that a much higher level of surveillance, particularly electronic observation, is the first step in fighting street crime. We may also need to consider recruiting a corps of informal police auxiliaries, like the Guardian Angels who have been so successful in some American cities, from the ranks of inner-city youth themselves; they, as much as any, are the chief victims of street violence, and they have the maximum interest in combating it.

But we need to combine all this human and mechanical surveillance, distasteful as it may seem, with improvements in design that reduce the opportunities for mugging and mayhem. Some of these, like removing the grosser errors in the big renewal estates of the 1960s, may be relatively easy; some, like designing the dangers out of underground subways, may be harder and more expensive. What we certainly need, as a start, are many more systematic and detailed studies of the Newman-Coleman type about the failures of our present urban designs, with the aim of mitigating or removing the grosser cases one by one.

All these spell the need for rather small-scale, detailed, incremental improvements. They all suggest a professional implication: the requirement for many more urban design professionals, neither architects nor town planners in the traditional sense but something in between, who are skilled in analysing problems and producing solutions that both work well and look good. In Britain we have not been very good at producing such people in the right numbers, almost certainly because no one gave the job a very high priority. With a few honourable exceptions, the planning schools, oddly, never seem to have been much interested. Neither have the colleges of art and design worried much about it, though it could have been a useful source of employment for their graduates.

Achieving this – the quality of *urbanity* – should now become some kind of national crusade. There is much at stake, not merely in London; it is nothing less than the question of whether we can maintain a decent and pleasant civic life in our great cities. Compared with our neighbours on the European mainland, such as the burghers of the great cities of Germany and Switzerland, we have never shown a particular talent for that art; the challenge now is whether we can show any at all. If we cannot, the consequences for millions of people, including the 2.5 million of inner London, could be very dire. But we should work resolutely to show that we can.

In doing this, we shall be putting the art of town planning back on course. Elsewhere, I have charted the strange story whereby the theoreticians of planning, those who taught it in the planning schools, steadily became less and less interested in basic questions of good practice (Hall 1988, Ch. 10). That perhaps reflected a demoralization and loss of credibility; but in turn it massively reinforced it (Reade 1987). The resulting irony is that, as argued in the preface to this book, planning is now attacked on all sides for actually contributing to our urban ills, when it was never more needed to help mitigate and obviate them. Only the planners themselves, and the schools that produce them, can demonstrate that they have put their house in order and can again do the job that society expects of them.

A central part of that job is the art of sensitive and humane urban design: the art of producing an urban environment that people feel good in rather than bad in, that encourages neighbourliness and solidarity rather than alienation and fear, that they want to respect and treat well rather than defacing and kicking down and trashing. It is not an easy art, and in part it has been lost; but the masters of the past could do it, and we can learn it from them again if we try.

7

Government 2001

In matters of governing London, an eternity seems to have passed in the quarter-century since *London 2000*. In 1963, the London Government Act had just been passed; London awaited one of the world's first experiments in strategic metropolitan planning through a directly elected, London-wide government. In 1988, the great experiment has been and gone: the Greater London Council, which assumed power on 1 April 1965, was officially abolished 21 years later. And the official reason for its demise, and that of the metropolitan county councils for the six provincial English conurbations, was provided in a government White Paper of 1963: these units of government had been set up during 'the heyday of a certain fashion for strategic planning, the confidence in which now appears exaggerated' (Secretary of State for the Environment 1983, 2); they had been engaged in 'a natural search for a "strategic" role which may have little basis in real needs' (p. 3).

The first part of that statement was a simple matter of truth. For the Royal Commission on Local Government in Greater London, which was established in 1957 under the chairmanship of Mr Justice Herbert, the overwhelming deficiency of the then system was the lack of an overall authority responsible for strategic planning, including transport planning. The planning of land uses and of the transport that connected and served them, in Herbert's view, demanded such a single authority for the whole built-up area of Greater

London. The Commission's report of 1960 gave telling case studies of the muddle and conflict that resulted from the lack of it (Royal Commission Local Government in Greater London 1960). Only a year afterwards, in an eloquent underscoring of the point, the government of the day was forced to make desperate *ad hoc* arrangements in order to set up a transportation planning study for the area.

The second part of the government's 1983 statement, in contrast, represented a value judgement which was certainly not shared by many other people, including many who styled themselves experts on the subject. In the huge debate that intervened between the White Paper of 1983 and the final abolition of 1986, very few such expert voices were heard defending the government's actions. Yet a worry remains. In the first place, no one save a few partisan zealots could swear in honesty that the Greater London Council had achieved all (or even most) of what had been expected of it at its birth. On the contrary, even its last-ditch supporters were in many respects seriously critical of it, and wanted to see it more or less radically restructured. And in the second place, the alarming fact is that the two years since abolition seem to have made precious little difference to the way London's government works day by day. It is as if the government has proved its own assertion that the GLC was a monstrous and expensive irrelevancy.

Retrospect: The 'Flawed Design'

The fact is this: in 1988, we start with a blank hole where strategic local government used to be. The onus of proof now lies on those who would seek to reinstate it. But before we come to that, it is clearly worthwhile to conduct yet another inquest: a cooler one, now that the dust of battle is settled.

In retrospect, the GLC's failure can be summed up thus: it did the things it was supposed to do badly or not at all, and it tried to do too many things it should never have tried to do. It was created as a slim, strategic authority for the co-ordination of land use planning and transport. If it was to do that effectively, it would clearly need to be in a position to tell the 32 London boroughs broadly what to do, through binding directives on their own plans and their own development control decisions. It would also need direct powers to build highways, to manage traffic, and to direct the development and management of the capital's public transport system. In practice, it did these things either inadequately or not at all.

On land use planning, it locked horns with the boroughs almost from the start. In inner London it took considerable direct planning powers from the old London County Council; in outer London it took them from a mosaic of county councils and three county boroughs, which had been jealous of their own rights and in one case (Croydon) had pursued a fiercely individual, pro–development strategy. Its relationships with the boroughs, as defined in the Act, were almost a perfect recipe for conflict: through its Greater London Development Plan it was supposed to produce binding guidelines for the boroughs; in the case of major developments crossing boundaries (as at Covent Garden) it could play a direct role, but the boroughs felt that they were fully competent in these matters.

In practice, because it took four years to produce the GLDP, another three to see it through a marathon public inquiry, and another four to get the Secretary of State's approval of a modified version, the boroughs were left without binding guidelines for over a decade. Subsequently, they took every opportunity to pressure governments – especially Conservative ones – to restrict the GLC's powers, accusing it of trying to act as a thirty-fourth borough, 'the LCC writ large' (Greater London Group 1985, 57). And this was a matter of real substance, since in some important respects the boroughs had interests that conflicted very directly with those of the GLC – as for instance on the question of large-scale public housing developments in the outer boroughs, where at first the GLC inherited the old LCC's housing powers and predatory instincts. When this occurred, invariably, it was the GLC that gave way.

Transport proved a more complex tangle still. At first the GLC got responsibility for main highways and traffic management, but in practice these powers were circumscribed: the GLC got 560 miles of so-called metropolitan roads, mainly from the old LCC, plus another 320 miles in 1969; central government kept responsibility for 143 miles of national trunk roads outside the old LCC area, such as the then-new motorways and the North Circular Road; the boroughs controlled the remaining 6900 miles of local roads, and were the effective agents for on-street parking schemes; the Metropolitan Police were responsible for regulation and control, including the deployment of the traffic wardens. All this provided another ripe source for demarcation disputes: in one of the most farcical, it proved impossible for a decade to implement a scheme for uniform traffic signs. And, throughout the GLC's life, there were continual protests from borough officials at unnecessary GLC interference in detailed matters like the location of pedestrian crossings, which required their approval. Meanwhile, after the GLC performed a *volte face* and abandoned its own road building plans in 1973, the government in effect ignored it and went ahead with plans to build or rebuild the highways in outer London, though in many cases it made haste exceedingly slowly.

The other anomaly was that, originally, the GLC was a *highway* rather than a new transport authority: it had no direct responsibility for public transport. That was remedied when Barbara Castle's Transport (London) Act of 1969 transferred responsibility for London Transport to it. After 1973, with the highway programme abandoned, the GLC's transport planners more and more turned their attention to public transport, achieving some success both in investment – the first stage of the Jubilee Line, opened in 1978, and the improved North London link of 1985 - and in revenue subsidy, with the development of the celebrated Fares Fair policy of 1981–3. Ironically, it was this policy, and the direct clash with government that resulted, that provided perhaps the single most important reason for the government's decision to close the GLC down. In any event, the extraordinary fact is that hardly at all during the GLC's history was it able to pursue a balanced policy towards both highways and public transport: it swung violently from emphasis on the one to emphasis on the other. But even during the latter period, it had only the most indirect responsibility for investment in British Rail's commuter services.

This last fact relates to another: the GLC's circumscribed geographical remit. The Herbert Commission tried hard to define a meaningful unit in terms of a continuous built-up area bounded by the metropolitan Green Belt. Subsequent to its report, politics intervened: several locations, clearly part of that built-up area, managed to extricate themselves. But that was marginal. The important fact was the one *London 2000* emphasized on its opening pages: even in 1963, Greater London was no longer great enough. The population growth was all outside, it was rolling progressively farther out, and London's own population was falling.

Since then, as seen, this paradox has simply been underlined and then double-underlined. The question that everyone was asking in the great debates of 1983–6 was whether it made any sense at all to attempt strategic planning over such a limited and essentially shrinking area. For, as the 1970 Strategic Plan for the South East so clearly emphasized, the really important strategic planning decisions now concerned the entire South-East region, a region that extended not 15 miles from Charing Cross, but 60, 70, even 80 miles distant. And, lacking any statutory body, the 1970 Plan had to be produced on an *ad hoc* basis, by a joint central–local government team especially brought into being for the purpose. Greater London was fast becoming as irrelevant a definition as the old London County Council had been.

Perhaps, then, the problem of the GLC is that it owed its existence to a 'flawed design' (Flynn *et al*. 1985, 64–5): the Herbert Commission had seen it as a slim strategic authority, but that ignored the problem of implementing the strategy. This may have been so. But the GLC added to the tragedy by another circumstance: the boundaries were so finely drawn that at every election political control changed hands. At first, with some bipartisan agreements, that mattered less. But eventually, it meant that virtually every major policy area became a political football, with huge reversals every four years. Coupled with the arrival of young politicians looking for new initiatives whereby they could make quick political reputations, this gave the GLC increasingly the quality of a political carnival rather than a serious strategic body for the management of the capital.

1988: A Hole in the Centre?

As everyone knows, at abolition the GLC's powers went three ways. Most, including virtually all planning powers, went to the City and the 32 boroughs, which were charged with producing so-called unitary plans and were also given responsibility for 825 miles of the former metropolitan roads and for traffic management, though in both planning and transport, the respective secretaries of state were given wide powers of discretion. These reserve powers were accompanied by the transfer of direct responsibility for London Regional Transport, and for some 70 miles of metropolitan road, to the Department of Transport. Finally, some powers not highly relevant to this tale (such as the Fire Service) went to new *ad hoc* bodies.

So far, it works. The rubbish gets collected and taken somewhere. London Transport still runs. The traffic lights still turn from red to green in some kind of sequence. The resulting traffic congestion is about as bad as ever, but no worse. There are even new things happening: a Docklands Light Railway, a new road in east London, major developments opening or in the offing. No one can see that the demise of the GLC has made much substantive difference.

More than that: the debate is now largely stilled, perhaps because everyone is exhausted; the decision is taken, and no one expects it to be un-taken in short order. There is a kind of unwritten law of public debate and public decision: issues swim into visibility, form the subject of intense controversy, get acted upon (or sometimes not acted upon), and then mysteriously go away. Especially, the media lose interest. Local government in London will not be an issue for the next half-decade, at least.

Yet underneath the surface, the problems that brought the GLC into being have not gone away. On the contrary: they are endemic, and if anything they have been intensified in the intervening 30 years. London's traffic is still stalled; its public transport still functions less smoothly than it might; there are major decisions to be made about the future pattern of the economy; huge developments are in the offing. We can be sure that before long – perhaps by 1995, almost certainly by the year 2000 – the spectre of London government will once again rear its head. Therefore, since this book is all about the medium-term future, it is right to anticipate the debate.

Prospects for the Future:
Two Models of Strategic Planning

When the debate again opens, alternative models, many of them aired in the hectic months before abolition, will be pulled from the file drawers and dusted down. There will be proposals for five or seven mega-boroughs to replace the present 32; for a reconstituted London County Council; for an indirectly elected London Assembly; for a Copenhagen-style indirectly elected slimline authority; for a strengthened GLC with powers to allocate finances between boroughs, as proposed by Sir Frank Marshall in his 1978 review of the GLC (Greater London Council 1978); for a directly elected wide-area regional authority on the model of Strathclyde in Scotland; even, doubtless, for the federalization of Great Britain (Forrester *et al*. 1985, 165–81). All these, and more, have repeatedly appeared over the decades, as successive political generations have wrestled with the problem of London's governance; we have been here before.

Unfortunately, most are non-starters, for the simple reason that they do not recognize political realities. An anecdote: in the University of California's computerized catalogue, there is no such subject as 'London Government'. The bemused researcher eventually finds the material under 'London Politics and Government'. For this, the California cataloguers might not win a prize in information science; but they might win one in political science. The fact is that in London, matters of government are first and foremost matters of politics. Any analysis that ignores the primacy of politics is not worth the time.

And these are big politics: as Ken Young and Patricia Garside remind us in their monumental history of Metropolitan London – significantly subtitled *Politics and Urban Change 1837–1981* – the primary fact about the government of London is that it represents a big potential threat to the government of the United Kingdom. That has been true ever since the medieval City and the medieval King stood eyeball to eyeball. Young and Garside make clear that the creation of the GLC was a gigantic historic anomaly, which occurred only because of Macmillan's typically audacious judgement that it would fall to the Conservatives (Young & Garside 1982, 308). For once, Supermac's political judgement proved wrong. Had Young and Garside waited a few more years to extend their story, they could have cited the latest dramatic illustration: the banner-bedecked County Hall of 1983-6, shouting defiance at a Conservative government on the other side of the river. With that in mind, no administration of any complexion is likely to contemplate again setting up a government-in-exile across the water.

So there are two ways. Either we seek to develop a slim, streamlined elected regional strategic authority such as Herbert presumably had in mind, an authority prohibited from performing any other function and presenting no real threat either to central government or to the boroughs, and this time making sure that it starts that way and stays that way; or, as the Joint Centre's expert Working Party declared in its review of the problem, we admit that central government is going to control London, and start to plan a structure on that basis: a Ministry for London, and a Grand Committee of the House of Commons.

The Slimline Elected Authority

There are precedents for the first solution, on the European mainland. As Alan Norton has shown in his useful review of metropolitan government abroad, 'Britain is an odd exception not only in proposing to abolish intermediate authorities which serve approximately half its population but also in paying scant regard to the case for decentralization' (Norton 1983, 2). True, events have shown that Britain is an extraordinarily centralized state, in which local government has no real defence against attack from Westminster (Flynn *et al.* 1985, 126). Nevertheless, the argument that London has been deprived of a democratic voice is an uncomfortable one, even for a centralist and confident government (Forrester *et al.* 1985, 148).

Norton's own examples suggest that some of these European-type authorities could potentially exist within such a centralist framework. Most of them are *ad hoc* creations, which have no clear constitutional status, but were set up to deal with special cases; they are fragile because they depend on agreement. But they can be very slim – Greater Copenhagen has only 115 employees, the Frankfurt Regional Union 187 – and some of them, at least, have shown a capacity to survive.

Such an authority, on the model of Greater Copenhagen, might be indirectly elected through the boroughs, with an admixture of members representing the wide interest: either MPs, or persons nominated by the Secretary of State. It might cover an area considerably wider than the old GLC, perhaps extending over the entire Metropolitan Area, perhaps even farther. It would thus begin to approximate to the regional prescription advocated by the Royal Town Planning Institute in their 1987 policy statement (Royal Town Planning Institute 1987). It would presumably take over all the functions of the Standing Conference, SERPLAN. Its remit would be to produce statements of regional guidance which, after approval by the Secretary of State, would be binding on borough and district authorities in drawing up their own unitary plans. It would also have a specific remit to advise on investment plans for both main roads and public transport in its area.

This structure would fit well with the revised planning system proposed by the government in 1986, in which county structure plans will be replaced by unitary plans, produced by district authorities, within a framework of strategic regional guidance (Department of the Environment and Welsh Office 1986). It would, however, raise two crucial questions.

The first is whether the necessary modicum of agreement would be forthcoming. Experience of the Strategic Conference, ever since the first version was set up in the 1930s, is that it is a good research organization and talking shop but is a weak decision–making body, tending to express the lowest common multiple of agreement among its members. The second, associated, worry is whether it would have any teeth. Strategic planning is fine so long as it gets implemented in real decisions on the ground; otherwise, it is a pure waste of time and money. The GLC's experience was that the implementing body is the one with the real executive power; hence the endless conflicts over apparent detail. A slimmed-down authority, restricted by statute, could find itself powerless.

There may be a way around this. OFTEL (the Office of Tele-communications), and the American regulatory agencies on which it is based, have no executive powers; yet they have proved surprisingly effective as watchdogs of the general public interest, even on matters of detail. So it might be possible to adopt that model. Maybe the problem with the GLC was not that it lacked executive powers, but that it tried to spread its activities too widely. Only an experiment would show.

The other possible objection is that an indirectly elected body, especially if diluted by nominees, is not a democratically responsible body. To that the answer is that it would be very difficult to ensure direct democratic answerability over such a vast geographical area, and on such general strategic issues; direct elections would hardly be likely to generate much excitement, save on rare occasions when some media-worthy issue cropped up.

Central Control

If a streamline Copenhagen-style authority is rejected, we are logically left with central control. Distasteful as it may seem to many, this may be the only practicable option. The argument, as the Joint Centre Working Party set it out, may be expressed as a series of propositions. The government in 1983-6 was determined to abolish the GLC, and it succeeded. Though many functions can and should go to the boroughs, there are certain functions that can be properly performed only on a London-wide basis. The question is how to do this effectively, economically, and accountably. If no one else can do them, they logically fall upon central government and its agents. This is underlined by the fact that, at the end of the day, central government pays for the key physical plant: main roads, public transport, basic infrastructure for major developments like Docklands. Therefore these powers should go to the Departments of the Environment and of Transport, where they will be overseen by Parliament (Greater London Working Party 1984, 5/1).

In detail, the Working Party suggested that a regional transport authority – similar in many ways to the Metropolitan Transport Authority proposed in an influential House of Commons Select Committee report of 1982 – would have powers over all major roads (including traffic management) within Greater London and all public transport (including BR commuter services) in an extended transport area, covering the London commuter field (House of Commons 1982, lxvii–lxix). The strategic planning responsibilities would encompass the present Greater London, and should be exercised ideally by a new Ministry for London, or, failing that, by a new London division

of the Department of the Environment, which would include officials seconded from the Department of Transport (Greater London
Working Party 1984, 5/1–5/4).

In retrospect, that prescription seems open to doubt. It does
not clearly enough relate land use and transport planning over the
same geographical area. And, because of the tight geographical
circumscription of the strategic planning function, it appears to
exclude major strategic decisions on matters like new communities,
which – as previous chapters have shown – are the truly crucial
ones for the region's future. That was understandable in terms of
the great debate of 1984, which was about government in *London*.
Now that debate is over, it is clearer that any new solution should
refer to an extended *region*.

I draw the conclusion that, under the centralist prescription, there
should be an advisory Metropolitan Planning and Transportation
Commission. It should cover at least the Metropolitan Area (the
zone within the 40-mile ring), if not the whole South East. Like its
indirectly elected equivalent, it would have a remit to advise the
Secretary of State on future main lines of development within the
region. The main difference would be that it would be 100 per cent
appointed by the Secretary of State, though it might – as of custom,
not as of right – contain some local authority members.

Such a body must be capable of balancing the concerns of the
local community against the needs of the wider community, in a
way that the present local government system in Roseland cannot
achieve. We might call it, for want of a better name, a Regional
Development Authority. It would be charged with producing a
regional framework for development and redevelopment, and
channelling public investment in inner-city regeneration. It would
identify the areas for major development and redevelopment within
the region, including sites for new communities. It would also
need to be centrally involved in co-ordinating regional investment
in transportation and communications, whether by road, rail, or
telecommunications. It would be the equivalent of a London Docklands Development Corporation on the scale of a whole region, but
it would not itself plan in detail: its job would end once action areas
were designated and the development rights sold.

It would be unique. It would correspond to no present level of
local government. So there is no easy way of ensuring its democratic
accountability. In a centralist system, there appears no alternative
to setting up such an authority through central government and
making it responsible to Parliament through annual reports, just as
the New Town Corporations and the London Passenger Transport

Board were in their day and the London Docklands Development Corporation in ours. Like all these, it would be a limited special-purpose authority; like them, it would sit side by side with the local authorities, which would keep nearly all their present powers save some strategic planning responsibilities.

Once this body had specified such locations, there would clearly be massive consequences in terms of enhanced land values and consequent land speculation. So, whether indirectly elected or appointed, it would exercise enormous influence. Yet if it did not do this, we should be left with planning by roulette. I draw the conclusion that it should specify locations, but that in consequence it should carry out its remit within a rather strict set of procedures, which I outline in Chapter 7.

The question of its areal remit is a difficult one. The so-called Metropolitan Area was a statistical convenience invented by government officials in 1960 to describe the belt of fastest population growth in the 1950s. As Chapter 1 already showed, that belt rolled progressively outwards from decade to decade, and now actually overlaps the boundaries of the official South East region. And this corresponds interestingly (albeit approximately) to the area of BR's Network SouthEast, its London-based commuter system: an area that extends up to 100 miles and more from London in certain directions, especially into East Anglia and the South West, the two fastest-growing regions of Britain.

This suggests that the appropriate region would be minimally the area of the present SERPLAN, and might indeed be the Greater South East suggested in Chapter 1 and used in subsequent statistical analyses in this book. This is a huge area, having around one-fifth of the area and more than one-third of the population of the entire country. (It is however comparable in many ways with the *Region Ile de France*, the corresponding unit for the Paris region.) And it must be underlined that, as Chapter 3 suggested, by far the greater part of it consists of reasonably self-contained labour market areas, only lightly touched by the outward ripple of London's commuter field. That was equally true of the Metropolitan Area of 1960. Now, as then, there is a critical contradiction between the region as defined in *functional* terms, as suggested by everyday movements, and that defined in terms of *planning* needs. London's outward growth throws a shadow that is far greater than the extent of its commuter field: it is this penumbra that requires strategic planning.

'Requires' strategic planning: that is a strong word for the late 1980s. For the government of the day has declared that there is no need for any such thing. In its Green Paper introducing the new unitary planning system, it was specific:

> Such arrangements would not represent a formalised regional structure, nor would they be a return to the type of large–scale regional planning which was attempted in the 1960's and 70's, but which proved largely ineffective and implied a degree of central direction and control that would not be compatible with today's conditions or with public opinion. (Department of the Environment and Welsh Office 1986, 14)

My argument is that soon enough, just as in the 1960s, there will be a call for the return of the strategic stance. Soon enough, planning by the turn of the roulette wheel will prove not satisfactory to anyone: not to the volume housebuilders, determined to press ahead with their plans for a score of new communities in the South East; nor to the beleaguered citizens and politicians of the shire counties, who live in fear of their depredations; nor to ministers, left in the hot seat with the need to take massively unpopular decisions. And this will prove particularly true if, as a quarter-century ago, the future estimates of regional growth undergo sudden radical upward revision. Then, strategic planning will suddenly become politically acceptable, even desirable, again. It lets the politicians, at least partially, off the hook. And that argument will be a clinching one.

From Strategy to Implementation: New Community Corporations

Within such a strategic framework, there is also a need for another kind of public body – or, rather, what the French would doubtless call a 'mixed entity'. That is for a new kind of development corporation to develop the new communities. We have long admitted the need for such public corporations to carry out large-scale development; ironically, in the 1980s the Thatcher government's Urban Development Corporations borrow directly from the model of the New Town Development Corporations used by the radical Attlee Labour administration in the 1940s. The basic reason is the one argued so forcefully by John Reith's New Towns Committee in its brilliant analysis for the incoming Attlee government in 1945: the need for speed and decisive action. There is no way that local authorities can achieve this: the melancholy early history of the 1952 Town Development Act shows that, as does the saga of the London docklands in the 1970s. Given the scale and complexity of local interests now, to try and achieve action through local agreement would be a forlorn hope.

Admitting the need for a corporation, nevertheless, no existing type exactly fits the bill. The old New Town Development Corporations are not the model, because they were posited on the assumption that they would do much of the development. The Urban Development Corporations are not the model either, because they would provide a framework for the activities of many different developers, whereas here we should assume that a very few developers will be involved, perhaps only one. This new kind of corporation would involve representatives of both the local authority and the developers, with some independently appointed members acting as arbiters of last resort. Its function would be to guarantee, as far as possible, a high-quality development carried through expeditiously. It would exist for as long as the development was taking place: normally, not more than ten years, perhaps a good deal less.

With these two levels of planning and development in place, there would at last be mechanisms for achieving large-scale change in an orderly and integrated way. The strategic authority would identify the areas of major planned change; the executive authorities would implement the plan. Both levels should be accountable to Parliament, not directly, in the daily hurly-burly of questions and debate, but indirectly, through the mechanism of the annual report. The critical decisions would be taken by ministers, who would be directly answerable. Local democracy would continue to exist, but clear special procedures would operate where experience has shown them to be necessary. It is a better way by far than the wheel of chance.

8

Money 2001

A new London will not come cheap. As so often in Britain, we
have tried to do things cut-price, and the results are all too plain
to see. That might read as a criticism of government policies, but
it is not: it is a comment on a far deeper trend, which affects
private development as well as public, and goes back decades if
not centuries. It shows in the all-too-rapid deterioration of the built
stock and the built infrastructure, in the cracked paving stones,
the decrepit street furniture, the litter-strewn streets and squares
that deface too many of our towns and are so shamingly evident,
to natives and visitors alike, in the heart of London: Third World
standards, and worse, in the heart of the First.

Now, we need to remedy two consequences of these cheapskate
policies: we need to ensure a much higher quality of new build, and
we need to spend more on maintaining what we have. The two go
together: if we had built better in the first place, as they did in some
European countries and also in the United States, then it would not
cost us so much to fix things up. But we have not spent enough
on either maintenance or renewal, and that is why so often London
seems to be coming apart at the seams.

Some of this money can and should come from the private
sector. In the coming decades, the majority of new housing will
clearly come from that source, as well as virtually all the commercial

development. If the proposals in Chapter 5 are followed, a significant proportion of transport investment could be financed privately also. In major commercial developments, it may make good sense for the developer to provide the whole of the basic structure in the form of local streets. And in residential developments, too, it is perfectly possible to ask the private developer to provide much of the overhead capital in the form of local roads and drains and pipes, which must provide the basic infrastructure for all other building. But, that said, there is an irreducible minimum part of our urban built environment that the public sector must provide.

More precisely, the public sector will need to provide it in close association with the private sector. How exactly they do it, in both a logistical and a financial sense, is the chief burden of this chapter. There are three main questions to be asked.

First, an apparent sidestep but in fact a necessary preliminary, which every recent investigation has had to ask: How independent a system of local government do we want? Should we seek to create truly independent authorities, with big differences in taxing and spending traditions, on the model of the United States and some other countries? Or should we in effect make local government into a mere agent to provide standardized services, determined centrally, across the entire country? This is a highly political, even ideological, question, which is how it will be treated here. And, because it is such, it will be best to get it out of the way first.

Second, how do we raise adequate taxes to ensure a good level of public built environment, at a time when all the pressures are to reduce public spending? That, again, may sound like a politically contentious statement, but it is not: the pressure on public expenditure was felt long before the first Thatcher government, and it has been felt across the world, in left-wing and right-wing regimes alike. It does focus on the currently controversial subject of local taxation, but it goes beyond the narrow question of rates versus community charge, to take in the far wider question of other possible sources of local tax revenue.

Third and finally, can we raise additional sources of revenue from the development process itself? Should we, and can we, seek to channel for public purposes some of the gains that come from development? If so, what is the fairest and most effective way of doing so? Is it, for instance, through so-called development agreements, whereby the developer contributes directly to the public costs? Or is it through some kind of tax on development?

183

Do We Truly Want Local Government?

It is, after all, a matter of choice. There is no God-given rule that local government is necessary. For the most part, no one ever asked the people whether they wanted it or not. People care that their dustbins are emptied every Thursday in the same way that they care that they get the post every morning. They care that their children get taught in school in the same way that they care that they will get treated if sick. They care that their car does not sink into a pothole round the first street corner in the same way that they care that it will not hit a rock on the M1. In each case, one service happens to come from local government, the other from the centre. Local authorities often act as agents of central government (as in the M1 case), and no one much bothers so long as the result is satisfactory.

The questions to be asked are really three: (1) In each case, is local government likely to be more efficient? (2) Is it likely to be more effective? (3) Is it likely to make people feel better? We have some evidence on the first two; on the third, it is not really a matter of rational choice at all.

On efficiency, we have plenty of evidence from the Redcliffe-Maud Commission, in the late 1960s, on different sizes of local authority (Royal Commission on Local Government in England 1969). Their report suggested that, for most services, medium-sized authorities were more efficient than very small ones. That was why, in the mid-1970s, we reconstructed local authorities outside London on the basis of bigger districts, (usual minimum size: 75 000 people), which is the system we have now. On the other hand, the evidence failed to reach clear conclusions on the critical question, Are really big authorities more efficient, or less efficient, than medium-sized ones? It might be that a monster authority – even up to the level of a Great Britain authority, though that question was of course not asked – might empty dustbins more cheaply than a medium-sized one. We do know that a fairly big authority is necessary to get rid of the rubbish efficiently, as was clear when the government abolished the GLC and had to give that function, in effect, to consortia of boroughs.

But Redcliffe-Maud was much more concerned about a different question, which was effectiveness. It might be cheaper to have the Borough of Great Britain come for your dustbin, but suppose the dustmen did not arrive one Thursday? Suppose you then had to phone the Directorate of Refuse, which had been decentralized – in a government efficiency exercise – to West Hartlepool? Suppose it then took you 30 minutes and £25 of your money to get through?

Everyone has plenty of horror stories like that, and they are not all in the public sector either. This suggests that, first, whoever runs the services, it is better to do so through local offices; and second, it is probably better to give these offices a considerable degree of autonomy as to how they run themselves. Given the fact that the economies of mega-scale are not all that clear anyway, this produces the perfectly conventional answer that it is best to leave local government well alone.

There is however a different point, which might be called the law of upward-ratcheting in public service provision. As the problems of running cities grow, there is a long-term historical trend for local government to extend into more and more areas. From 1870 to 1975, GDP rose on average 1 per cent a year, local authority spending between 2 and 3 per cent a year (Foster *et al.* 1980, 600). For a long time, in fact, Parliament encouraged and enjoined it to do so; and even now, there is the same upward pressure. (Consider for instance the implications of recent well publicized child abuse cases for social services staffing.) Further, as the Layfield Committee on Local Government Finance pointed out in 1976, local government is inherently labour-intensive, and wage agreements are reached nationally, regardless of the state of the local economy; voluntary and professional organizations put constant pressure on local authorities (who need little prompting) to do better; and the performance of other authorities always provides a goad to do at least as well (Committee of Inquiry into Local Government Finance 1976, 237-8). If, then, there is pressure to cut costs, the inevitable result is the decline of certain services which are among the oldest and most basic functions of local authorities, such as the upkeep of the streets; hence all those potholes and pavement cracks. The paradox thus emerges that these services are now actually worse than they were when we were much poorer and local government was much slimmer. And these happen to be just the ones on which the quality of our common civic life so much depends.

One way out of this was a major option investigated by the Layfield Committee: centralize the whole system. Leave local government, but make it effectively an agent of central government, delivering a more or less standard package of local government services across the entire country (though with room for minimal variations). This, Layfield stressed, was a realistic option, quite in line with historic trends. The critical question was 'whether all important government decisions affecting people's lives and livelihood should be taken in one place on the basis of national policies; or whether many of the decisions could not as well, or better, be taken in different places, by people of diverse experience, associations, background and political persuasion' (Committee of Inquiry into Local Government Finance 1976, 299). The choice, the Committee stressed, was a difficult one; it was not for them to make, but for the government (p. 300).

How Do We Find The Tax Money?

That brought them, and brings us, straight to the second question. If the choice was for centralism, then – they thought – most money would logically come from central grants; there would be a small area in which local authorities could still exercise some discretion, and for this the rates would be good enough. (Central government might want to limit this discretion, though.) The alternative, they stressed, was to make local government more clearly local, by reducing the amount of central government grant. And that must logically mean finding a new source of local tax revenue to make up for it. The best for this purpose – indeed, Layfield thought, essential for it – would be a local income tax (LIT), levied by the main spending authority in each area: non-metro counties, metropolitan districts and Scottish regions. LIT would not replace rates, and the other authority in each area would continue to depend on rates. (Layfield thought that London was such a special case that it would not exactly fit this model, so special arrangements would need to be made.) Central government would still want to give grant so as to manage the overall economy; the best way would be through a unitary grant, which could be clawed back if local government exceeded a set spending target (Committee of Inquiry into Local Government Finance 1976, 246-9).

The Labour government of the day drew back from local income tax, and so did the succeeding Thatcher governments, despite their repeated manifesto commitment to abolish the rates; the Treasury objections evidently proved too strong. And, as Layfield recognized, there are problems with it: deducted through PAYE, it could appear almost invisible to the taxpayer, and so would prove an ever-present source of temptation to free-spending local authorities; if central government cut national income tax, as Thatcher governments have done, local government would have an inbuilt incentive to make compensating increases in LIT (Committee of Inquiry into Local Government Finance 1976, 263-7); there would be big administrative complications in introducing it; and it would still give problems of equity as between one authority and its neighbour, since rich areas would be able to provide better levels of services at lower costs to their residents than poor ones (Foster *et al.* 1980, 483, 507).

But the first Thatcher administration, in 1981, did implement the Layfield proposal on unitary grants (Foster *et al.* 1980, 613). That is interesting, because it suggests that at that time it was still thinking in terms of a Layfield-style localist solution – though in fact, such a grant is also compatible with a centralist solution. And then, finally, it opted for the poll tax: a proposal so right-wing radical that back in 1976, in those far–away middle-of-the-road days, Layfield never even considered it.

It needs saying, in fairness, that the poll tax is more respectable, in terms of fiscal theory, than anyone would gather from the storm of controversy that has inevitably surrounded it. To appreciate that, some elementary economic theory is needed (Foster *et al.* 1980, 39-49). Governments exist to provide what economists call public goods: goods that either will not be provided by the market, or cannot be produced efficiently by it. There are two cases, one called *non-excludability* (a good like a lighthouse or a street, which must be provided for all comers); the other called *non-rivalness* (a service that can be provided in greater quantity at zero extra cost, like a park or a museum); many public goods, like street lighting, have both these characteristics. But there is another way of classifying public goods: in a seminal essay of 1980, Christopher Foster used the old-fashioned terms 'beneficial' and 'onerous'; the Government Green Paper of 1986, directly based on it, substituted 'beneficial' and 'redistributive'.

Beneficial goods are goods that are non-excludable or non-rival, but where no element of redistribution, from richer to poorer people, is involved: the aim of government must be to provide them so as to maximize the surplus of social benefits over social costs. Ideally, we should pay for such goods directly, by means of user charges, but the problems of non-excludability and non–rivalness make this impossible. So the aim should be to find a tax that gets as near to user charges as possible; citizens would pay for the benefits they got from the service. The poll tax is precisely this tax. With poll tax, different authorities would provide different amounts of services at different levels of poll tax; people would move to the authority that provided the bundle closest to their preferences. This, in an economic sense, would be efficient; people, once they had moved to their preferred area, would get no more and no less of services than they were willing each to pay for, which would be what the economists call a Pareto-optimal outcome (Foster *et al.* 1980, 221-2).

But, as Amartaya Sen once well said, an economy can be Pareto-optimal and still be perfectly disgusting (Sen 1970, 22). The problem with this solution is that it takes no account of redistribution. The other bundle of services, which the Victorians called *onerous* and we prefer to call *redistributive*, has this redistributive quality: some citizens pay to provide benefits for others, either for motives of equity (to transfer income, in money or kind, to the poor), or for reasons of paternalism (to provide so-called merit goods, like education, to those who otherwise might not get them). Traditionally, while beneficial goods have been paid for on the basis of benefits enjoyed, onerous goods have been provided on the ability-to-pay principle, which means some kind of tax on income or wealth – income tax, capital tax, or property tax, for instance.

The problem, however, is that in practice the distinction has not been clearly made. Rates are clearly an ability-to-pay tax, but not a very accurate one as compared with (say) local income tax. To make it more complicated, the role of redistribution looms much larger at national level than at local level, because local populations are likely to be more homogeneous in character than populations of entire countries. And this is particularly true if we assume – a big assumption, this – that people are free to migrate locally to live among their own kind, thus making it possible for them to choose as between local governments that provide local bundles of beneficial services that fit the needs of their residents (Tiebout 1956; Foster *et al*. 1980, 43-4). This suggests an impeccably logical principle: leave the job of redistribution to central government, which will raise national income tax and other taxes (including a national non-domestic rate), and will use them to provide grants to local authorities so as to produce standardized levels of redistributive services like education and welfare; then, leave local governments with the job of providing beneficial services like emptying dustbins and sweeping streets, for which purpose a bob-a-nob poll tax will be most efficient (Foster *et al*. 1980, 233, 240).

There is an historic irony here: in 1980 Foster and his colleagues rejected their own logic, thinking it too inequitable in its implications (pp. 240-1); in 1988 the Thatcher government has no such inhibitions, and has taken over the Foster prescription *tout court*. Here is the logic, spelt out in the 1986 Green Paper:

Moving from rates to a flat-rate community charge would mark a major change in the direction of local government finance back to the notion of *charging* for local authority services ... although there is scope for extending user charging, most local authority spending will inevitably not be financed by such charges. For the element of local spending paid for by local taxpayers, a community charge would provide a closer reflection of the benefit from modern people-based services than a property tax. (Secretary of State for the Environment, 1986, 25)

The logic here is centralist: far from moving towards greater local autonomy, the poll tax essentially represents Layfield's centralist solution, enforced through the ballot box. Redistributive services will come from the centre; here, local authorities will act merely as agents of central government, and to ensure this Whitehall will lay down national norms, particularly through the Great Educational Reform. This being so, with a poll tax, the large middle majority, having presumably little interest in redistributive local services, will simply refuse to vote for anyone who proposes them. Local government will therefore confine itself to its proper job of providing beneficial services. The theoretical logic behind this, though harsh, is impressively impeccable; it has just not been very clearly spelt out by the government, either because it is too harsh or because it is too theoretical for the average voter, or both.

It is in fact very theoretical indeed. For the Tiebout article on which the Foster thesis is based, which is one of the most frequently cited in undergraduate courses on public finance, is justly titled 'A Pure Theory of Local Expenditures'; it is all posited on the notion that everyone is perfectly free to migrate to the place that provides the optimum bundle of beneficial services. This might be an accurate description of Middle America in the mid-1950s, or perhaps small parts of Yuppie Britain today; it does not seem to describe very well the behaviour of the average person in South-East England in the late 1980s, though perhaps it describes the way the government would like to see us behave. It all seems to confirm two theses: first, that economists are indeed prone, as legend has it, to begin by saying 'Imagine a model of a person'; second, as Keynes once said, that 'Practical men, who believe themselves to be quite exempt from any intellectual influences, are usually the slaves of some defunct economist' (Keynes 1936, 383).

The average voter, who has had the misfortune of never taking a course in the Pure Theory of Public Finance, may like this, or like it not. The fact is that it is coming to pass, because the elected government of the day is hell-bent on it. And, in fairness, it does represent a very clear response to a national (and, indeed, international) problem which has been long in the making; witness

189

developments like California's Proposition 13 of the 1970s, which was essentially an answer to the same problem of ratcheting local expenditures. The gains will be economic but also political, in that major policy choices, being centralized, will thereby be simplified. The losses will be political, in that voters will no longer be able to choose alternative styles of redistribution within the boundaries of the same nation-state. The choice finally is a very basic one, between two very different political philosophies. The irony is that it should have been the Tory party, long the defender of local rights against the bureaucratic centre, that should have taken the initiative. But, from Peel onwards, it has been a Tory tradition to dish the Whigs. From now on, at any rate, it seems likely that this will become a major line of political cleavage in British life.

Do We Need a Development Tax?

There is another strange and obscure twist to this tale: though the Thatcher government has thus bought one important argument from Christopher Foster, it is more surprising perhaps that it has not bought another. For the final conclusion of Foster and his colleagues in 1980, after exhaustive examination of the alternatives, was that, on balance, the best source of new local revenue was a very old idea: site value rating (SVR). Though less economically efficient than user charges or poll tax, it was much more so than rates or local income tax. (Local income tax, the Layfield favourite, they found particularly inefficient because it would encourage many people – the rich, the old, minorities – to move to rich areas to enjoy high levels of redistributive services at low cost to them.) Site value rating was less equitable than LIT, but had many advantages.

In particular, assuming – a large assumption – that central government decided to allow local governments to continue to operate at least some redistributive policies, SVR would be the least objectionable way of getting them locally financed. The reason is that, as a tax on economic rent, it would not give people any incentive to move to other areas; house prices would adjust in consequence, removing the incentive (Foster *et al.* 1980, 228-9). It would also have the special beneficial effect that it would encourage the redevelopment of run-down areas like London Docklands, by giving owners the maximum incentive to recycle their land quickly; an argument particularly telling for the first Thatcher government, which was wrestling with precisely that question. And it could be combined with user charges, LIT, and central government grants. Its main disadvantage would be the practical problems of getting it started: in particular, the problem that valuers might tend to make their assessments not on real market values, but on the over-optimistic expectations of planners (Foster *et al*. 1980, 480-1).

The Case for an Auction

We have probably missed the opportunity for site value rating now, if indeed it ever existed. And there are undoubtedly problems in combining it with the kind of comprehensive planning system we have had since 1947, in which site values essentially reflect the planner's decision as to what will be allowed to happen on the site. But there may be an alternative, simpler, way of achieving the same end. This is to auction planning permissions: a proposal originally suggested by the American land economist Marion Clawson (Clawson 1967).

In a British context, it would work like this. A regional planning commission, such as proposed in Chapter 7, would produce a regional structure plan, identifying two major kinds of action areas: inner-city areas, to be revitalized through government leverage; and greenfield sites, to be developed as new communities. (It would also identify necessary transportation and communication services, such as new motorways or commuter lines, to bring these areas into better relationship with each other.) For the latter, the Treasury would then auction the development rights in the form of Development Bonds. At this stage it would be a gamble, because the designation would not yet be confirmed; there would be the usual public inquiry. Owners of the land, at this point, would have first refusal, but only at the going bid price. They could then sell their land with the rights or not, as they chose; of course, they could sit on their land if they wished. As and when the designation were confirmed, clearly there would be intense market activity in the rights; the owners would presumably make quite a lot of money. If the designation were not confirmed, they would get their money back, rather like a failed share issue; as with a premium bond, they could never lose their investment but they could win a lot.

There are several good reasons for auction. But they are different reasons, and it is important to distinguish them. One is that the community has a right and almost a responsibility to tax betterment, the increase in the value of land that occurs because of the community's actions, which is therefore an unearned increment to the landowner in a very strict sense. This might be disputed; the entire history of British planning, ever since the great 1947 Planning Act, has been littered with periodic attempts by Labour Governments to collect betterment and regular reversals by succeeding Tory administrations (Reade 1987, 16-23, 58-9, 63-4). The other reason, more crudely, is that this is a potential source of tax revenue that the Treasury ought not to miss, since it is buoyant and easy to collect, and since it would allow other taxes – especially income tax – to be further reduced.

In any case, there is a final clinching argument for it: it is a way round Reade's devastating criticism of the entire post-1947 British system of planning – or, as he more accurately calls it, the post-1953 system (the date when the Conservatives repealed the financial provisions in the original 1947 Act). This is 'the inherent contradiction ... produced by the attempt to operate land-use planning in the absence of an effective tax on betterment', which 'seems guaranteed to lead to pseudo-planning, the appearance of planning without the reality' (Reade 1987, 23). It would base itself on the impeccable theoretical basis that the development value in large-scale developments had been created through (and only through) public action and should therefore pass to the public purse.

But it would do so in a way that might just be attractive to quite a number of people: to the owners of the land; to developers, and certainly to the Treasury, which would find it an instant and buoyant source of revenue, like premium bonds but better. It might thus provide a way at last of ending the dreary game of political football that has run into massive extra time these last forty years, whereby Labour governments (in 1947, 1967, and 1975) pass laws to collect so-called betterment, and succeeding Conservative governments (in 1954, 1971, and 1980) promptly repeal them (Reade 1987, 58-9, 63-4). It might secure a way of breaking the log-jam on development in the South East. And, additional attraction to the Thatcher government, it might even pave the way to further cuts in income tax.

It has another advantage: as Foster and his colleagues recognized, a charge of this kind can be used to finance redistributive local services. Assume, as suggested earlier, that from now on in Britain a major line of national political cleavage develops regarding the proper functions of local government: the Conservatives support central control over redistributive policies; Labour supports the principle of local autonomy. Then a future Labour government could modify the auctioning of development rights so as to give a share to local government, which could do with it what it wished; the Conservatives could continue to take it all centrally, preferring to distribute money through grant. This, hopefully, could guarantee a degree of political stability for the plan: a consummation devoutly to be wished.

There are, of course, obvious objections, some theoretical, some practical. One side will say that, just like site value rating, it will encourage overdevelopment; to which the answer is: that is for the planning system to deal with. The other side will say that it will nationalize values that are already embodied in land prices. The answer to that is quite simply that these values were nationalized in 1947, compensation was paid, and that part of the Act has never been rescinded. If prospective developers have foolishly paid hope value, that is their problem; we need not lose sleep over them.

The most powerful objection is that, in theoretical terms, it is very much a second-best to site value rating. It does not tax potential development value all the time, but only at one special point of time. Thus it does not provide the same built-in incentive to develop, especially in run-down urban areas. It might even meet with the same resistance as greeted those earlier attempts to collect betterment. The reason is that both land seller and land buyer expect to share the development value, and they will object to paying it to the state (Reade 1987, 19). However, it is crucially different from all these earlier attempts in one respect: it is not a levy; no one need pay it; it will settle at its equilibrium level, being whatever level landowners and land buyers decide is worth their while. This could be virtually zero, as it might well be at first; it could be much higher. There will be no built-in reason to wait for the repeal of the legislation – particularly, of course, if it were introduced by a Conservative government.

In any case, there is an argument that might prove the clinching one: politics is the art of the second-best. Auctioning development rights doubtless would not secure many of the good things that – *vide* Foster *et al.* – site value rating could achieve; but it is perhaps possible in the short term, in a way that site value rating certainly is not. The third Thatcher government has nailed its colours to the mast of poll tax, and the new system of local taxation is going to be built on that, not on a hypothetical alternative. Precisely the beauty of the development auction is that it could act as a useful supplement to poll tax, providing a buoyant source of central government revenue at a time when one has never been more sorely needed. That is the main reason why it is put forward here.

There will also be practical objections to it. One will come from part of the development industry. This will be that it will prove much easier to proceed through so-called development agreements: Section 52 agreements, named after the clause in the 1971 Planning Act. In recent years the number and scope of these agreements has hugely grown, not least in those proposed for private new communities in the South East. The idea is that the developer directly carries much of the infrastructure costs necessitated by the development: roads, water, sewers, even schools. Thus, one of the most potent sources of local objection to such schemes is removed from the start.

Further, an additional attraction to any local authority in the 1980s, these contributions entirely escape all government restrictions on local authority spending. Auctioning development rights would automatically make developers unwilling to continue reaching such agreements, since they would thereby be paying their contribution twice. We could arrive at a similar outcome to that of auctioning by the present route, if the inspector at each inquiry – who might need to become a panel of experts – were given wider powers to negotiate as between developer and local authority about the level of developer contributions; there would in effect be a public bargaining session on the Section 52 agreement. The answer to that is that it would still prove enormously complicated and expensive and time-consuming – more so, even, than the present protracted proceedings. An auction would be far simpler. But to have an auction, you have to have something to auction. That logically demands that the planning system take the initiative.

Another conceivable objection is that the proposed procedure is undemocratic. To that there are three answers. One is that, ultimately, the responsibility will rest with the Secretary of State, who will continue to be accountable to Parliament. Another, related, answer is that the national Parliament, or at least a regional forum within it, is the right level of accountability for this kind of decision. The third is that the present system of accountability, which entails every community in the South East trying to shift development into someone else's backyard, is really a very poor way of reaching a democratic and equitable set of decisions as between conflicting interests. This may not be perfect, but it is better.

A further objection is that the Treasury will object. (After all, it usually does.) It would be a device for increasing public expenditure, outside Treasury control. Therefore, the question would arise: Where and for what purpose would the proceeds go? If into general Exchequer funds, then the local community would not get the benefit, and would be even more opposed than now. If directly to the local community, then the Treasury might try to claw the proceeds back. In any case, the question would arise as to what local community we are talking about. The development may cause congestion on roads 10 or 20 miles away. It may fill schools administered by a county located at a similar distance, or hospitals run by a health authority even more distantly located. Finding the right apportionment formula, as between country and district, would be a work of art. That is accepted; but it does not seem an insuperable objection. Proceeds of the sale should presumably be divided: first, so much for spillover effects (plus a *douceur*) to the local community, to be further divided between county and district according to a general formula; second, the rest as general community gain to the Treasury.

A *douceur* may savour slightly of corruption. But it is a very important element of any workable scheme. We have often admitted the principle with regard to individuals, who may thereby be induced to make a voluntary sale rather than going through the palaver of compulsory purchase. The same ought logically to apply to communities. By paying enough, and a little more, to overcome inconveniences, we might make local communities a little less resistant to development. Of course, it would be a pipedream to imagine that all opposition will cease; some will not be compensatable at any price. But we should make it easier. At present we make it maximally difficult.

This should help deal with another practical objection: that the local authorities, who will not want it, will ensure that it will not work. After all, by dragging their feet they seem to have ensured the demise of the 1976 Community Land Act, or at least that part of it that involved them directly in land purchase. But the present proposal does not involve them actively. By creating a Regional Development Authority, the onus of making designations of development land is removed from them. By having the Treasury or its agent conduct the auction, they are not involved in the subsequent procedure. They merely receive a grant to pay for the infrastructural consequences of the development. The objection might well be a different one: that this is a way of completely bypassing the local authority planning system in respect of major development decisions. In one sense that is true and undeniable; but in another it is not. The local authority, both the county and the district, will be able to object to the designation, which will presumably go in every case through the mill of a public inquiry. There, the case for and against the development will be completely argued through; and the final decision, as always, will lie with the Secretary of State. This is an argument not about the substance of this particular chapter, but about the whole hierarchy of planning powers. But, by making it crystal clear that major new urban developments will be accompanied by the means to bear the resultant costs to the community, the proposals in this chapter might at least soften some of the objections.

The final objection, I am sure, is the weightiest. It is that the proposal, resting as it does on a return to central strategic planning, would be ideological anathema to the present government. Additionally, ultimate heresy, it appears to represent a return to discredited Labour policies of the 1960s, if not the 1940s: what is the auctioning of development rights, but a veiled return to the Development Charge of 1947? The answer is, not quite: this charge, recall, would not be centrally determined, but would be voluntarily paid by the developer on the basis of his own estimate of what the permission was worth. And the very pervasiveness of the Section 52 agreement shows just how willing developers are to make such voluntary payments.

In summary: we are going to get the poll tax, and with it a massive change in the role of local authorities: they will become mere agents for providing redistributive services, otherwise restricting themselves to basic beneficial services. That in turn is likely to create a major new line of cleavage in British political life, between centralizers and defenders of local autonomy. In the meantime, both sides might agree on the case for additional revenue that might be used either for cutting existing taxes, or for again extending the redistributive role of local authorities. Auctioning of development rights is such a source of revenue.

It has major political advantages. The political heat will be in part taken off the hapless Secretary of State. Since there will effectively be a market in planning permissions, we shall immediately find out what such planning permissions are really worth, in a way that we never can now. And there will at last be an orderly supply of development land. As *Which?* magazine might say, as compared with site value rating it might not be Best Buy, but it is Worth Looking At.

9

London 2001

This book, like its predecessor 25 years earlier, has been a call for effective regional planning. The argument has been the same, now as then: that planning of the right kind, done well, is better than not planning. Better, in fact, for almost everyone: for producer and consumer, for buyer and seller, for richer and poorer, for individual and society, for red-blooded entrepreneur and red-flagged collectivist. The background has been the same, too: as in the early sixties, so in the late eighties, all too little planning of the right sort, and the woeful results all too plain to see. We are come full circle, and this book is intended to help slide the wheel around again.

Looking Back and Looking Forward

At this point, some reader may have the morbid curiosity to ask, How consistent is all this with what you wrote a quarter-century ago? To save him or her a trip into the library's reserve stacks, here is the answer: In some respects remarkably similar, in some very different, but in spirit, I hope, identical.

At the equivalent point in *London 2000*, I argued that there were areas of certainty and areas of choice. The certainties 'occupied a much larger part of the planners' calculations than they have generally cared to admit in the past'. I assumed, 'almost as a matter of certainty, that by the end of the twentieth century, there will be in the London Region one and three-quarters to two million extra jobs and nearly four million more people, in one million extra households'; three in four would own their own homes, of which there would need to be a million more in that part of the region outside London; they would own some 8 million cars, about three times the 1961 total; and they would commute farther, on average, than they did then.

These predictions have proved wrong in one sense, right in a wider sense. There will not be more jobs or more people in the London region, as defined in *London 2000*: there were 27 000 fewer people there in 1986 than in 1961. But that was because the growth of population has been accompanied by an outward roll of both people and jobs far more radical than anything I imagined. The Greater South East, the revised regional definition used here, had added some 2 million people in the quarter-century between 1961 and 1986, and was expected to add another $1\frac{1}{2}$ million between 1986 and 2001. Jobs – the big surprise – had not grown notably, because of the holocaust of deindustrialization in the 1970s; but households were forming much more rapidly than ever imagined in the 1960s, with more than a one million additional units projected in the years 1986-2001 alone. The home ownership projection looked like being close to target: the car ownership projection, reapplied to the extended region, likewise.

The areas of policy choice, I suggested in 1963, were five. First, employment: by taxing employers in London, we could produce a more rapid outflow of jobs than would otherwise occur. Second, homes: I argued for many more new towns and a new kind of public development agency. Third, transport: through a new charging system for road use, people should be encouraged to show that they are willing to pay more for a better level of service; in any case, though public transport would continue to carry the great majority of London commuters, more and better roads would be needed. Fourth, redevelopment: we needed a new mechanism for more effective comprehensive development of the inner city. And fifth, administration: the Greater London Council, then not yet in being, now come and gone, would prove inadequate and should be replaced by a new kind of government, like a German *Land*.

Some, very small, bits of all this happened; most did not. But some of the events happened anyway, policy or no policy. Employers did not need taxing to leave London: they left in their thousands, leaving an industrial wasteland. There were three monster new towns, not many smaller ones; but they are getting finished, after a fashion.

There was no road pricing, despite a couple of half-hearted attempts (after one of which, ironically, Singapore borrowed the scheme and made it work); new roads got built, but not enough of them, and very few in London itself. We have no new redevelopment mechanism, and comprehensive redevelopment is widely distrusted and disliked. We do not have federal government, though once in the 1970s we seemed to be nudging gently towards it; instead, we have increasing centralization of an already centralized system.

So: not a record of conspicuous success. And yet: the fact is that, instead, we did try large-scale regional planning in the 1960s, abandoned it all too soon in panic, have muddled through for a decade and a half, and now find the chickens come home to roost. A churlish author might say that he told you so, but that would be no help. Instead, let us start from where we are. It is 1988: a very different Britain from that of 1963. We have collectively lost much, though not all, of our belief in planning. We do not officially believe in regional government. We believe in setting the people free to earn their own livings, own their own homes, drive their own cars – let nothing stand in their way! How, on that basis, do we develop a strategy for the development of the region?

Start by asking the question, Why did planning again get discredited, then? For very good reasons. It produced a massive and a niggling bureaucracy, which did not remotely justify its keep. At strategic level, Abercrombie produced his historic Greater London Plan of 1944 with a staff of precisely eight professionals and eight cartographers, as the buzz-bombs flew overhead; it changed the face of London irreversibly for the better, and could have done so even more and even better if there had been the money and the political will at the right time. The GLC produced its Greater London Development Plan of 1969 with a cast of thousands; it achieved almost nothing, and has been consigned to the footnotes of history.

At local level, we have the same phenomenon: enormous efforts spent mainly in stopping and stifling all initiative, all too often that of other planners. Within London, especially, the planners in the GLC and the planners in the boroughs began to fight each other, until it seemed that most of their energies were thus spent. Planning, in the public mind, came to be associated with everything that was negative. No wonder, then, that successive Thatcher governments have spent huge efforts in trying to cut it down to size. Like so much else in Thatcherism, this reflected the spirit of the times.

We need no more of that kind of planning, the kind that gave planning a bad name. We need a strong, slim strategic plan, Abercrombie–fashion, that will tell everyone what is going to happen and then allow them to get on and do it. This book has not been that plan, but it has suggested what kinds of things it would contain and how it would look. The job remaining is to pull it all together: to suggest how such a planned London would work and look and feel. What would London 2001 be like to live in?

One answer, which simply must be correct, is: not that much different from the present London. There is a limit to what we can do in 13 years, or even treble that. The broad structures will remain the same. People will still commute by train and tube to offices in the City and the West End, live in distant suburbs, shop in their local town centres, seek recreation in London's country or on London's coasts. What matters is the increments, which gradually cause one London to change, imperceptibly and chameleon-like, into another. Abercrombie well understood that organic character of all good planning; hence his success. We will do well if we achieve the same degree of incremental and organic change in the next forty years as was achieved in the four decades between then and now.

What would such an organically planned city region look like? How would it feel to live and work in? We can pick out four main elements. For work, and also for services and entertainment, it would be a *many-centred city*. For living, including community services and the education of children, there would be *real communities*. For moving about, we would have *a choice of transport systems from any A to any B*. For recreation or the plain enjoyment of looking, there would be *a continuous green backcloth*. And, behind them all, a *slimline regional planning system*.

These elements are startlingly unoriginal. So, in a sense, is the argument of this whole book. The great names in the pantheon of British planning – Ebenezer Howard, Raymond Unwin, Patrick Abercrombie, Jimmy James – all made these elements the keystones of their planning philosophy. But they need reinterpreting, and reasserting, for each successive generation. This is what we must now do.

The Many-Centred City

The first essential, once again, is precisely that argued in *London 2000*: to make London progressively into a polycentric city. To the two existing cities around which London has been shaped down the centuries, we now need to add a third, a fourth, a fifth, perhaps a twentieth and a thirtieth. Each should have its distinctive function and character. Each should feel like a city. And not just any city, but part of one of the greatest urban complexes of the world.

Some of these new cities would in effect be wrapped around the old, forming subsidiary nodes at the edges of the City and West End: King's Cross, Spitalfields, the South Bank downstream from London Bridge. Others – Canary Wharf, Deptford Park, Old Oak – will form new complexes apart from the old, thus helping to create a truly polycentric structure within the built-up mass of Greater London. Yet others – Reading, Milton Keynes, Chelmsford, Cambridge, Ashford, Bournemouth, Swindon – will perform more specialized functions for their surrounding sub-regions towards the edge of the region, thus reinforcing and enhancing its multi–centred character. All will be tied together by a regional transportation network, built through upgrading and extension of what we have now, which will interconnect the nodes both with the existing centres of this vast sprawling region, and with each other.

These will be nodes for working and also for entertainment and public life. Each will be surrounded by residential areas which will also contain local jobs and services. Thus, increasingly, people will find a wide range of employment, services, and entertainment opportunities within easy reach. But that does not mean a slavish pursuit of self-containment, which was an unattainable goal in the London of 1963, let alone that of 1988. Many inhabitants of the extended London of 2001 will have the means of mobility and will exert their right to exploit the fact. What it does mean, what planning should always mean, is *choice*: if people dislike long-distance commuting, if they tire of it, then they should be able to avoid it. That is what the polycentric structure is intended to achieve.

Real Communities in Real Places

There is another quality it ought to be able to produce: a great variety of places to live in, some more urban in feel, some more rural; some big and bustling, some small and intimate; but all distinctive places, with a sense of community. Planners, in planning them, should above all strive to avoid Gertrude Stein's over-quoted epitaph on her native city of Oakland: 'There's no there there.' Or, in the California Department of Transportation's lesser-known but equally devastating words, 'Oakland: Next Eleven Exits'.

There is the ever-present danger that new communities, however labelled, will acquire just that last quality, and thus be no communities at all. They will be too homogeneous in age (both of buildings and of the people in them), in socioeconomic class, in life-style, in political sympathies. They will be all too tidily planned, like with like. It is not easy to avoid this: the postwar New Towns certainly did not, and the privately built new communities may be even more prone to fall into the trap. Variety in planned provision will help: some housing for old folks, some affordable housing, some bits of old urban structure (though that, if anything, will make achieving them politically harder). At the very least, every such place should be a place. You should know when you enter it and leave it, and if perchance you leave the motorway at the wrong exit, you should immediately know you are in the wrong place.

The same goes for London itself. In Chapter 6 I suggested a new battle to achieve what Abercrombie strove for but what was seldom achieved: a reshaped London, in which the structure of the village-like communities emerged more clearly, and within which people could make safer, quieter, more comfortable lives for themselves. It does not need drastic urban surgery: on the contrary. It does mean reshaping the pattern of both vehicle and pedestrian movement, to keep through traffic away from front doors and playing children, and to give people security and solidarity when they emerge from their houses. Traditional urban structures do this not badly, though by gentle management they can be persuaded to do it even better. Untraditional structures, of which we seem witlessly to have built all too many these last three decades, may require more change.

A Choice of Transport From Any A to Any B

A polycentric region, I argued above, would give people choice: choice to work nearer home, choice to commute if the job were worth while. And a range of varied types of community would give them choice of another critical kind. But, equally, the entire region must be connected by a transportation lattice which will enable them to get from any node to any other, quickly and conveniently. Once again, the idea is not novel. It was inimitably spelt out by Ebenezer Howard, in that famous diagram of the polycentric Social City in the first edition of his book (Howard 1898); all we should be doing is to build his Inter-Municipal Railway, on a scale appropriate to the present-day South East.

The latter-day equivalent is a new kind of commuter rail network, which the Parisians have invented and which we should be emulating: a Regional Express Rail, passing under and through central London, connecting the inner nodes and the outer nodes, and linking both with London Underground, the existing BR Network SouthEast, and local light rail systems such as that in Docklands. We need to make it as sleek and attractive as we can, because without it the congestion on the orbital highway system may become intolerable. But we need to recognize the challenge for transport planners on the roads, too, because most people – wisely or not, selfishly or not – will continue to take to their cars.

The key to that will lie as usual in a combination of two policies: investment and management. Investment, because, given the projected growth of population and employment in the Greater South East, there is going to have to be a lot more roadspace. The radials will have to be widened from two lanes to three and from three to four, as the Department of Transport has proposed for the M4 between Maidenhead and the M25. The M25 will have to be duplicated by an outer orbital between 30 and 40 miles from London, and also duplicated by an express toll motorway along the M25 right-of-way. There will need to be a lot of investment on other roads, especially those that feed into the existing motorway and primary route system.

But – as London itself has shown for decades and Roseland is beginning to show now – no amount of investment will in itself deal with congestion: traffic will grow to fill all available space. Therefore, in London and outside it, we shall need to manage scarce roadspace to best effect. With a limited-access network such as we have in the motorways and improved trunk roads, it becomes easier: we can ration access to the system at congested hours, giving priority to buses, to minibuses, ride-sharers, and other travellers who use roadspace efficiently. On the most congested stretches, which we would widen, we should dedicate the extra space to these groups. If we build tollways, we should again give priority access, toll-free too, to these users. This works in California and it can work in South-East England.

It can even work on some roads within London itself, like a reconstructed North Circular and a future South Circular. But here, because the problem is so endemic, more drastic solutions will be necessary. Here too, there is a need for new roads: in east London, where the penny has dropped, and in south London, where as yet it has not. But the main need is comprehensive traffic management through pricing. There is an irony here: *London 2000*, in 1963, was way ahead of its time in arguing for such a solution, which was then technically not feasible. But with advances in electronics, it is more than feasible now. And, given the exasperation of London's road users, which means all Londoners, it may now be politically feasible also. That is one of the major arguments this book offers.

There may of course be an old, tired counter-argument: 'The motorist will not stand for it.' In London, the motorist does not even figure in a majority of all households, let alone a majority of all people. The people who sit fuming on the motionless bus are far more numerous and therefore politically influential. And even drivers can be brought to see the point. Since they are fully accustomed to paying as they go for electricity, gas, and telephone services, and may soon be paying the same way for water, no one can argue that it is a novel principle.

Charging for scarce roadspace – not, notice, all roadspace at all times – would bring many incidental benefits. Not least, it would allow better comparisons between investments in roads and investments in public transport, above all in railways. And it should thus make clear what at present is obscure: how much we are collectively willing to pay for a good-quality regional transport system. At present, compared with major city regions on the European mainland, like Paris and Munich, we do not pay much and we get correspondingly little back. There, the population at large pays a lot in taxes to subsidize a good system. We might pioneer a different approach: by charging properly for scarce roadspace, we might demonstrate that users are willing to pay for the right level of service. Here, too, ever since the Greater London Development Plan of 1966-9, we have been floundering. We should flounder no longer.

A Backcloth of Open Space

Reading the acrimonious debates of 1988, a visitor from another country or another planet might well think that South-East England was in imminent danger of being concreted over; that the Green Belt, that most sacred cow of British planning philosophy, was about to be sacrificed on the altar of speculation; that school parties would soon need to be ferried to Devon or Derbyshire to see a cow. It is of course sheer fantasy. The South East is, as it always has been, by no means the most heavily urbanized part of England; that distinction belongs to the North West. Some one-fifth, at most, of its territory is covered by bricks and mortar, and much of that consists of the giant blob of Greater London. No one in authority has seriously proposed to follow the Adam Smith Institute in even nibbling at the Green Belt. Proposals to that end, like Consortium Developments' ill-judged proposal at Tillingham, or the retail development at Wraysbury, immediately become objects of the most intense controversy.

The sound and fury obfuscate the real issue, as perhaps they are intended to do. The real issue is the extent and shape of new urban development outside the Green Belt – or, more accurately, Green Belts: not merely London's, but also those around smaller places like Oxford. There is plenty of open land in the South East that is, in the planners' expressive parlance, 'White Land'. We could cater for the most ambitious estimates of the House Builders Federation and still leave more than three-quarters of the region in fields and woodland, now and for the foreseeable future.

The real questions are different. Should we crowd the new developments into certain parts of the region, or scatter them more or less equally, sharing the agony as between Berkshire and Essex, Northamptonshire and Kent? And then there is a subtly different question: *Within* each of these areas, should we concentrate the development in rings around the existing towns? Or build new towns in the open countryside? Or extend a large number of villages just a little? Or some combination of these? Whichever choice we make, at either the larger regional scale or the local scale, there will still be plenty of green space left; that is not the question at all. The question at both scales is whether we want a greater *degree* of concentration or of scatteration.

There are of course arguments both ways; there always have been. In favour of concentration: better access to a wide range of local jobs and services, not merely for the present generation, but also for their children; a better chance of maintaining a good public transport system as an alternative to universal motorization; bigger continuous green spaces elsewhere, good not merely for those living in them, but also for those who come out from the towns at weekend. In favour of scatteration: modern technologies, which allow people to work in smaller units, even at home; more people within walking distance of green fields, good both for adults and children; a greater sense of village community, which meets many people's preferences; less traffic concentration, and less congestion.

Of course, they are not either/or choices. And the answer will prove to be one of balance. We will not be able to crowd the whole of the population growth into a few mega-growth zones, because people will be getting born and growing up and marrying all over the region, and plans must make provision for that. But, since people will also be moving on a large scale, and since some parts of the region are much more accessible and are already more developed than others, and since there are such qualities as economy of scale and economy of scope, some concentration of growth makes perfectly good sense.

We come back, then, to the argument of Chapter 4. It will prove right to put, say, about three in every four of the new houses and the new people into growth around the existing towns in Roseland, and in the South East fringe; and to put another tenth into new communities within a few major growth areas. Since many of the existing towns are also in the major growth areas, that means that we can expect upwards of 40 per cent of overall growth to be there – 20–30 per cent around existing towns, 10 per cent in new communities – and perhaps 20 per cent in medium growth areas, leaving another 30–40 per cent to be scattered across the extended region.

What this means, for the way the Greater South East region will look and feel in the early 21st century, is, again: not much different from now. Most of the region will remain deeply rural: a landscape of fields, fens, woods, villages, dotted with country market towns. At widely spaced intervals of 30 or 40 miles, as now, there will be bigger – properly, medium-sized – towns, typically county towns like Cambridge, Colchester, Maidstone, Guildford, Oxford; some of them, designated medium growth centres, will have grown appreciably, some less so. Additionally, there will be perhaps a score of new communities built by private enterprise, especially close to towns like Oxford and Cambridge, which are themselves subject to exceptionally strict containment policies. But Green Belt and other restrictions will ensure that these are kept quite separate from their parent towns, surrounded by green countryside.

Then, somewhat different in feel, there will be the major growth areas. These will be based on the areas identified in the 1970 Strategic Plan, because they were the places best suited – by their location on the major motorway and inter-city rail corridors, by the scale of their existing urban development – for large-scale growth. But now, some at least may take a different form. Southampton-Portsmouth will be extended out to Bournemouth-Poole, as a kind of *Randstad* around the green heart of the New Forest. Reading–Wokingham–Aldershot–Basingstoke will be extended eastwards to include Bracknell, and perhaps westwards to take in Newbury. Crawley–Gatwick will also embrace Horsham immediately to the west. Milton Keynes-Northampton will logically extend eastwards and northwards in a linear development to include Wellingborough, Kettering and Corby. South Essex will form another *Randstad* together with Chelmsford.

Several of these extensions, very importantly for the region's future development, take in fast-growing cities and towns at the fringe of the extended region, like Bournemouth-Poole and Northampton-Wellingborough. And two other major planned developments in this fringe belt – the expanded town of Swindon and the New Town of Peterborough – should be further developed as major growth centres; the latter, additionally, incorporating further growth around Huntingdon-Godmanchester and one or more new communities in the Cambridgeshire Fenland, immediately to their east. Finally, without doubt, there will need to be a further look at two growth centres identified, but then not pursued, in the planning studies of the 1960s: Ipswich and Ashford, each of which may well need satellite new communities around them to help house their growth.

The alarm sirens, doubtless, will start to wail. But before someone presses the button, let this be stressed and again stressed: *major growth centres do not mean urban sprawl.* On the contrary: here, as elsewhere, we are talking about that classic phrase first coined by Unwin, *Towns against a background of open country.* A town like Swindon or Northampton or Peterborough might well expand further; a town like Ipswich or Ashford may not. Instead, much of the growth, both of homes and of job opportunities, will take place in discrete communities some distance away. Local road networks – partly in place, partly to be developed – will ensure that the resulting traffic flows bypass the communities rather than overwhelming them. The great majority of people will have open countryside within a few minutes' drive, even a few minutes' walk.

A Slimline Planning Authority

It will not be achieved by osmosis. It will need a tougher approach than anyone has shown, these last twenty years, to plan the development of the entire region in the best interests of the people in it; above all, to balance the claims of the established populations against those of the new generations and the generations still unborn. It will not be achieved in talking shops representing sectional local interests, wherein decision–making resembles that of the ancient Polish parliament where any member, by lifting a finger, may block any motion he pleases. Too long in the South East, things have fallen apart; too long, the centre has not held. Now, the centre must reassert itself; the necessary action can come only from the centre, or so close to the centre as to make no difference.

It could be a Regional Planning Commission, rather like a standing Royal Commission, if those had not gone so utterly out of favour. It could be like the old Regional Planning Council, if those had not gone out of fashion too. It would need to be insulated from local political pressure, though it would have to take account of it. So it would need to be stuffed with the Great and the Good, even the Grand: people of a fiercely independent cast of mind. It would be there to advise the Secretary of State for the Environment, and thus act as a kind of political lightning conductor, diverting much of the opprobrium for unpopular decisions away from him; he could hide behind its ample coat-tails.

Its main job would be to produce and then revise a plan for the broad development of the region: nothing too detailed, nothing too fancy, above all nothing expensive to prepare. But it would have to say fairly definitively where development should occur and where not. And it would need to relate this to a long-term transportation plan, both road and rail, which would necessarily carry a hefty price tag; hence, it would have to be agreed with the Department of Transport, within Treasury guidelines.

Once it was approved – through either an Examination in Public, or scrutiny by a Commons Select Committee – it would, like any ministerial guidance now, provide guidelines to the planning authorities in drawing up their local plans. In perhaps 90 per cent of the region, that should be enough. But in the other 10 per cent, where substantial development is expected – above all in the major and medium growth areas, but also wherever new community developments were proposed – a special planning regime should come into operation. A planning brief would be drawn up, and the development rights would be auctioned. Thence, a mixed public–private development corporation would come into existence, incorporating representatives of the local authority and the developers as well as independent members, to bring the scheme to completion.

Such a system, and nothing much short of it, is needed to bring order out of chaos in the South East. Once again, as in 1963, the question is, Which?

A Day in London 2001

Suppose we achieve it. What would life be like, for the average household in the extended London region of the early 21st century? Consider a day in the life of the Dumills.

Edward Dumill, 55: registrar, *Polytechnic University of the South Bank* (*PUSB*)
Mary Dumill, 52: market researcher, *Kent Surveys, Maidstone*

London 2001

Sebastian Dumill, 25: management trainee, *Channel Software*
Chloe Dumill, 21: biotechnologist, *Master's student in food technology*

We met the Dumills, those of us who remember, in *London 2000*. Some few details have changed since then, but not many. Edward Dumill's job turned out at first to be not in a university, but in one of the new polytechnics of the 1960s; but that got put right in 1994, when, in concert with the others, it decided to restyle itself a polytechnic university. Mary Dumill relocated herself to a new job in Maidstone. Sebastian, the electronics manager, discovered that his real penchant was for software development. Chloe, similarly, had found that by the turn of the century, biotechnology was a necessary basis for her chosen career in food technology, which especially involved research on the spoiling qualities of foods in large catering establishments.

Their new town of Hamstreet has become one of four satellites around Ashford, closely linked to the giant European Freight Centre located between it and Ashford. Most commuters to Maidstone and London therefore commute by the new High Speed Rail link which runs parallel to the old Tonbridge Line from Ashford, travelling to it by the automated light rail system which was created during the 1990s as part of the plan to develop Ashford as a medium growth centre at the gateway to the Tunnel.

In this transmogrification, the town has changed its physical form too. It is only one-third of the size, 30 000 instead of the 95 000 expected in 1963; growth around Ashford is shared between the town itself and its four satellites. The big central pedestrian deck is far less vast, though part of the town centre is built over a parking garage. The segregation of car traffic and pedestrians is less dramatic, though it is still evident.

But, at a larger scale, the pattern is still there. The people of Hamstreet live lives that are not circumscribed either by the boundaries of their new community or even by the greater Ashford area, a mini-conurbation of some 150 000 people. They commute freely across south-east England, to London, to other locales in Kent, even across to France. As predicted in 1963, at Ashford, Mr Dumill joins the 08.28 from Boulogne to London via the Channel Tunnel, changing at Bromley to a train that takes him to the new campus of PUSB in complex at Deptford Park. Mrs Dumill drives up the M20 to her campus-style office on the edge of Maidstone, another medium growth centre under the 1990 plan, now a town of some 100 000 people. Sebastian, who has a job in an Anglo-French software company based in St Omer, has already taken the 07.20 train to Lille, uttering thanks for the British Parliament's recent decision to join European Standard Time; like other trans–Channel commuters, he had found that early Monday morning start a really bad opening to the week. And Chloe's Master's course takes her by car to the University of Kent at Canterbury.

For Edward Dumill, travelling by train, the major change compared with his youth is the large number of people who leave and enter at the major intermediate stops: many alight at Headcorn, another new community halfway between Ashford and Tonbridge; at Bromley, now a giant office and commercial centre, about one in five passengers leaves or changes trains.

Deptford Park, once a vast area of derelict railway land south of the Surrey Docks, is now another huge office and campus complex, at one of London's biggest rail interchanges: main-line trains from Kent via Bromley here meet the Bakerloo and Jubilee Lines, and the East London branch of the Docklands Light Railway; this last links the complex with the Surrey Docks redevelopment immediately to its north. It is also next to the inner South Circular, which here swings north into the approach to the duplicated Rotherhithe Tunnel. The Deptford Park complex employs 40 000 people; the whole of the Surrey Docks complex employs 100 000. Many of them are with financial institutions which left the City of London in the great shake-out of the 1990s, when the search for lower rents began to dominate the minds of corporate executives. The South Bank University relocated some of its operations here during its expansion during the late 1990s, finding it exceptionally convenient for both students and staff. The other campuses are the original one in the Wandsworth Road, plus new centres at Dartford and Croydon, also opened during the last decade.

Edward and Mary Dumill are celebrating their twenty-eighth wedding anniversary tonight. But, since electronic pricing makes it expensive to use the London streets until 18.30 – and impossible unless your car is equipped with a transponder – Mary Dumill waits until then to bring the family car up to town and then take her husband, via the inner South Circular, across the new Battersea Bridge to dinner on the other side of London. One or two observers had predicted as early as the 1960s that London's restaurant belt would spread west from Chelsea and Kensington, but they got the details slightly wrong: it went in one direction down to Fulham, while in the other, leaping over the big office and shopping centre of Hammersmith, it landed in the Chiswick High Road and adjacent streets. After the great and much delayed rebuilding of Hammersmith Broadway in the 1990s, indeed, there was not much

room for restaurants. The activities that have been attracted here –
big construction and civil engineering companies, computer companies – typically do a lot of business abroad, and have colonized the
main route to Heathrow, here in Hammersmith, farther west along
the Chiswick High Road, and on the Great West Road.

When it is time to go home, the Dumills have only a few minutes'
drive to join Southway, the South London tollway, at its start
under the Chiswick Flyover. Diving in an immersed tube under the
Thames, it continues in a three-mile tunnel under Richmond Park
and Wimbledon Common, emerging into a clear moonlit night in
Wimbledon. But not for long: it dives again into a long double–deck
tunnel under Mitcham Common to Croydon, where the Dumills
leave it for the A23 link road that takes them out to the M25.

It is past midnight, but traffic on London's motorway and expressway system is still heavy. When the first of these motorways were
built, in the late sixties, the storm of protest was so great that the
programme was put into cold storage for the next twenty years.
Instead, the Department of Transport channelled the money into
producing the M25 London orbital motorway, the world's longest
bypass, which opened in 1986. By the time that the upgrading of the
North Circular Road to motorway standard was completed, in 1994,
south London boroughs were complaining that they had been left out
in the cold. It was then that advances in tunnelling technology, and
the injection of private capital into tollway construction, provided
an answer. Now, the call is for an even bolder enterprise: a scheme,
first mooted in the 1980s, for a 12-mile east–west motorway in an
immersed tube under the Thames, from Chiswick to the new East
London River Crossing.

There is heavy traffic along the M25, the M26, and the M20 all
the way down to Ashford – and beyond, because some people are
going to their weekend cottages in Normandy. Most are travelling
out, from theatres and cinemas and restaurants in central London.
But some are coming back in, from country eating places or friends
up to 60 miles distant. This is a highly mobile society; distance is
no big barrier. As in the 1980s, as in the 1960s, Londoners of 2001
live without the car during their working day, but in the evenings
and at weekends the car is an integral part of their lives. Just as
they no longer work in isolated communities, so they can no longer
form their friendships and their social lives within tightly bounded
communities. For them, Chiswick to Dover has no more significance
than Hammersmith to Hampstead when they were young.

Most of the towns you see from the M20 – Britain's High Road to
Europe – are big, old-established towns, important sub-centres for the

211

areas 15–20 miles around them. Maidstone and its suburbs by now have 100 000 people, Ashford – which boomed after the opening of the Tunnel – about the same number. Each has its contingent of London commuters, its local factory, shop, and office workers, and its quota of commuters to other places in the extended London region. The lights that illuminate the sky to the south mark a new town: Headcorn, started next to the Channel Tunnel High Speed Train route at the same time as Hamstreet. Twenty miles nearer to London, its houses were snapped up by London commuters. Its architects, finding they had to build on ill-drained Weald clay, made a virtue of the fact and designed the town around a series of canals which divide the town into islands. The style of the housing, fashionably post-modern and formal, ironically followed the suggestion of an academic who had originally suggested the idea of the town in the early 1960s, but who could not have seen that by the 1980s everything would look like that. The uncompromising functionalists who had planned the original Hamstreet were of course routed; Hamstreet went the same way, and Edward Dumill – who originally thought it frivolous – has come to quite like it.

And so back to the far corner of Kent. It does not seem such a far corner now that it is Britain's gateway to Europe: the mouth of the Tunnel is a mere ten miles away, and already they are talking of the bridge–tunnel for cars that will supplement it. It seems strange for a family that moves so easily across the face of southern England and northern France, but the Dumills think of themselves quite unconsciously both as Londoners and as Kentishpersons. Hamstreet is their town, and when they stroll next morning along its pedestrian pathway system to do their weekly shopping, they will feel as much at home, and a part of it, as they felt themselves Londoners the night before.

Last Questions

The Dumills have made a return visit in this book. They were created for the original *London 2000*. When I came to regenerate them, as I reopened the old book to refresh my memory, I had some trepidation. Here was the proof of the prediction, a quarter-century later. How well would it stand the test of time?

The answer is rather an odd one. For the prediction was an unusual one too: it was a prophecy not of what *would* happen, but of what *might* be possible if certain trends continued, and if, also, certain policies were pursued. What has happened, I believe, is that the trends have continued; in fact, they have been stronger and more embracing than I dared expect. The people did move out; so did their jobs; they did become mobile, both in their commuting patterns and even more so in their social patterns. But the policies have, on the whole, been pursued at best half-heartedly, at worst not at all. Much of the time, we did not have the 'positive planning actions'; we did not have the New Towns, the motorways, the new shopping and office sub–centres. We did 'turn the blind eye'. Consequently, as I already suggested in Chapter 1, we have the dire consequences I predicted: the 'formless, inadequately planned sprawl of offices'; the 'traffic congealing to a stop'; the 'ugly, dispiriting, demoralizing suburbs sprouting like fungi from every old town' (Hall 1963, 209).

Not quite, of course. As said at the outset, we have some planned decentralization: three New Towns; some expanded towns that are new in all but name; some sub-centres. But mainly, it has happened willy-nilly, and the grievous results are all too plain.

And now, we do not have much time. Back then, I thought that we had a generation or more to do what we needed to do. It was my generation, of course. At first, in those expanding, optimistic, euphoric 1960s, we seemed to be getting it all right. There was the creation of the Regional Planning Council and Board. Goaded by them, there was the quick progress towards a definitive regional plan – the first for more than three decades, and an excellent one too. And then everything fell apart, in a slough of cancellation, expenditure cuts, policy reversal, recrimination.

Now, there are faint signs that – ironically, in an era devoted to nonplan – we could snatch some kind of a victory from the jaws of defeat. Docklands are a triumph of planned inner-city regeneration, of a kind. The private enterprise new communities at last promise the kind of development I was calling for then, albeit thirty years on – but better late than never. The development industry is entrepreneurial and imaginative. There is a new willingness, of an almost Victorian kind, to venture big money to create new infrastructure. It only needs harnessing and guiding.

The problem is that no one is giving it a lead. I happen to believe that this is an odd way to run a mature capitalist economy. It does not correspond to my understanding of how any such economy works in the late twentieth century. Outstandingly successful examples of such economies – France in the 1960s and 1970s, Japan and Singapore and Korea in the 1980s – have prospered through an *economie concertée* in which the state planning system and the private corporate planners have worked hand in hand. MITI may not run Japan, but MITI and the giant corporations do. Singapore's planners

– both economic and physical – have provided the framework for the successful growth of private enterprise. We should be doing the same.

I do not want to argue, from this, that a comprehensive physical development plan is an inevitable prerequisite for economic success. The Tokaido megalopolis is a notable example of the contrary. But it may well be the exception that proves the rule: it is a fact that many of the most successful of these countries – France, Sweden, Hong Kong, Singapore – are outstanding cases of planned large-scale urban development. Planned design may not be absolutely necessary, but it powerfully helps. And for the same reason that developers spend money on the design of their business parks, or the London Dock-lands Development Corporation pours funds into environmental improvement: decision-makers, especially those whose decisions matter, prefer to locate in good physical circumstances. What is right at the local scale is equally right at the regional.

Again, the choice stares us in the face. If we continue to succeed economically, if we remain Europe's outstanding success story, we are going to continue to see a dizzying rate of physical development in South-East England down to the end of the century and beyond. We can handle it well or handle it badly. We can have more badly located and badly designed office blocks in town centres that are congealing to a stop. We can once again have ugly, formless, dispiriting suburbs that no one wants to inhabit for more than a few months. We can have miles of physical dereliction and human decay in our inner cities. It will profit no one: neither the witless developer, nor his hapless erstwhile tenant or buyer. Or we can have a strong, slim regional plan such as Abercrombie once gave us, with the infrastructure that will regenerate the inner cities, with town centres that work, new communities that feel good to be alive in, a green and pleasant land around.

The case for regional planning, then, remains as powerful now as it did a quarter-century ago. And the fact is that, contrary to our reputation for muddling through, when we really commit ourselves to the grand design – Brunel's Great Western Railway, Frank Pick's tube system, Abercrombie's 1944 plan, the New Towns – we do it superbly well. Sadly, we lack confidence in ourselves, because sometimes the follow-through on the ground has been poor. Yet, if we really harnessed the resurgent entrepreneurial spirit of Britain to the creative powers of the planner, what a splendid city, what a splendid country, we could create for ourselves.

As in 1963, so in 1988, the question is the same.

Which?

References

Abercrombie, P. (1945) *Greater London Plan 1944*. London: HMSO.

Adams, J. G. U. (1974) ...and how much for your Grandmother? *Environment and Planning, A* 6, 619–26.

Advisory Committee on Trunk Road Assessment (1977) *Report* (Chairman: Sir George Leitch). London: HMSO.

Begg, I., B. Moore, & J. Rhodes (1986) Economic and Social Change in Urban Britain and the Inner Cities. In Hausner, (1986, I, 10–49).

Best, R. H. (1981) *Land Use and Living Space*. London: Methuen.

Buchanan, J. M. & R. D. Tollison (1972) *Theory of Public Choice: Political Applications of Economics*. Ann Arbor: University of Michigan Press.

Buchanan, J. M. & G. Tullock (1962) *The Calculus of Consent: Logical Foundations of Constitutional Democracy*. Ann Arbor: University of Michigan Press.

Buck, N., & I. Gordon (1987) The Beneficiaries of Employment Growth: An Analysis of the Experience of disadvantaged Groups in expanding Labour Markets. In Hausner (1987, II, 77–115).

Buck, N., I. Gordon, & K. Young (1986) *The London Employment Problem*. Oxford: Oxford University Press.

Cervero, R. (1986) *Suburban Gridlock*. New Brunswick, NJ: Rutgers University Center for Urban Policy Studies.

Champion, A. (1987) Momentous Revival in London's Population. *Town and Country Planning* 56, 80–2.

Champion, A. G., A. E. Green, D. W. Owen, D. J. Ellin, & M. G. Coombes (1987) *Changing Places: Britain's Demographic, Economic, and Social Complexion*. London: Edward Arnold.

Chisholm, M. & P. Kivell (1987) *Inner City Waste Land: An Assessment of Government and Market Failure in Land Development*. (Hobart Paper no. 108). London: Institute of Economic Affairs.

CILT (Campaign to Improve London's Transport) (1987) *Railways for London: Investment Proposals for the LR Tube and BR Network*. London: CILT.

Clark, C. (1957) Transport: maker and breaker of cities. *Town Planning Review* 28, 237–50.

Clawson, M. (1967) Why not sell zoning and rezoning? (legally, that is). *Cry California* 2, 9, 39.

Cohen, S. & J. Zysman (1987) *Manufacturing Matters: The Myth of a Post-industrial Economy*. New York: Basic Books.

Coleman, A. (1976) Is planning necessary? *Geographical Journal* 142, 411-30.

Coleman, A. (1985) *Utopia on Trial: Vision and Reality in Planned Housing.* London: Hilary Shipman.

Committee of Inquiry into Local Government Finance (1976) *Local Government Finance: Report of the Committee of Inquiry.* (Chairman: Frank Layfield), Cmnd. 6453. London: HMSO.

Conway, J. (1985) *Capital Decay: An Analysis of London's Housing.* SHAC Research Report no. 7. London: SHAC.

Countryside Commission (1987) *New Opportunities for the Countryside: The Report of the Countryside Policy Review Panel.* CCP 224. Cheltenham: Countryside Commission.

Damesick, P., N. Lichfield, & M. Simmons (1986) The M25: a new geography of development? *Geographical Journal* 152, 155-75.

Department of the Environment (1977a) *Inner London: Proposals for Dispersal and Balance: Final Report of the Lambeth Inner Area Study.* London: HMSO.

Department of the Environment (1977b) *Inner Area Studies: Liverpool, Birmingham, and Lambeth: Summaries of Consultants' Final Reports.* London: HMSO.

Department of the Environment (1988) *1985 Based Estimates of Numbers of Households in England, the Regions, Counties, Metropolitan Districts and London Boroughs 1985–2001.* London: Government Statistical Service.

Department of the Environment, Water Data Unit (1978) *Water Data 1977.* Reading: Department of the Environment.

Department of the Environment and Welsh Office (1986) *The Future of Development Plans: A Consultation Paper.* London: Department of the Environment.

Donnison, D. & D. E. C. Eversley (1973) *London: Urban Patterns, Problems, and Policies.* London and Beverly Hills: Sage.

Evans, A. W. (1987) *House Prices and Land Prices in the South East – A Review.* London: House Builders Federation.

Flynn, N., S. Leach, & C. Vielba, (1985) *Abolition or Reform? The GLC and the Metropolitan County Councils.* Local Government Briefings no. 2. London: Allen & Unwin.

Forrester, A., S. Lansley, & R. Pauley (1985) *Beyond our Ken: A Guide to the Battle for London.* London: Fourth Estate.

Forshaw, J. H. & P. Abercrombie (1943) *County of London Plan.* London: London County Council.

Foster, C. D., R. A. Jackman, & M. Perlman (1980) *Local Government Finance in a Unitary State.* London: George Allen & Unwin.

Gershuny, J. & I. Miles (1983) *The New Service Economy: The Transformation of Employment in Industrial Societies.* London: Frances Pinter.

Gillespie, A. E., & A. E. Green (1987) The changing geography of producer services employment in Britain. *Regional Studies* 21, 397–411.

References

Greater London Council (1978) *The Marshall Inquiry: Report to the Greater London Council*, by Sir Frank Marshall. London: Greater London Council.

Greater London Council and Department of the Environment (1974) *London Rail Study Part 1*. London: GLC.

Greater London Group (1985) *The Future of London Government: Report*. London: London School of Economics.

Greater London Working Party (1984) *The Government of London: Response to the Government's White Papers Public Transport in London and Streamlining the Cities...* Reading University/ College of Estate Management, Joint Centre for Land Development Studies.

Hall, P. (1962) *The Industries of London since 1861*. London: Hutchinson.

Hall, P. (1963, 1969) *London 2000*. London: Faber & Faber.

Hall, P. (1987) The anatomy of job creation: nations, regions and cities in the 1960s and 1970s. *Regional Studies* 21, 95–106.

Hall, P. (1988) *Cities of Tomorrow: An Intellectual History of Urban Planning and Design in the Twentieth Century*. Oxford: Basil Blackwell.

Hall, P., M. Breheny, R. McQuaid, & D. Hart (1987) *Western Sunrise: The Genesis and Growth of Britain's Major High-Tech Corridor*. London: Unwin Hyman.

Hall, P., R. Thomas, H. Gracey, & R. Drewett (1973) *The Containment of Urban England* (2 vol). London: George Allen & Unwin.

Hart, D. A. (1976) *Strategic Planning in London: The Rise and Fall of the Primary Road Network*. Oxford: Pergamon Press.

Hass-Klau, C. (ed.) (1986) New ways of managing traffic. *Built Environment* 12, 5–106.

Hausner, V. (ed.) (1986, 1987) *Critical Issues in Urban Economic Development* (2 Vols). Oxford: University Press.

House Builders Federation (1987) *Private Housebuilding in the Inner Cities: A Report by an Independent Commission prepared for the House Builders Federation*. London: House Builders Federation.

House of Commons (1982) *Fifth Report from the Transport Committee, Session 1981–2: Transport in London*. Vol. I, *Report, Appendices, and Minutes of Proceedings*. London: HMSO.

Howard, E. (1898) *To-Morrow*. London: Swan Sonnenschein. Reprinted as *Garden Cities of To-morrow*. London: Faber & Faber, 1946.

Howard Humphreys & Partners (1987) *Heathrow Surface Access Study Report: For Department of Transport*. Leatherhead: Howard Humphreys.

Hughes, M. (1987) Railways muster their forces. *Railway Gazette International* 143, 383–6.

ILEA (Inner London Education Authority) (1987) *Ethnic Background and Examination Results 1985 and 1986* RS 1120/87. London: ILEA.

Kasarda, J .D., & J. Friedrichs (1986) Comparative demographic-employment mismatches in US and West Germany. In H. J. Ewers, H. Matzerath,

& J. B. Goddard (eds), *The Future of the Metropolis: Economic Aspects*, 221–49. Berlin: de Gruyter.

Keeble, D., P. L. Owens, & C. Thompson (1982) Economic potential and the Channel Tunnel. *Area* 14, 97–103.

Keynes, J. M. (1936) *The General Theory of Employment, Interest, and Money*. London: Macmillan.

Killingworth, C. M. (1968) The continuing labor market twist. *Monthly Labor Review* 91, 12–17.

London Planning Advisory Committee (1988) *Strategic Planning Advice for London: Policies for the 1990s: Draft Document for Discussion*. Romford: LPAC.

London Regional Transport and British Rail Network Southeast (1986) *Light Rail for London?* London: LRT and BR.

Marmot, A. & J. Worthington (1987) Great Fire to Big Bang: private and public designs on the City of London. *Built Environment* 12, 216–33.

Minister of Transport, Steering Group and Working Group (1963) *Traffic in Towns: A Study of the Long-term Problems of Traffic in Urban Areas*. London: HMSO.

Mogridge, M. J. H. (1986) *A Strategic Transport Plan for Inner East London*. London: Docklands Forum.

Mogridge, M. J. H. (1987) The use of rail transport to improve accessibility in large conurbations, using London as an example. *Town Planning Review* 58, 165–82.

Movement for London (1987) *Wheels of Change: The Londoner's Journey to Work*. London: Movement for London.

NEDO (National Economic Development Office) (1986) *Directions for Change: Land Use in the 1990s*. London: NEDO.

Newman, O. (1972) *Defensible Space: Crime Prevention and Urban Design*. New York: Macmillan.

Newman, O. (1980) *Community of Interest*. Garden City, NY: Anchor/ Doubleday.

Norton, A. (1983) *The Government and Administration of Metropolitan Areas in Western Democracies: Survey of Approaches to the Administrative Problems of Major Conurbations in Europe and Canada*. Birmingham University, Institute of Local Government Studies.

Office of Population Censuses and Surveys and Registrar General, Scotland (1984) *Census 1981: Key Statistics for Local Authorities, Great Britain*. CEN 81 KSLA. London: HMSO.

Office of Population Censuses and Surveys (1987) *Mid-1986 Population Estimates for Local Government and Health Authority Areas of England and Wales*. OPCS Monitor no. PP1 87/1. London: HMSO.

Office of Population Censuses and Surveys (1988) *Mid 1985–based Population Projections for Local Authority Areas in England*. OPCS Monitor no. PP3 88/1. London: Government Statistical Service.

References

Pennick, N. (1983) *Early Tube Railways of London*. Cambridge: Electric Traction Publications.

Potter, S. (1987) New towns around the world. *Town and Country Planning* 56, 289–97.

Rajan, A. (1987) The riddle of unemployment. *New Society*, 30 January, 10–12.

Rasmussen, S. E. (1937) *London: The Unique City*. London: Jonathan Cape.

Reade, E. (1987) *British Town and Country Planning*. Milton Keynes: Open University Press.

Regional Studies Association (1983) *Report of an Inquiry into Regional Problems in the United Kingdom*. Norwich: Geo Books.

Roberts, J. (1988) *Quality Streets: How Traditional Urban Centres Benefit from Traffic Calming*. London: TEST.

Roger Tym & Partners (1987) *Land Used for Residential Development in the South East: Summary Report for Department of the Environment and SERPLAN*. London: Roger Tym & Partners.

Royal Commission on the Distribution of the Industrial Population (1940) *Report*, Cmd. 6153. London: HMSO.

Royal Commission on Local Government in England (1969) *Report*, Cmnd. 4040. London: HMSO.

Royal Commission on Local Government in Greater London (1960) *Report*, Cmnd. 1164. London: HMSO.

Royal Town Planning Institute (1987) *Strategic Planning for Regional Potential*. London: RTPI.

SEEDS (South East Economic Development Strategy) (1987) *Trade Winds: The Changing Face of Retailing and Retail Employment in the South East – An Alternative Strategy*. Stevenage: SEEDS.

Secretary of State for the Environment (1983) *Streamlining the Cities: Government Proposals for Reorganising Local Government in Greater London and the Metropolitan Counties*. Cmnd. 9063. London: HMSO.

Secretary of State for the Environment, Secretary of State for Scotland, and Secretary of State for Wales (1986) *Paying for Local Government*, Cmnd. 9714. London: HMSO.

Self, P. (1975) *Econocrats and the Policy Process: The Politics and Philosophy of Cost-Benefit Analysis*. London: Macmillan.

Sen, A. K. (1970) *Collective Choice and Social Welfare*. San Francisco: Holden-Day.

SERPLAN (London and South East Regional Planning Conference) (1982) *The Impact of the M25*. SC 1706. London: SERPLAN.

SERPLAN (1985a) *Regional Trends in the South East: The South East Regional Monitor 1984-85*. RPC 369. London: SERPLAN.

SERPLAN (1985b) *Developing SE Strategic Guidance: South-East England in the 1990s: A Regional Statement*. RPC 450. London: SERPLAN.

SERPLAN (1986a) *Regional Trends in the South-East: The South-East Regional Monitor 1985-86*. RPC 535. London: SERPLAN.

SERPLAN (1986b) *The Regional Basis for Planning for Housing:*

Statement by the Regional Planning Conference. RPC 561. London: SERPLAN.

SERPLAN (1986c) *House Prices in Perspective: A Review of South-East Evidence*, by W. S. Grigson. RPC 572. London: SERPLAN.

SERPLAN (1986d) *Regional Trends in the South East: The South East Regional Monitor 1985–86*. RPC 535. London: SERPLAN.

SERPLAN (1986e) *Housing Land Supply in the South East (outside London)*. RPC 590. London: SERPLAN.

SERPLAN (1986f) *Implementing the Regional Strategy for the South East*. RPC 630. London: SERPLAN.

SERPLAN (1987a) *Development Potential in the Eastern Thames Corridor*. RPC 700. London: SERPLAN.

SERPLAN (1987b) *Regional Trends in the South East: The South East Regional Monitor 1986-87*. RPC 800. London: SERPLAN.

SERPLAN (1987c) *House-Building Progress and Structure Plan Provisions in the South East Region: 1981-86*. RPC 803R. London: SERPLAN.

SERPLAN (1987d) *Housing Land Supply in the South East (outside London)*. RPC 805. London: SERPLAN.

Simmons, M. (1985) Orbital motorway that reinforces the South-East. *Town and Country Planning* 54, 132–4.

Simmons, M. (1987) The impact of the Channel Tunnel. *The Planner* 73, 16–18.

South East Joint Plan Team (1970) *Strategic Plan for the South East: A Framework*. London: HMSO.

Tiebout, C. M. (1956) A pure theory of local expenditures. *Journal of Political Economy* 64, 416–24.

TCPA (Town and Country Planning Association) (1987) *North–South Divide: A New Deal for Britain's Regions*. London: TCPA.

Tripp, H. A. (1938) *Road Traffic and its Control*. London: Edward Arnold.

Tripp, H. A. (1942) *Town Planning and Road Traffic*. London: Edward Arnold.

Tullock, G. (1976) *The Vote Motive: An Essay in the Economics of Politics, with Applications to the British Economy*. Hobart Paperback no. 9. London: Institute of Economic Affairs.

Vickerman, R. W. (1987) The Channel Tunnel: consequences for regional growth and development. *Regional Studies* 21, 187–97.

Wates, N. & C. Knevitt (1987) *Community Architecture: How People Are Creating their own Environment*. Harmondsworth, Middx: Penguin.

Young, K. & P. L. Garside (1982) *Metropolitan London: Politics and Urban Change, 1837–1981*. Studies in Urban History no. 6. London: Edward Arnold.

Index

Numbers in italics refer to figures in text

221

Index

motorways 18, 123

Neighbourhood Watch schemes 158
new communities
   Consortium Development proposals
      47, 94, *14*, 99
   from existing towns 108
   hopes for 213
   location proposals 105-7
   need for public provision 103
new Covent Garden 154
New Towns
   achievements 22, 213
   Act (1946) 35
   list Table 3, 23
   Mark II 38
   Milton Keynes 22, 38, 104
   Northampton 5, 22, 38, 104, 207
   Osborn, Frederic 16-17
   Peterborough 22, 38, 104, 207
   twenty-five for London (Appendix)
      110-18
Northampton 22
North Circular 17

office
   building boom 12-13
   design controversy 12
   limiting demand for 13
   promoting movement outside 13-14
Office Development Permits 13
Osborn, Frederic 16-17, 32
outer boroughs
   difference in employment 59
   employment rates *8*
   population gain 90
   unexploited development sites 70
Outer London
   defined Table 1
Outer Metropolitan Area 2, 5, 22-3, 38,
      56, 123, 145
Oxford 5

Paris
   Metro 128
   RER trains 128
park-and-ride *17*, 139
parking
   control 142-3
   off-street 144
   penalties 143
Peterborough 22, 207
Peterborough-Huntingdon 4, 71
Pick, Frank 31, 121
planning
   balance sheet 156
   change of approach 161

changes *6(a)*, *6(b)*, *6(c)*, *6(d)*, Table 11,
   Table 12, Table 15
controversies 16, 24, 25, 26
development agreements 48, 194
for employment 67
guidance to district authorities 48
impact 102
issues 28
land supply 101
land use 171
local balance 78
London streets 120
policies 38, 45-6, 108
post-war system 21
regional commission 177, 191, 207
relaxation of controls 110
return to strategy 180, 196, 199
safe design 161
strategic objectives 98
turning points 154, 168
poll tax 187, 188-9
polycentric cities 44, 77, 200-1, 202
population
   birth rate 36, 44
   changes *6(a)*, *6(b)*, *6(c)*, *6(d)*, Table 11,
      Table 15
   forecasts Table 13
   growth and decline 2-3, 4, 30, 38, 104
   growth Table 12, Table 14, Table 16, 86
   movement 46, 79
   numbers of Table 1, 3
   projections Table 17, *11(a)*
   relationship with jobs 79
   stemming the outflow 28
public transport
   as jobs benefit 67, 69-70
   buses 30, 135, 145
   Fares Fair policy 172
   investment package 124, 146, 204
   planning 170
   trams 31

Rasmussen, Steen Eiler 16, 29
railways
   bottleneck 12
   commuter-line closures 135
   Docklands Light 14, 15, 125
   expansion 32
   in central London 120
   Inter-Municipal railway 202
   InterCity 24, 72
   light rail proposals 140, 203
   Network SouthEast 179
   park-and-ride stations 127
   planned systems 72, 124, 125
   Southern Railway 32, 121, 122-3
   Thameslink 125

224

Postscript

London 2001 was delivered to Unwin Hyman in July 1988 on two floppy disks, which carried the author's own laboriously two-finger-generated text. It was published almost exactly six months later from that same text: a process that bypassed a small army of secretaries, typesetters and proofreaders. As a result, there were some modest negative consequences for employment in the London region. More significantly, because of the speed of publication, relatively fewer things than usual occurred in the interim to make a topical book out of date. Rather more has occurred in the last six months, between initial publication and this new paperback edition.

Most important have been developments in transport. During the autumn of 1988, the chorus of complaint and frustration about London's transport reached an absolute crescendo, which did not much mitigate during the winter of 1989. Congestion on the roads appeared to get worse; official figures appeared, confirming that indeed it had, but not by much (Department of Transport 1988). Services on the Underground further disintegrated, with over-crowded trains and scores of escalators out of order. Finally, in January 1989 came the long-awaited Central London Rail Study from a joint working group of the Department of Transport, London Transport and British Rail (Department of Transport *et al*. 1989).

It was a curious document that seemed to stop where it got interesting. It evaluated several proposals for major new lines and finally plumped for three schemes, which seemed to show a good cost-benefit ratio. One came from London Transport: predictably, it was their old favourite, the Chelsea–Hackney line, which they had been trying to build since 1949, if not earlier. The other two were more novel, though not entirely so. They were two main-line tubes to be built by British Rail's Network Southeast, one running west-east from Paddington and Marylebone to Liverpool Street (and connecting with Thameslink at Farringdon), the other linking either Euston or King's Cross–St Pancras with Victoria. The point, which would not be lost on anyone, was that the London Transport

227

proposal and the second British Rail proposal were competitors for the same pot of gold; no one would build both. No wonder the joint working party stopped there.

What seems certain is that the east–west line is hot favourite. It would connect with the new Heathrow link from Paddington, which the privatized British Airports Authority will build, so there is a prospect of private finance. It could be associated with massive redevelopment of the run-down area around Farringdon station, which would become the great transport crossing of London, equivalent to Chatelet–Les Halles on the Parisian RER; an area that includes the City of London's Smithfield meat market, now one of London's greatest redevelopment prizes. It is, ironically, a superior (that is, very much more expensive) version of the Brunel Line suggested in *London 2001*. The north–south line is an alternative version of the Kingsway Line suggested here; while a third British Rail option, not chosen as a priority project, represents an alternative version of the book's Garden City Line.

The study also evaluates a number of proposals for tube lines and extensions in south and south-east London; so the similarities are close, though the details are different. In particular – a symptom, surely, of the institutional divisions within the working group – in very few cases are there proposals for London Underground to link up with Network Southeast inner suburban lines in South London; the two are treated effectively as separate systems. Frank Pick, 54 years ago, did better than that.

Still, the study represents some kind of limited breakthrough. Though it never mentions the term, it could mean a real start on an RER for London, which is one of the main messages in *London 2001*: a system that could bring outer suburban and exurban commuters speedily and conveniently to central destinations. By June 1989, Chris Green – Director of Network Southeast – was openly talking about plans for a London RER. If it gets built, the location of the stations on the new system will have profound implications for the pattern of intensive commercial development in the next half-century. So watch Old Oak Triangle.

Meanwhile, the era of commercial toll highways edged nearer. In May 1989 Paul Channon, the beleaguered Transport minister, produced a government statement endorsing the principle and saying that they would not compete with publicly-financed roads for public money (Department of Transport 1989a). Almost simultaneously, he announced a doubling of public expenditure on roads, with a widening of the newly-finished M25 and many of the radial motorways that feed into it (Department of Transport 1989b). The plans stopped at the M25, leaving London still a gaping hole in the programme. Here, presumably, the private contractors would step in.

Predictably, both the Conservative-controlled London Boroughs' Association and the Labour-controlled Association of London Authorities attacked the government's London road plans – which would probably be a major target for private funding – as environmentally obtrusive and badly conceived; in June, neighbourhood opposition resulted in a big public demonstration. So the really big battles on toll roads for London will be some time in the future. The Labour group also announced that it was backing electronic road pricing: a precursor, perhaps, of a major policy shift at some future date.

One transport proposal brought forth the biggest howl of protest since the historic days of the plans for London motorways. All three alternatives for the high-speed rail link from Central London to the Channel Tunnel were attacked with equal venom. 10 000 Kentish-persons marched on Downing Street. Then came an environmental compromise: a new plan that put 25 of the 68 miles in tunnels. The opposition continued to simmer, giving a foretaste of what was in store for the London road proposals. Meanwhile, the new plan included a proposal for a 'parkway' station close to Detling near Maidstone, which could carry high-speed Kentish commuters either to London or to Paris.

On the wider issues of housing and new community development, there was little progress. Major schemes for an out-of-town shopping centre at Wraysbury in the Berkshire green belt, and another for Bricket Wood between Watford and St Albans, were rejected after inquiries. The Director of the Town and County Planning Association, David Hall, called for more garden cities on greenfield sites. Environment Secretary Nicholas Ridley pondered his response to the public inquiries into new community proposals at Foxley Wood south of Reading and Stone Bassett east of Oxford. In July 1989 it came: in the jargon reserved for such occasions, he said that he was 'minded' to approve Foxley Wood, but two weeks later he rejected Stone Bassett.

In mid-March, Ridley issued his long-awaited strategic planning advice for Greater London. It said almost nothing that was new or unexpected. It merely repeated the old formula that London would be expected to provide almost one-third of all the new homes, 260 000 to be precise, in the South East from 1987 until the year 2001 – an exceedingly tall order, given the winding-down of the London Docklands Development Corporation during the 1990s. It gave open permission for the conversion of large old houses into flats.

It urged inner east London boroughs – Labour boroughs – to open their arms to developments associated with the financial sector, and boroughs everywhere to make special provision for new start-up businesses. It gave due notice that the green belt would be maintained. It said that the vitality of town centres shoud be a consideration in judging large new out-of-centre developments. And that, apart from a statement about hotels around Waterloo station's new Channel Tunnel terminal, was about that.

So there are plenty of things due to happen, but not tomorrow. This far, for a book about a subject that often seems to move at approximately the speed of light, *London 2001* remains topical.

PETER HALL
June 1989

References

Department of Transport (1988) *Transport Statistics for London*. Statistics Bulletin (88) 51. London: HMSO.

Department of Transport *et al*. (1989) *Central London Rail Study: A Joint Study by The Department of Transport, British Rail Network SouthEast, London Regional Transport, London Underground Ltd*. London: Department of Transport.

Department of Transport (1989a) *New Roads by New Means: Bringing in Private Finance. A Consultation Paper* Cmnd. 698. London: HMSO.

Department of Transport (1989b) *Roads for Prosperity* Cmnd. 693. London: HMSO.